U.S.-JAPAN MACROECONOMIC RELATIONS

INTERACTIONS AND INTERDEPENDENCE

IN THE 1980S

U.S.-JAPAN

INTERACTIONS AND

MACROECONOMIC RELATIONS

INTERDEPENDENCE IN THE 1980s

Edited by

YUKIO NOGUCHI

and

KOZO YAMAMURA

UNIVERSITY OF WASHINGTON PRESS

Seattle and London

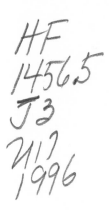

Library of Congress Cataloging-in-Publication Data
U.S.-Japan macroeconomic relations : interactions and interdependence in the 1980s / edited by Yukio Noguchi and Kōzō Yamamura.
    p.   cm.
    Includes index.
    ISBN 0–295–97551–2 (alk. paper)
    1. United States—Foreign economic relations—Japan.   2. Japan—Foreign economic relations—United States.   I. Noguchi, Yukio, 1940–   .   II. Yamamura, Kōzō.
HF1456.5.J3U17   1996   96–23280
337.52073—dc20   CIP

Contents

U.S.-Japan Macroeconomic Relations

INTERACTIONS AND INTERDEPENDENCE

IN THE 1980S

Introduction

YUKIO NOGUCHI AND KOZO YAMAMURA

THIS VOLUME PRESENTS eight studies, ranging from political-economic to econometric, on the macroeconomic policies of the United States and Japan during the 1980s and on capital flow and other significant effects of those policies. Broadly stated, the overlapping motivations for this volume are to offer analyses and descriptions that will help us better understand (1) domestic and international reasons for the macroeconomic policies of the two nations; (2) reasons for, and effects of, the large flow of capital from Japan to the United States; and (3) the direct and indirect effects the macroeconomic policies of the 1980s in both nations continue to have on their respective economic policies and performance and on bilateral economic relations today and in the coming decades.

In presenting such studies, our hope is to suggest that, while studies of bilateral trade issues focused on many forms of Japan's trade barriers and various bilateral agreements and unilateral sanctions are valuable, we need more studies on policy and analytic issues relating to bilateral international capital movements and on macroeconomic factors affecting the movements. To be sure, trade and capital flow are closely linked because in the long run capital exports must be financed by current account surplus. But, as this volume hopes to demonstrate, further studies of bilateral capital flow and macroeconomic factors that determine the timing and magnitude of capital flow can help us significantly in better understanding the reasons for, and the character of, U.S.-Japan economic relations as well as in analyzing how bilateral economic relations affect the economic performance of both nations.

We believe also that the insights and analyses offered in this volume will be

3

useful in our collective efforts to confirm or reject various hypotheses offered on such questions as:

1. What were the causes of the "bubble"—the rapid increase in the prices of shares, land, and other assets—in Japan in the 1980s? Were the causes purely domestic or, because Japan's monetary policy was influenced by international— especially bilateral—considerations, were they both international and domestic?

2. Does a difference in tax rates cause international capital movement? There were arguments in the mid-1980s that the high corporate tax rate in Japan induced capital outflow from Japan. It was also argued, for example, by the Maekawa Report in April 1986, that preferential treatment for interest income caused excessive saving in Japan and hence its current surplus. Are these arguments valid?[1]

3. Does capital movement really matter? Are Feldstein and Horioka correct in suggesting that it does not because a nation's investment rate is correlated with its saving rate? Did the seeming irrelevance of large capital flow to the magnitude of investment still hold in the 1980s when international capital movements increased so rapidly?[2]

4. What are the dominant determinants of exchange rates?

Of course, the principal underlying reason for this volume is that we believe the economic performance of the United States and Japan and harmonious economic relations between them are of global significance. Since these two most technologically advanced economies, jointly producing just about $9 trillion of GDP amounting to almost 31 percent of the world's total GDP in 1993, are the largest suppliers of technology and capital in the world, their performance in this decade and into the next century cannot but shape the future course of the global economy. Should they fail to minimize the economic conflicts between them, not only the performance of both economies but also the future of the world trade regime can be seriously compromised.

Few would contest the observation that how well the two economies perform and how they can minimize economic friction between them today and for some years to come are to a very significant extent determined by what transpired in and between these economies during the 1980s. As we are all familiar, this was the decade during which the United States, accumulating over $1 trillion of fiscal deficit and recording large annual trade deficits, became the largest international debtor, while Japan, making large investments in productive capacity and earning large trade surpluses, became the largest net creditor. In the 1990s, how well the American economy performs and what policy can be or needs to be adopted to sustain its performance are substantively determined by the magnitude of American debts. Japan's economic performance and policy in this decade is also determined by the large investment and other legacies of the "bubble" and its "bursting" in the first years of the 1990s.

This volume is a collaborative effort of a binational study group that was organized in 1993 and held conferences in 1993 and 1994. Participants wrote and revised their respective chapters on various aspects of U.S. and Japanese monetary policy and capital flow in the 1980s to achieve two goals: to shed collective light on many important analytic questions still inadequately analyzed, and to provide descriptions and discussions of the policies and institutions of both nations during the decade. We allocate much more space for such descriptions and discussions relating to Japan than those relating to the United States because yet only a limited amount of the former are readily available in English.

At one level, each participant was asking one or more of such principal questions as: What were the domestic and international reasons for the contrasting macroeconomic policies adopted in the 1980s, i.e., a tight money, loose fiscal policy in the United States and an easy money, tight budget policy in Japan? To what extent can the U.S. policy be explained as a reflection of its waning but still-remaining political and economic power while Japan's policy as that of a more export-reliant economy supporting the American-led trade regime and supplying American markets? How did the Reagan policy change during the decade and how did the Black Monday of October 1987 affect the domestic and international motivations of the macroeconomic policies of each nation and with what demonstrable consequences? What were the domestic and international motivations and consequences of the Plaza and Louvre Accords of the mid-1980s? How did the major developments in the financial markets of both nations (such as the liberalization of financial markets in Japan) affect the capital flow and economic relations between the two nations? And, why did similar tax policies in the two economies yield such different results?

At another level, participants were asked to wrestle with two very fundamental economic-analytic and policy-related issues that are relevant not only in examining the performance and policies of the two economies and their relations but also in analyzing and discussing global economic developments. Of course, we are aware that the world consists of many nations, although the analyses we present focus on the United States and Japan.

One is whether we should focus our attention more on demand or supply factors, i.e., do we see Japan's very large external surplus of the 1980s as detrimental to the interests of the United States and other economies because it signifies a reduction in demand in these economies, or do we emphasize Japan's large capital exports in the decade as beneficial to the United States and other nations importing capital to ease their own shortages of capital? The answer depends on which of the two factors is constraining the economic performance of many economies over time. Although the effects of demand factors should not be underestimated, we believe the relative importance of supply factors has been increasing in the world economy to justify closer studies of economic-analytic and political-economic issues relating to capital movement across national boundaries.

The other issue relates to the effects of macroeconomic policy on capital movement, i.e., how we see the effects of fiscal policy on the exchange rate would differ depending on whether we believe the current account surplus or capital flow is to be seen as the force majeure in determining the exchange rate. If the current account surplus is regarded as the principal determinant, an expansionary fiscal policy that would increase income and reduce external surplus would be seen as the main cause for the depreciation of the currency. On the other hand, if capital flow is seen as the major determinant, the opposite conclusion must be drawn. This is because an expansionary fiscal policy would raise domestic interest rates and invite an inflow of capital from abroad, thereby increasing demand for the currency of the nation experiencing the capital inflow.

The first two chapters, by Yamamura and Noguchi, provide broad political-economic and economic overviews of the reasons for the capital flow in the 1980s from two different perspectives. Yamamura's international political-economic study sees the large twin deficits of the Reagan years and Japan's "bubble"—the major, closely intertwined reasons for the large capital flow from Japan to the United States—as the legacies of "the last hurrah" of the postwar "bargain" struck between the United States and Japan. The bargain he refers to enabled, within the framework of the IMF-GATT system of the Pax Americana, the United States to consume by continuing to inflate its economy and enabled Japan to opt to save and export to maintain the high performance of its economy. He argues that the 1980s was the last decade during which the bargain could be kept by the United States, which justified its twin deficits by neoliberal Reaganomics rhetoric, and Japan, which continued to reduce its official discount rate in order to maintain its export performance by accommodating U.S. overconsumption.

Yamamura's argument is supported by his examination, in broad strokes, of inflation, fiscal deficit, productivity, and the trade balance of both economies during the 1960–90 period. In these decades, the United States continued to overconsume and steadily lose international competitiveness while Japan pursued its developmentalism—promotion of growth by industrial and other policies as well as by distinctive practices of Japanese firms—to increase its international competitiveness and accumulated trade surplus. He concludes that the current and near-future macroeconomic policy and performance of both nations as well as their bilateral economic relations are substantively determined by the legacies of the bargain.

Noguchi's chapter analyzes Japanese macroeconomic policy and the political-economic reasons for the policy that brought about a major investment boom, the "bubble" in land and stock prices, rapid accumulation of current account surplus, and a large capital outflow from Japan in the second half of the decade. For Noguchi, the principal causes of the "bubble," the sharp rise in the current account surplus, and other related developments were Japan's easy money policy adopted to cope with the rapid appreciation of the yen and the tight budget policy adopted to reduce the budget deficit.

The fundamental reason for these developments in the 1980s, Noguchi argues, is the neglect of the interests of consumers who gained little from the "bubble" and the stronger yen while being subjected to various unwelcome effects including sharply rising land prices that made house-ownership impossible for many, excessive investment in productive capacity, and a rapid increase in exports. Noguchi believes that the producer/investor-oriented "biases" in the Japanese political economy are being rectified in the 1990s. But he also believes that, if Japan is not to repeat the policy errors of the 1980s, the transformation of the structure of the Japanese political economy needs to proceed more rapidly and more fundamentally than is seen today.

In the next two papers, Hamada and Ito focus their attention on capital flow from Japan to the United States during the 1980s. Hamada's study is the more broad-gauged of the two and offers historical perspective as well as discussions of related analytic works. His chapter contains a review of the magnitudes and patterns of capital flow between the two nations during the 1980s; analytic discussions of the relationships between the current account and the role of various components of capital movement; discussions of institutional developments, including various legal changes affecting capital flow, in both economies but especially in Japan during the past few decades, that worked as push or pull factors; analytic appraisals of political-economic issues behind the capital flow and changes in the balance of payments; and his view that the future prospects of both economies can only improve slowly because of the legacies of the 1980s.

Hamada is explicit in characterizing the efforts at U.S.-Japan policy coordination, especially in the forms of the Plaza and Louvre Accords in the mid-1980s, as having been less than successful because they resulted in Japan's adoption of an easy money policy which triggered the "bubble" and the depreciation of the dollar which in turn slowed the adjustment of the U.S. current account. He notes also, as does Noguchi in his chapter, that the efforts produced a change in the political balance in favor of the Ministry of Finance which would place priority on reducing the fiscal deficit over the Bank of Japan attempting to achieve a stable monetary policy. The "bubble" and its varied consequences were the outcomes, Hamada argues, of the combined forces of the ministry and of politicians wishing to pursue an expansionary monetary policy, also using international coordination as a pretext.

Ito's contribution offers a quantitative overview of the Japanese current and capital accounts in the 1980–92 period and regression analyses of the effects of

Japanese securities investment in U.S. financial markets and the principal determinants of Japanese direct investment abroad. The most important among
his findings and conclusions include the following. During the 1980s, current
account surpluses and long-term capital outflows moved together but the
relationship changed in the 1990s: in contrast to the preceding decade, fluctuations in the capital account and its components (e.g., securities and direct
investment) are no longer necessarily related to fluctuations in the current
account. In the American financial markets, bond investment was favored by
Japanese investors in the first half of the 1980s but the preference changed to
direct investment in the latter half of the decade. Capital outflow from Japan
to the United States from the mid-1980s to the beginning of 1990 had the effects
of reducing long-term interest rates in the United States by 150 to 200 basis
points. And, Japan's direct investment has been closely linked to Japanese export
behavior; the United States was the major destination for both Japanese exports
and direct investment in the 1980s but as exports to Asian economies began to
increase in the 1990s, so did Japanese direct investment.

Iwata's and Slemrod's studies follow, offering analyses of the effects of taxation on capital flow. Iwata argues that, under several assumptions, tax reform
in both nations during the 1980s had significant effects on capital movement,
i.e., the change in capital cost due to changes in the corporate tax wedge induced
a significant amount of international capital movement ranging from $9 billion
to $34 billion. His findings include the recent narrowing of the binational gap
in the corporate tax wedge, thus the corporate tax burden. He welcomes this
development because he hopes it will continue to minimize tax-distorted international capital movement.

Iwata also argues for implementation and strict enforcement of the residence
principle in levying foreign-source corporate income because the principle, if
adopted as an international taxation system, will assure efficiency of production
in the world economy and will also make income-shifting through transfer
pricing and thin capitalization unprofitable. However, since the actual international taxation system is closer to the source principle, his second-best preference is to adopt corporate tax rates, standards in calculating transfer prices,
and rules on thin capitalization that are as similar as possible.

Slemrod's contribution examines the empirical and analytic links between
the large capital flow from Japan and other nations to the United States during
the 1980s and the changes in American tax laws. Closely analyzing the changes
in the laws from the Economic Recovery Tax Act of 1981 to the Omnibus
Budget Reconciliation Act of 1990 and the effects of each law, he makes findings
that can be broadly summarized as follows: (1) the 1981 tax cut was a significant
reason for the capital inflow in the decade because of the large fiscal deficit it
created; (2) the net effect on capital investment in the United States by multinationals due especially to the Tax Reform Act of 1986, containing various

significant changes that affected their incentives for foreign direct investment, is not unambiguous; and (3) capital outflow from the United States to Japan and elsewhere in the 1990s will be likely to diminish as the American fiscal deficit in the 1990s remains appreciably below that in the 1980s.

In making each of the above findings and others, Slemrod carefully analyzes contrasting theories and examines the possible effects of various technical legal provisions on incentives for portfolio and direct investment by American and foreign multinationals and for individual savings. In the process, the insights and findings by such scholars as Martin Feldstein, Myron Scholes and Mark Wolfson, Han-Werner Sinn, and others are closely scrutinized for their analyses and empirical evidence. Like Iwata's, this study too sheds valuable light on how the tax laws of the United States and other advanced nations affected the capital flow in general and the bilateral capital flow in particular in the 1980s.

The final two chapters are ambitious econometric efforts in which macroeconomic policy and its internal and external effects are analyzed. Yoshino focuses on the "bubble" in Japan while Turnovsky and Bianconi focus on American expenditure policy.

Yoshino's paper first analyzes how and why the banking, corporate, and individual behavior changed as monetary policy changed especially during the "bubble" of the 1987–90 period to cause banks to extend huge, speculative loans to real estate and non-bank financial institutions, many of which subsequently defaulted on these loans. The behavior of banks is analyzed using balance sheet data of all banks, thus identifying heretofore little-examined differential patterns of asset composition, costs, and loan practices of various types of large and small banks. Corporate behavior is examined analyzing the structure of assets and liabilities to establish that corporate asset-holding shifted from ordinary deposits to stock-related products and deregulated financial instruments and that liabilities shifted from bank loans to the issuance of stocks and bonds during the bubble years.

Second, Yoshino, using a structural vector autoregression model and other econometric techniques, examines the changes in monetary policy to find that in the monetary policy reaction function, the exchange rate and price level became important determinants during the 1980s. And, lastly, he analyzes the impact of monetary policy and the exchange rate on asset prices and other macroeconomic variables such as money supply and establishes that land prices were most affected by changes in the money supply after 1980.

The chapter by Turnovsky and Bianconi accomplishes two goals. One is to build a benchmark macroeconomic model to interpret part of the recent performance of the U.S. economy. In their model, special attention is paid to increases in U.S. spending and to the relationship with Japan. The former is seen as a potential source of imbalance with the rest of the world in general and Japan in particular. Their model, adopting a rigorous equilibrium macroeconomic framework based on a representative agent who maximizes utility subject to intertemporal budget constraints, tracks well the behavior of real output, exports, the real interest and exchange rates, employment, the net asset position, and the current account.

The other goal of their contribution is to offer an empirical analysis based on their own and other models in the literature. In particular, they compare the qualitative dynamic properties of the model with the dynamics spelled out by the data through the vector autoregression methodology. One of their most significant findings is that expenditure shocks in the United States in the 1980s were transmitted between the United States and Japan more through the real exchange rate than through the current account.

An important lesson from the experience of the 1980s is that considerable international factors influenced domestic economic policies, especially those in Japan. It cannot be denied that, as the 1980s progressed, the monetary policy of both the United States and Japan was increasingly influenced by the significant effects it had on international capital movements. We had not previously witnessed interaction between international factors and domestic policy formation to the extent observed in the second half of the decade. This interaction, we believe, will increase in the future.

Although this does not directly imply the necessity of policy coordination, we may say that the exchange of information and a mutual understanding of the policymaking process in both countries have become very important. In recent years, the U.S. attitude toward Japan seems to have changed significantly. The United States seems to be shifting its attention away from Japan toward the rapidly growing Asian countries, especially China. It has also begun to put more emphasis on multilateral linkages such as those through the WTO and APEC rather than on bilateral ties. This shift may be a natural one in view of the slow (or virtually zero) growth of the Japanese economy in recent years and the disenchantment on the part of the United States concerning the outcome of bilateral trade negotiations. It must be noted, however, that these arguments place too much emphasis on trade issues. If we look at the capital movement side, the linkages between the United States and Japan are still very important, and hence the bilateral tie between the two countries remains crucial for the long-term performance of both economies.

We express our sincere appreciation to Kokusai Kōryu Kikin, Nichibei Center (the Abe Fund) for the generous financial support that made this volume possible and to Zaisei-keizai Kyōkai (The Institute for Economic and Financial Research) in Tokyo and the Society for Japanese Studies in Seattle for the administrative support they provided for the conferences we held. We are especially grateful to Yoshiyuki Takahashi of Zaisei-keizai Kyōkai for capably administering our project. And we must also acknowledge that this binational volume would have been impossible were it not for Martha L. Walsh's editorial skills and effective "administrative guidance."

NOTES

1. The Maekawa Report refers to a report on Adjustments in the Economic Structure for International Cooperation prepared by a private study group headed by Haruo Maekawa and submitted to then Prime Minister Nakasone in October 1985. For a description and discussion in English, see Takatoshi Ito, *The Japanese Economy* (Cambridge, Mass.: The MIT Press, 1992), pp. 373–75.

2. See Slemrod's contribution in this volume for full citations of the study published in 1980 by Martin Feldstein and Charles Horioka, and Feldstein's 1994 article, based on the 1980 study.

The Legacies of a Bargain

The Reagan Deficits and Japan's "Bubble"

KOZO YAMAMURA

TO SUPPLEMENT AS well as to complement the other essays in this volume, this study examines the political-economic motivations for American and Japanese macroeconomic policies since the 1960s, which substantively affected the fundamentals and trade performance of each nation. Although most attention is paid to the 1980s, I examine the macroeconomic policy of the preceding decades as well in order to better understand both (1) the political-economic reasons for the American and Japanese macroeconomic policies of the 1980s, a principal cause of the large capital flow in the decade, and (2) the reasons for, and the likely effects on bilateral economic relations of, the macroeconomic policy being pursued today by the Clinton administration and the Japanese coalition government. Given the goal of this chapter, I also present an abbreviated discussion of the broad characteristics and patterns of technological change which determined, along with macroeconomic policy, the fundamentals, thus trade performance and capital flow, of both nations.

Based on this examination, this chapter advances three central arguments. First is that the trans-Pacific capital flow occurred because of the existence in the 1980s of two governments that can be characterized as follows. The Reagan administration adopted a "supply-side" macroeconomic policy that sharply reduced tax revenues while increasing the "absorption" level—the sum of consumption, domestic investment, and government expenditure—of the United States.[1] The main reasons for the Reagan macroeconomic policy were domestic and international political economic motivations: gaining and retaining the White House by increasing absorption, and preserving, while exploiting, the U.S. status as a "hegemon" in the international political economy. The last of the cabinets of the Liberal Democratic Party (LDP) maintained the historic low official discount rate of 2.5 percent for 27 months (from February 1987 to May 1989), thus helping to create a "bubble" in asset prices and to cause a large capital outflow. The closely intertwined reasons for such a macroeconomic policy include the efforts of these cabinets, which faced increasing political and economic costs of Japan's postwar "developmentalism," to retain power by pursuing a policy course that would continue to enable Japan to remain a "supporter" in the international political economy.

The second argument, which can be seen as an elaboration of the first, is that the macroeconomic policies of the Reagan administration and the final LDP cabinets can only be understood in a long-term perspective, that is, as "the last hurrah" of the policy course the United States as a "hegemon" and Japan as a "developmentalist-supporter" had respectively followed since 1945 and especially in the preceding two decades. The Reagan administration's conservative rhetoric and "supply-side economics" are more readily understood as necessary outcomes of the macroeconomic policy of an administration following the example of those from Kennedy to Carter that chose to finance overabsorption by inflating the economy. In their respective decades, those earlier administrations too followed varying versions of a macroeconomic policy exploiting or trading on the "hegemonic" power of the United States at the costs of the fundamentals and trade performance of its economy.

The macroeconomic policy of the final cabinets of the LDP must be seen as due substantively to two main factors. One is that postwar Japan's "developmentalism" had succeeded in creating a large, internationally competitive and export-dependent manufacturing sector for which access to international markets, especially to the American market, was indispensable. The second is that, for the LDP cabinets and the bureaucracy, the wide range of developmentalist policies, institutions, and practices that had helped to nurture such a manufacturing sector were difficult to change even after their contributions to economic performance had declined and their political and economic costs had begun to mount both at home and abroad.

My third argument is that the macroeconomic policies of both nations and their economic relations today and for some years to come can only be understood when we realize that both the United States as a "hegemon" and Japan as a "developmentalist-supporter" have had their respective "last hurrahs." That is, the 1980s which saw the large bilateral capital flow was an important political-economic watershed for both nations. Recognition of this fact, I argue, is essential if we are to better understand the character and effects of the macroeconomic, trade, and other policies of the Clinton administration and of Japan's coalition cabinet as well as the likely future course of bilateral economic relations in coming years. Put differently, I argue that (1) the large bilateral capital flow of the 1980s was an unintended offspring of the postwar political-economic bargain between the United States, which continued to overabsorb by exploiting its hegemonic privileges, and Japan, which underabsorbed in pursuit of its developmentalist goals; and (2) what we see today and will see into the future—in both nations' macroeconomic and other policies and in bilateral economic relations—are and will continue to be substantively shaped by the offspring.

This study proceeds as follows. To pave the way for the analyses to follow, Section I presents (1) brief discussions of what is meant by "hegemon" and "supporter," (2) an abbreviated characterization of "developmentalism," (3) a discussion of the long-term, broad characteristics of technological change that I believe useful in various evident ways in this chapter, and (4) a statistical exercise demonstrating the importance of the fundamentals in determining the magnitude of Japanese direct investment in the United States. Section II offers analyses of the political-economic reasons for and various consequences of the American macroeconomic policy during the 1960–90 period. Section III does the same for Japan during these years. The concluding Section IV presents reflections on the significance of the legacies of the 1980–90 period for both nations in their respective economies and in the bilateral economic relations of today and in the coming years.

I. AN ANALYTIC AND STATISTICAL PROLOGUE

By now, an extensive literature on the theory of hegemonic stability offers highly nuanced and subtly varied definitions of, and roles expected of or actually played by, a hegemon (Webb and Krasner 1989; Keohane 1984). However, for the purpose at hand, by a hegemon I refer, following Kindleberger, to a state possessing predominant economic power, committed to maintaining a liberal international trade order, and able to assume the costs of providing public goods that are necessary in maintaining the liberal trade order (Kindleberger 1975, 1981). The definition just given is for a "strong" hegemon; a "weak" hegemon in contrast is a state whose relative economic dominance has diminished, one that is significantly less committed to maintaining a liberal trade regime and decreasingly able to provide public goods. A weak hegemon can be a "predatory" hegemon in that it uses, in some circumstances, its remaining hegemonic power to its own gain at the cost of others in the international trade regime (Lipson 1983). Most specialists of the hegemonic stability theory argue that the United States turned from a strong hegemon to a weak (and even predatory) hegemon between the early 1960s and the early 1970s. Unlike many specialists of the hegemonic stability theory who discuss the political-military power of a hegemon, my concern in this chapter is limited to the political-economic power of the United States as a hegemon.

Supporter is a term first used by David Lake in analyzing the workings of the international trade regime in the absence of an effective or strong hegemon. His definition of supporters is "the middle size countries of high productivity . . . which cannot unilaterally lead the international economy . . . [but are] willing to accept high short term costs for long term gains." He characterized supporters more fully as follows:

> When a hegemonic leader exists within the international economy, sup-
> porters will free-ride, protecting industries at home and expanding exports
> abroad. They assume, in short, that the hegemonic power will carry the
> burden of preserving their export markets while they remain free to pursue
> self-seeking policies at home.

But, when no strong hegemon exists and two or more supporters are present in the international economy, their mutual desire to export will constrain their respective desire to protect home markets. This is because of their high relative productivity which causes them to "value export markets more than protection at home" and they "will sacrifice the latter only if necessary to obtain the former" (Lake 1991, 124; see also Inoguchi 1986).

Referring readers interested in a full economic analytic and political-economic discussion of "developmentalism" to Yasusuke Murakami's recent seminal work, I present here a highly abbreviated summary of what I refer to in this chapter as developmentalism.[2] Developmentalism can be seen as a version of capitalism in which the state participates in the economy substantively more than it does in free-market (neoclassical) capitalism. This is because the central premise of developmentalism is that, so long as the firms in a nation attempting to catch up with the advanced nations face decreasing long-run cost (i.e., have successively new technology to borrow), the state can and should aid firms' efforts to increase productive capacity and efficiency by adopting new technology. To do so, a developmentalist state is to adopt industrial policy (a wide range of policies that affect the investment and disinvestment decisions of firms in numerous direct and indirect ways), a progrowth macroeconomic policy, and education and other policies to deal with politically and/or socially undesirable effects of growth (e.g., income redistribution).

Several facts are also important relating to developmentalism. I identify only the most important among them without elaboration.

(1) For developmentalism to work, a bureaucracy that is not "captured" by interest groups must be able to implement industrial, macroeconomic, and other policies to achieve its goals. However, given that significantly more formal and informal powers are possessed by the bureaucracy in a state adopting developmentalism than in a "neoclassical" capitalist economy, the bureaucracy when "captured" by interest groups, as occurs sooner or later, can create serious political and economic problems. Thus, one significant problem faced by de-

velopmentalism is how to minimize the risks of the bureaucracy being "captured" and to ensure that the power of the bureaucracy remains limited to the amount necessary.

(2) Developmentalism pursued in a nation in which the government is dominated by a single political party over a long time faces an inevitable problem of the principal actors (politicians, business, and bureaucracy) allocating a large amount of resources to maintain the close relationships among themselves. This is because the relationships in a developmentalist state yield high returns for their investment of resources. For example, campaign contributions by business to politicians who are certain to be reelected and possibly occupy ministerial positions yield economically significant returns in numerous well-known ways. Bureaucracy can better maintain turf and power by catering to the wishes of politicians in the dominant party and of businesses enjoying the patronage of these politicians. The results are often outright corruption at worst and non-transparent policymaking and administrative processes at best.

(3) Developmentalism that is justified as a means to "catch up" with the advanced industrial nations is likely to continue even after the catch-up process has ended. The main reason for this is that the developmentalist policies adopted and governmental or quasi-public institutions created and the institutions and practices of firms that emerged and were maintained to pursue developmentalism are difficult to dismantle even after their costs begin to exceed social gains. And, of course, this is especially the case when many resources are invested to maintain them by the main actors as noted above.

(4) Developmentalism can become a significant source of trade conflict when developmentalist policies, institutions, and practices are continued even after an economy practicing it has "caught up" with the most advanced nations and its largest firms, at the frontier of world technology and having access to necessary resources (financial and human), are able to make significant innovations.

Let me now turn to the following broad discussion of technological change which I believe is useful not only in discussing Japan's postwar developmentalism but also in gaining insights on the reasons for (1) the decline in the economic predominance of the United States as a hegemon (thus giving rise to a weak hegemon that is predatory); (2) the oft-discussed "structural" problems of the industrial economies; (3) observed trends toward increasing disparity in income distribution, and growth with a high unemployment rate (the "mismatch" of required vs. existing labor pools) in the industrialized economies; and (4) the ongoing and seemingly intensifying trade conflicts among the advanced industrial nations.[3]

One can, I believe, reasonably argue that what can be called the twentieth-century technological paradigm emerged from the 1880s into the first decade of this century. This paradigm, which followed the preceding nineteenth-century paradigm (of large-scale use of steam energy, the cotton textile industry, and railroads), can be characterized by its increasingly sophisticated uses of electricity and manmade materials (e.g., cement, glass, rubber, polyethylene, and many other increasingly complex chemical products).

In its breakthrough phase, i.e., during the first 25–30 years of the century-long twentieth-century paradigm, slow and uncertain productivity increases were achieved by only a small number of industries adopting the new paradigm. The total amount of investment was yet small and productivity increases for the economy as a whole remained stagnant or were even declining. The result was what economic historians called the Great Climacteric of the 1880–1913 period during which all industrial economies suffered prolonged recession, thus experienced intense international competition and conflicts as evidenced by that between England and Germany.

In the maturation phase of this paradigm after the First World War, an increasing number of industries adopted new technology. New industries combining the products of the new paradigm emerged and grew to produce automobiles and then a wide range of products using electricity, ranging from radios, refrigerators, washing machines, and the like to increasingly more complex electronic products for industrial and consumer uses such as television sets and computers. Even with the experiences of the Great Depression and the Second World War, the maturation phase gained momentum during the interwar years and reached its most productive stage during the postwar decades. Aided by pent-up demand, Keynesian policies, and the increasingly liberal trade regime of the Pax Americana, international trade increased rapidly. Investment, productivity, and real wages too continued to increase.

The United States was the first to reap the harvest of the maturation process beginning in the 1920s, and its leadership in the process continued well into the 1960s. But, Europe and then Japan recovering rapidly from the war soon followed. Japan, adopting developmentalism and benefiting most from the international trade regime of the Pax Americana, rapidly produced more and more increasingly internationally competitive products of the technological paradigm and increased its share in global markets.

Technology easily crossed national boundaries and the followers had little difficulty in imitating. Knowing the paths the United States had taken, targeting industries was not difficult for the followers. Developmentalist Japan was the most effective pursuer of the United States and caught up or even surpassed the latter in one industry after another beginning in the late 1960s.

By the early 1970s, however, the twentieth-century paradigm was spent and it became increasingly evident to many that a new twenty-first-century paradigm was emerging. The new paradigm differs qualitatively from its predecessor because its distinctiveness consists of using and depending crucially on degrees of precision measured in millionths of seconds and millimeters, on digital analytic constructs that have no visualizable analogues, and on multifaceted and complex scientific discoveries that are understood only by a small number of scientists. And the new paradigm differs also in many other ways. It uses less energy and fewer raw materials, requires new skills and education, new modes of work, and even new concepts of property rights. As yet we are uncertain how the emerging paradigm will change our economies.

It is evident that we are today in the period of breakthrough into the twenty-first-century paradigm and are experiencing, as we did in the 1880–1913 period, a climacteric, the birth pains of a new technological paradigm. Since the early 1970s, increases in productivity, thus the real wage level, among the industrial economies have slowed. This is more evident in the United States because it had been the richest and most advanced. And, as during the breakthrough phase of the twentieth-century paradigm, the industrial nations are likely to continue to experience seemingly intensifying trade conflicts among them; the conflicts will continue to be most pronounced between the United States and Japan, the leaders in the new paradigm. If the lessons of the past served as a guide and if the new paradigm takes a longer period to reach its maturation phase because of its technological complexity, it is quite possible that the conflict will last well into the beginning of the next century.

The final input providing the underpinning for the discussions of this chapter is the following statistical exercise attempting to demonstrate the importance of (1) the below-identified proxies for the fundamentals for the United States and Japan and (2) Japan's excess saving ("negative" absorption) in determining the magnitude of Japan's foreign direct investment (FDI) in the United States.[4]

Figure 1 presents a time series of relative productivity indices in the United States and Japan and relative unit costs (unit labor costs [ULC]) in Japan and the United States. The former is constructed using Bureau of Labor Statistics output per worker data and is the ratio of Japanese productivity to that of the United States. The time series should not be interpreted as a comparison of absolute productivity levels but, rather, a comparison of growth rates with 1982 as the base year. As during the rapid growth period (1950–73), even in the decelerated growth period (to 1982) following the oil crisis of 1973, Japanese productivity grew appreciably faster than that of the United States. In the mid-1980s the rate of increase of American productivity accelerated slightly relative to that of Japan until 1987 when the trend reverted to that of the 1970s.

Relative unit labor costs were constructed using Bureau of Labor Statistics indices of ULC and are the ratios of Japanese ULC in dollars to that of the United States. Exchange rate fluctuations play a critical role in this series. The dip in the early 1980s is due to the strong dollar in these years and the relative growth in Japan since 1985 can be attributed to the strengthening of the yen after the Plaza Accord of 1985.

Figure 2 displays a time series of relative output in manufacturing in Japan

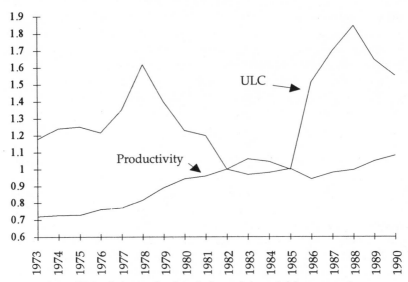

FIG. 1. Japan/U.S. relative productivity index and the unit labor cost ratio

and the United States.[5] Japanese output increased steadily faster than that of
the United States over the period in question, and by 1990 Japanese output had
increased by approximately 25 percent more than the United States from the
base year of 1982.

Figure 3 shows the portfolio and foreign direct investment flows from Japan
to the United States as a percentage of GNP of the United States. While portfolio
investment flows were highly volatile over the period (with a marked increase
in inflows from 1983 to 1988 and substantial disinvestment in 1989), flows of
FDI on the other hand have been on the rise since 1982.

The following regression was run in order to ascertain the correlation between Japanese foreign direct investment flows and the manufacturing fundamentals of the Japanese economy relative to those of the United States. The
dependent variable is the ratio of Japanese direct investment in the United
States and U.S. GNP. This was regressed on the output ratio, productivity ratio,
unit labor cost ratio, the Japanese domestic savings-investment balance, the
ratio of high-tech balance of payments between Japan and the United States,[6]
and the real exchange rate.

Some of the proxies for the fundamental variables were lagged three years in
order to represent their long-term nature as determinants of FDI. These are
the productivity ratio, output ratio, and Japanese savings-investment balance.
The length of the lag was set somewhat arbitrarily though the results are robust
to changes in the lag from two to five years, with the exception of the output
ratio which loses significance at different lags. These variables combine to

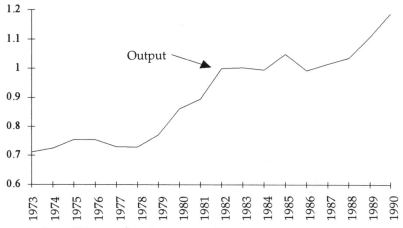

FIG. 2. Japan/U.S. manufacturing output ratio

represent a proxy of economic strength rather than incentives to invest abroad. If the lags were set shorter than three, the distinction between incentives and proxies of strength would become less evident. In the case of the savings-investment balance the lag is assumed to be long enough to insure exogeneity.

Unit labor costs are lagged one year as they are assumed to represent a financial incentive to invest abroad rather than a symptom of economic strength. Japanese costs are measured in dollars in calculating this ratio. A proxy for relative technological strength at the time of investment is the ratio of high-tech balance of payments deflated by the GDP deflators and the real exchange rate expressed in yen per dollar. Balance of payment accounting implies endogeneity of this variable; however, it is assumed that as there are many items included in balance of payment accounting, it is possible that fluctuations in FDI will not affect the technology balance of payments in the same period. Due to possible endogeneity of these variables, a Hausman specification test was performed and endogeneity was rejected in each case.[7]

The regression was performed using data of the 1973–89 period for two main reasons: Japanese FDI in the United States before 1973 was relatively small and consistent data for all the independent variables are not available after 1989.[8] Table 1 presents the results.

The signs on the productivity, output, and savings-investment coefficients are all positive.[9] Thus, these results are consistent with the notion that the relative performance of the two economies should be considered in addition to financial incentives when examining FDI flows. The sign on the unit labor cost ratio coefficient is also positive. This demonstrates the importance of relative cost as an impetus to invest. As labor costs increased in Japan relative

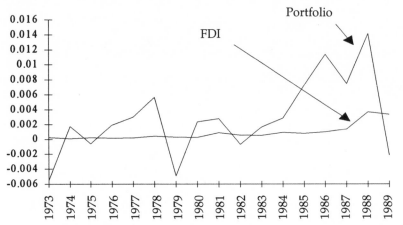

FIG. 3. Japanese portfolio and direct investment in the United States as percentage of
U.S. GNP

to those in the United States, Japanese firms took advantage of this incentive.
The real exchange rate coefficient is insignificant but is the correct sign.[10]

Financial incentives are important when considering FDI flows between
Japan and the United States. The cost-lowering benefits of FDI clearly played
a key role in determining the timing of the outflow of investment from Japan.
However, the fundamentals add valuable information as they provide a picture
of the events leading up to those of the 1980s. Changes in the relative fundamentals put Japanese firms in the position to invest and take advantage of the
financial incentives afforded by the market. This is to say that we must keep
firmly in mind the fact that the fundamentals—Japan's strong productivity
growth, the rapid increase in the output of its manufacturing industries, and
the continued high saving rate—do matter along with Japan's macroeconomic
policy in explaining the magnitude of Japan's direct investment in the United
States.

A caveat that I must mention here is that, given its goals, the remainder of
this chapter discusses macroeconomic policy, trade, exchange rate, capital flow,
and the like focusing on the United States, Japan, and bilateral relations. The
more desirable exposition that would also examine bilateral relations in a global
context is not attempted.

II. U.S. MACROECONOMIC POLICY

Most will agree with scholars of the theory of hegemonic stability that, in the
1960s, the United States was a hegemon playing the central role in maintaining
the Bretton Woods system. The economic power of the United States was

TABLE 1
Regression Results

Dependent Variables	Coefficient
Output ratio, Japan/U.S. (lagged three years)	0.00955
	(2.20)
Productivity ratio, Japan/U.S. (lagged three years)	0.00277
	(1.75)
Savings-investment, Japan (lagged three years)	0.0306
	(2.93)
Unit labor cost ratio, Japan/U.S. (lagged one year)	0.00183
	(2.26)
Technology balance of payments, Japan/U.S.	0.00789
	(1.36)
Real exchange rate	−0.000006
	(1.05)
Constant	−0.0028
	(1.00)

NOTE: The numbers in parentheses are t-ratios, DF=10. Durbin-Watson Statistic=2.09024; adjusted R^2=0.8108.

predominant in virtually all dimensions, and the roles it played, for example, in the Kennedy Round (1962–67), as well as in many other international trade regimes, attest to the yet strong hegemonic status of the United States.

However, at the same time, what could not be denied was the fact that even in this decade "absorption" was steadily rising; the pace of increase was even more rapid if the meaning of the term "absorption" was expanded to include that made by American forces abroad (net military transaction). Thus, that the United States was "overabsorbing" was becoming increasingly evident, as its basic balance deteriorated as a trend from $−1.138 billion in 1960 to $−3.891 billion in 1970 despite the positive, if declining, trade balance and a still relatively large net income investment which rose from $3.378 billion in 1960 to $6.233 billion in 1970.[11]

Of course, in the Bretton Woods system, continuing "overabsorption" of this magnitude in the 1960s posed no serious problem to the international trade regime. Rather, it was seen as a necessary course that the hegemon of the system had to follow to perform the role of the sole provider of international liquidity. That is, the United States was permitted to finance its deficit in the basic balance of payments by creating more credit at home and exporting it. This meant that increased credit provided demand at home without commensurate saving, and exporting dollars was amply justified to create the needed liquidity abroad. But the United States indulged in this justification and continued to export dollars; a result was the increasing trend toward inflation in Europe during the 1960s. This was why de Gaulle already in 1965 was expressing his sharp criticism against what he believed was the fundamentally unstable and "exploitative" character of the Bretton Woods system.[12]

The United States did try to slow the outflow of capital by controlling corporate investment abroad. But, bent on achieving rapid growth, neither President Kennedy nor President Johnson pushed for the sufficiently high interest rates that could have achieved the purpose much more effectively. Instead, to mitigate the trade deficit, Americans chose to apply political pressure to Germany and Japan, the largest surplus earners who had the most to gain by being cooperative "supporters." Thus, credit creation—the hegemonic easy money strategy—by the United States continued throughout the 1960s.

Kennedy's neo-Keynesian advisers popularized and managed to "sell" to the president and the Democratic Congress the idea of a full-employment budget (anticipating what tax revenue would be if full employment were attained) which took the form of the tax cut of 1964. The budget seemed to realize its goal at least partially but only at the cost of the rising prices that began in 1965. Then Johnson chose to wage the War on Poverty and the Vietnam War without increasing taxes. A necessary consequence was inflation, and it grew increasingly evident that the dollar was steadily becoming overvalued.[13] Although "benignly neglected" by the United States, the strong dollar of course was the reason the exporting "supporters" were willing to take a little political pressure from Washington. But, finally, in 1968, the last year of the Johnson administration, when prices climbed faster and the current account surplus shrank to less than one-quarter of the preceding year (from $2.59 billion to $590 million), tight monetary and fiscal policies (including a temporary surcharge to raise tax revenues) were adopted abruptly. The result was a recession which enabled Nixon to capture the White House.

The productivity gap between the hegemon and the supporters narrowed steadily during the 1960s because of American exports of capital and technology, inflation creating an uncertain climate for vigorous investment, a continuing high level of absorption (including hegemonic military expenditures) relative to saving, and the inevitability of the followers (and especially developmentalist Japan) catching up with the technological leader in the maturation phase of the twentieth-century paradigm. For example, the index (1982 as the base year) of output per person employed in manufacturing industries rose between 1960 and 1970 by 18.7 for the United States as against 33.6 for Japan.[14]

In addition to facing the task of extricating the United States from the Vietnam War, Nixon found in 1968 an economy in recession, an overvalued dollar, the declining competitiveness of American industries, and a pool of liquidity posed for inflation. The hegemon had been seriously weakened. The temporary tax increase of 1968 had lapsed by 1970, and a painful fiscal squeeze had begun. For reasons of bracket creep, any tax increase would be extremely costly politically, but the fiscal burden of the Great Society program, especially that of Medicare, was growing rapidly. Demographic change was adding to the costs of education and pensions as did Nixon's new Federalism which put some of its costs on the federal budget. Keeping an eye on the Congressional election of 1970, Nixon abandoned deflation and by 1971 the fiscal deficit along with prices began to rise sharply. That is, the deficit which stood at 0.3 percent of GNP in 1969 rose to 2.2 and 2.0 percent in 1970 and 1971, and the CPI was rising at 6 percent in 1971.[15]

This was the background against which a run on the dollar began, forcing Nixon to adopt his "New Economic Policy" on August 15, 1971 which suspended the convertability of the dollar to gold indefinitely, added a surcharge of 10 percent on about half of imports, levied new taxes, and rolled back expenditures and froze prices and wages for 90 days. Nixon made devaluing the dollar sound like a victory. He argued that the United States was not abandoning the Bretton Woods system because of American economic weakness (due to continued overabsorption while its productivity was rising more slowly than that of its trading partners) but to make the free-loading allies, especially Japan, pay their share. The dollar declined gradually but steadily and, as a result, exports rose during the next few years, turning the current account deficit into a surplus beginning in 1973. Thus, the Nixon plan seemed to work for a while. Devaluing the dollar pleased exporters and floating dollars relieved banks and others from controls on investment abroad.

But the Nixon program of devaluation was not accompanied by deflation. It was a cosmetic act. The economy did not deflate, and absorption (including only marginally reduced military expenditures) remained untamed; imports, now more expensive, continued to flow in; and prices rose, offsetting much of the deflationary effect of devaluation. Of course, inflation was also fostered because of the large fiscal stimulus injected into the economy by Nixon to help recapture the White House (Tufte 1978).

The increasing expenditures for all the reasons just noted had kept the federal deficits large both in 1971 and 1972 as already noted. In the latter year when the presidential election was over the wage-price control came off and the price level again rose sharply. But Nixon maintained an easy money policy; monetary restraint in 1973 was an exception forced by the fact that the CPI that year was rising at 8.7 percent.

Nixon's America was realizing the hegemonic seigniorage exploiting the special international privilege of being a printer of dollars (and being able to supply much of the raw materials and food it needed). Had other nations done the same, i.e., continued to devalue and consume, inflation would have risen very rapidly due to the import of increasingly expensive goods. Nixon's America in short was exploiting a comparative advantage in a beggar-thy-neighbor policy. Japan, like European nations, was not able to retaliate. Had they bought dollars to support its value, they would have been importing inflation; if they did not and the dollar fell, their exports suffered and this would have been the case especially for the increasingly high value-added products for which the United States was the major market. Given this fact and because Japan still depended on the United States for defense, Japan chose to import inflation and continue to export its products. This was the bargain between the United States and Japan (and Europe) that enabled the Bretton Woods system to last as long as it did. But by 1971 the bargain could no longer help the system to withstand its fundamental dilemma and the system had to end when Nixon "delinked" the dollar from gold.

Thus, Joanne Gowa's analysis is accurate when she concludes that the United States chose to destroy the Bretton Woods system in order to increase its political and economic freedom of action (Gowa 1983). Gilpin's words summarizing the reasons for the demise of the system are apposite here:

> The growing power of Western Europe and Japan was threatening to place restraints on American autonomy, because the vast holdings of dollars by Europeans and Japanese meant that if the dollar were to hold its value and the dollar-exchange system was to be preserved, the American policy would have to conform to their wishes. Rather than see its autonomy curbed, the United States chose to abandon the system. (Gilpin 1987, 140–41)

Nixon's strategy, which could only be a short-run strategy supported by inflation and a mounting deficit, was essentially continued by Presidents Ford and Carter for the remainder of the decade. When Europeans and Japanese complained that Carter was continuing the Nixon strategy of beggar-thy-neighbor devaluation of the dollar, his administration suggested the "locomotive theory." Simply put, the theory demanded, in terms of the hegemon-supporter bargain, that supporters stimulate their respective economies instead of letting the United States do all the work of "absorbing" in the post-oil crisis global recession. Inflation-phobic Germans complied grudgingly but Japanese were more obliging. They were eager to export more to the United States to buoy their economy out of the post-"oil shock" recession and stay the course of their developmentalism.

As evident in the large fiscal deficit, the weakening dollar, and the fundamentals (especially in contrast to those of the supporters), the hegemon was further weakened throughout the 1970s because it lived beyond its means by financing its debt by inflation. By 1979—the year of the second oil crisis, brought on by OPEC attempting to recoup its loss due to a decline in dollar-denominated oil revenue—the inflation rate in the United States reached 13.3

percent and the price of gold hovered around $875 per ounce. Some economists began to seriously discuss the possibility of the hard landing of the dollar.

Against this backdrop, Carter appointed Paul Volcker to the Fed. He immediately adopted a stringent monetary policy, reducing the double-digit growth rate of the money supply of most of the 1970s to a mere 4.5 percent. Volcker's goal was to wring inflationary liquidity out of the economy and bring about stability in prices and try to achieve balances in the budget and trade accounts. Volcker's surgery caused real interest rates to climb sharply from 1.6 percent in 1979 to 2.5 percent in 1980 and 4.5 percent in 1981.[16] The result was predictable. A recession ensued and it, as was the case at the end of 1960s, changed the occupant of the White House.

These events of the 1960s and 1970s determined Reagan's rhetoric and macroeconomic policy, thus their political and economic consequences. Reagan's rhetoric or ideology was necessary to justify the Reaganomics that produced the twin deficits (and the large capital inflow especially from Japan), distributional consequences, and the weakening of the fundamentals of the economy. To justify the rhetoric and Reaganomics, he claimed that he had "the conservative mandate." But in reality, he had no such mandate (as I endeavor to show below). Instead, his rhetoric and economics were an anodyne administered by Reagan for himself, and to the Congress and the electorate to minimize the pains of trading yet more of the remaining responsibilities of a hegemon and of justifying American efforts to maintain or increase absorption without matching savings and exploiting the privileges of the hegemon. Reagan's neoliberal rhetoric and the supply-side economics which James Tobin dismissed as "fraudulent economic programs" of a "simplistic ideologue" (Tobin 1988, 103) were no less and no more than the last hurrah of the hegemon who once shouldered the burden of the Bretton Woods system but who had become too weak and even predatory.

An examination of the carefully crafted, detailed quantitative analyses of the 1980 and 1984 presidential elections that were made by many political scientists clearly demonstrates that Reagan cannot claim to have had a "conservative mandate." What these careful studies show is the following. The most important determinant of the election outcomes of 1980 and 1984 was "the electoral fortune," how the economy, as measured by unemployment and changes in the purchasing power of wages, was doing just before and at the time of the election. "The difference in the electoral outcome for Carter and Reagan in 1980 is not really how much they increased consumer purchasing power or reduced unemployment but when" and "Mondale lost [in 1984] because the economy was booming, unemployment was falling, inflation was under control, and Ronald Reagan was president" (Chubb and Peterson 1985, 71, 73). Indeed, these scholarly findings demonstrate virtually in unison that the economic conditions just before or at the time of election mattered more (followed by party affiliation) in deciding the outcome than many other factors (Markus 1982).

Even in the 1980 election which was much closer than the one in 1984, Carter lost because he did not have "electoral fortune" despite the fact that he had advantages over Reagan in personal qualifications and in non-economic (e.g., human rights) issues. The election outcome substantially depended on the economic conditions and only "minimally" on "the Reagan mystique" (Miller and Shanks 1982, 351–52). That is, in the words of a report issued by the 1980 National Election Survey Panel of the *American Political Science Review,* "the analysis yields support for the retrospective voting model and provides no evidence for the contention that Reagan's victory was the result of his policy or ideological positions," thus "there is no evidence at all to argue" that "Reagan's victory represented a mandate" for his ideology or policy (Markus 1982, 538, 558). Without the benefit of these studies, then speaker of the House Thomas O'Neill was also aware of this fact as evidenced in the following wry observation he made just after the Economic Recovery Tax Act of 1981 passed the Congress: "The record shows there was no mandate, but Congress thinks there is one and is acting in that manner" (Greider 1981, 30). In support of the arguments of this chapter, I need to add only the following on Reagan macroeconomic policy and its macroeconomic consequences as both are already extensively documented and debated.[17]

During the 1981–85 period, the policy was tight money and loose fiscal policy. The rhetoric justifying the policy was to get rid of excess liquidity and create a smaller government, i.e., stop the rising trend of taxes and trim expenditures. Based on supply-side "economics," the policy was to reduce inflation and taxes while increasing investment, employment, and income in due course. The policy appealed to voters, especially those in the middle class, who had seen their taxes rise and income stagnate during the Nixon-Ford-Carter years of easy money and inflation.[18] Thus even the Democratic Congress voted for the Economic Recovery Tax Act of 1981.

However, what ensued differed from the rosy scenario envisioned by the Reagan administration. The tax reduction did stop the rising trend[19] but when the increased state and local taxes were also considered, the total tax burden rose instead of declining during the same four-year period (32.2 to 32.5 percent of net national product) (Tax Foundation 1990). And, the promised trimming of federal expenditures failed to materialize because of the significant increase in defense expenditures and a steady rise in entitlement and interest outlays. The result was increased federal expenditure and a rapidly increasing federal deficit. While the former rose from 22.1 percent of GNP in 1980 to 24.3 of GNP by 1983 and 23.1 in 1984 and 23.9 in 1985, the latter climbed from 2.6 percent of GNP to 4.1 in 1982, 6.3 in 1983, 5.0 in 1984, and 5.4 in 1985 (U.S. Government 1992, Part Seven, 15). The burgeoning deficit brought the Reagan boom of these years. Americans were now absorbing even more than before under the new label of Reaganomics.

Of course, by pursuing a tight monetary policy and financing absorption by debt instead of inflation, a necessary result was a rapid increase in borrowing from foreigners, especially from the Japanese, who found the high interest rates in the United States attractive. (The Japanese had their own additional reasons as will be discussed in the next section.) But the prosperity financed by foreign debt—the prosperity that enabled Reagan to defeat Mondale handily in 1984— could not but lead to serious overvaluation of the dollar. Based on the IMF index, the value of the dollar rose by 28.2 percent against the average index of the major currencies. The dollar that was worth ¥220 in 1981 bought ¥244 by early 1985. American exports declined and cheaper imports rose sharply. The American current account balance that was $1.2 billion in surplus in 1980 deteriorated very rapidly and steadily to record a deficit of $122.2 billion—3 percent of GNP—in 1985. Japan, playing a major role in this development, tripled its trade surplus against the United States from $13.6 billion in 1981 to $39.5 billion by 1985.

Again, predictable results followed. Many Americans, including those managing the industries facing increasingly potent competition from foreign firms taking advantage of their weaker currencies, chose to invest in the service sector, real estate, and tax-sheltered investments. And, others, often on borrowed funds, chose to engage in mergers and acquisitions of firms more to reap quick financial reward than to increase the productive capacity and efficiency of the firms they absorbed or acquired. The 1980s thus became well known for financial manipulations and instability as typified by the acquisitions and mergers relying on "junk bonds" and by the failure of Continental Illinois, a large regional bank, in 1984.

The call for protectionism increased. Even Reagan was forced, for example, to impose voluntary export restraints on Japanese steel and automobiles in 1981 and to begin the U.S.-Japan High Technology Group negotiations (which led to the 1986 agreement on the American market share in the semiconductor market of Japan). Reacting to the seemingly rising tide of protectionism in the United States and the pressure directed against Japan, the latter issued in October 1985 the so-called Maekawa Report which promised greater efforts to liberalize trade and to stimulate domestic demand.[20] But with the rising fiscal debt and high value of the dollar, balance of payments rapidly and steadily deteriorated as noted above. The boasts of the Reagan administration officials that the high value of the dollar reflected the strength of the American economy sounded increasing hollow.

Numerous other problems were being created by the deficit-financed boom of the 1982–85 period. For example, the net saving rate (as a proportion of national income calculated on the OECD basis) in these years hovered between

2.2 and 4.3 percent (in contrast to the 8 to 11 percent range of a decade earlier), the index of real hourly compensation remained stagnant (ranging between 98.1 and 99.5 in comparison to 100 in 1982), and the unemployment rate never fell below 6.5 percent even though real before-tax average hourly and weekly earnings continued to decline.[21] The boom was on borrowed time and money.

As 1985 proceeded, the risks of the financial crisis presaged by the failure of Continental Illinois were becoming real. Faced with the crisis and the evident signs of weakening in the major economic indicators, the Fed relented and eased the money supply. But this only encouraged speculative booms, corporate take-overs, and increases in consumption. (The net saving rate of 3.32 percent in 1985 continued to decline to 2.20 percent in 1986 and 2.08 percent in 1987.) Inflation still did not pose a problem thanks to the high dollar (i.e., cheap imports) and to the level of investment in manufacturing that remained far from robust (private gross fixed capital formation as a proportion of national income steadily declined from 17.66 percent in 1985 to 16.66 in 1987). In short, "the macroeconomic record of Reaganomics" in 1985 was "not good" because "almost all major macroeconomic indicators other than inflation have shown a deterioration" (Branson 1987, 51).

This was the reason for the Plaza Accord among the G5 in the fall of 1985 to bring about a coordinated lowering of the value of the dollar. Aided also by monetary and fiscal policies adopted by the Japanese as will be discussed below, the dollar's value fell very rapidly from ¥244 at the time of the accord to ¥153 by the summer of 1986.[22]

By most indicators, the U.S. economy continued to slump. Despite the weakened dollar, the balance of payments deteriorated further, the trade deficit reached $105.7 billion, and the current account balance was −$142 billion in 1986. But the weaker dollar was now adding the risks of inflation, and thus interest rates, which had been showing signs of moderating, began to be raised. However, at the same time, the budget deficit was refusing to decline. In 1986, it stood at $212.6 billion, even more than the highest nominal level ever, $212.2 billion, that had been reached in 1985.

This was because the borrowing from abroad was continuing to rise and the total burden of interest was continuing to mount both to government (federal and local) and private firms. By the end of 1986, the ratio of overall debt, private and public, reached a level seen just before the Crash of 1929 (Cleveland 1990, 165–66). It was difficult to maintain confidence in the dollar. But with the governments of the major industrial nations cooperating based on agreements made at the Louvre in February 1987, the dollar now hovered around the ¥140–150 range. One result was that Japanese exports to the United States of manufactured products that had become competitive at the ¥120 level (as frequently stated by the executives of Japanese automobile and electronics firms) continued to increase. Japan's trade surplus against the United States rose to $51.4 billion in 1986 from $39.5 billion the preceding year.

Then, because of the conditions in the financial markets already noted, Black Monday came in October 1987, forcing the United States to ease its monetary policy and to maintain the reduced interest rates to March 1988. A result was a weakening of the dollar to around ¥120 (and at times even higher during late 1987 and in the early months of 1988). But Japanese exports continued to increase. The trade surplus which stood at $56 billion in 1985 rose to $92.8 billion in 1986 and kept on rising to $96.4 billion in 1987 and remained at $95.0 billion in 1988. The American share of Japanese exports did decline during these years. But, despite the sharp rise in the yen, the United States was still importing 33.8 percent of total Japanese exports in 1988. This sent many economists scrambling for explanations (as will be discussed in the following subsection).

An important reason for the firmness of the yen was the very large American federal deficit still in excess of 3.0 percent of GNP and Japan's large capital exports to the United States. Following a tightening of the monetary policy in March 1988 by the monetary authority, which feared inflation due in part to the weak dollar and was concerned with the need to maintain the inflow of capital, the dollar firmed into the spring of 1989. But, as the federal deficit remained at such a high level, the American current account balance in 1989 still showed a deficit of $106.4 billion.

The debt-fed boom of Reaganomics sputtered on until 1990, aided by increasing exports made possible to a significant extent by the cheaper dollar and by the expansionist policies of Japan and Europe. But by 1990, the American economy was in a recession brought on by several factors, including a further weakening of investment, a debt crisis throughout the economy, and the faltering of the Japanese and European economies. With the dismal record of the Bush years—the GDP recording an average growth rate of 2.2 percent, the hourly wage level failing to rise at all, while the rate of unemployment exceeded 7 percent—and the cumulative effects that Reagan policies had on income distribution, Bush's "electoral fortune" dictated the outcome of the presidential election of 1992.

The hegemon's "last hurrah" indulged in by Reagan's United States, it should be emphasized, enabled the nation to overabsorb more than in the preceding decades and the absorption was financed by debt, an increasing proportion of which was held by foreigners. In constant dollars, the federal expenditures, which had risen by 35 and 36 percent respectively in the 1960s and the 1970s from the preceding decade, rose in the 1980s by 41 percent from that in the 1970s. This was financed by the large fiscal debt which caused foreign portfolio investment in the United States to exceed American portfolio investment abroad in 1985 and caused the United States to become a net international debtor in 1987. And, as we see below, Japan, a major supporter, played a principal role in making this hegemonic debt-financed overabsorption possible for reasons of its own.

III. JAPANESE MACROECONOMIC POLICY

As in the case of the United States, what occurred in the Japanese economy in the 1980s, including the "bubble" and large capital exports to the United States and elsewhere, can only be better understood when seen as the last hurrah of the policy course that postwar Japan as a developmentalist-supporter had pursued since 1945 and especially in the preceding two decades.

Even with the recessions of 1961, 1964, and 1967 that were caused by tight monetary policy adopted to reduce a mounting trade deficit (resulting from rapid growth dependent on import of raw materials and capital goods), Japan achieved a high real annual growth rate in excess of 10 percent during the 1960s. Few knowledgeable analysts dispute the fact that this growth performance was made possible by a combination of several reasons including: effective entrepreneurial responses to market signals both at home and abroad in the trade-promoting Bretton Woods system; various efficiency-increasing institutions and practices of firms (e.g., management-labor cooperation); and Japan's developmentalist policies, institutions, and practices. The last, which have been well documented, included direct and indirect subsidies that took the forms of loans at below-market rates, various forms of assistance to R&D, de jure and de facto cartels to enable firms to invest in new technology ahead of demand, the fixed exchange rate at ¥360 to a dollar, various prosaving policies, a small government, "administrative guidance," and other policies and practices. Also, that Japan, benefiting from the American nuclear umbrella, spent less than one percent of GNP for defense must not be forgotten.[23]

To keep the discussion of the importance of the hegemon-supporter bargain for Japan's economic performance in perspective, we need of course to be reminded that government involvement even in the forms of sanctioning de facto or de jure cartels did not limit competition except for a short period. Even while price cartels were in effect, competition for market share continued by offering better and more diversified products and by providing better services, more reliable deliveries, etc.[24] An outcome of such a competition was a steady increase in the international competitiveness of Japan's manufacturing industries. Indeed, principally because of rapidly increasing productivity, the WPI rose appreciably less than did the CPI which was rising moderately. This fact and the rapidly increasing output meant that the relatively rapid pace of increase in the money supply, needed to maintain the rapid pace of the investment race by firms adopting new technology, could be continued. But, as Japan's exports continued to increase rapidly aided by increase in productivity and the overvaluation of the dollar as noted in the preceding section, the persistent trade deficit turned to a steady trade surplus as the decade neared its end. Thus, by 1969, a tight money policy had to be adopted for the first time, not to reduce imports but to curb inflation.

As the growth performance continued to increase real income (and tax burdens on earned income were not increased and the effective taxes on interest and dividends were reduced to promote saving), the LDP had little difficulty in remaining in power. This was the decade during which developmentalism was continuing to achieve its intended goal with yet minimal political and economic costs. Bureaucracy had little difficulty in selecting industries to "target," and firms were eager to follow the guidance of ministries in exchange for the various benefits the targeted industries received. Thus, to characterize this economy that was successfully pursuing its developmentalist policy as Japan Inc. was to capture significant aspects of the realities of the Japanese political economy in the decade.

The picture changed significantly in the 1970s. The decade began with the first major jolt to the hegemon-supporter bargain: the adoption in 1971 of the New Economic Policy by Nixon, or "the Nixon shock" as the Japanese called it. Other shocks and unwelcome developments followed in succession: the Smithsonian system of ¥308 (from December 1971 to February 1973) that made the bargain a little less attractive, the oil "shock" of 1973 that triggered the major recession of 1974–77, the second oil "shock" of 1979, and a rapid increase in the budget deficit throughout the decade (for reasons discussed below). The costs of developmentalism, appearing in forms ranging from escalating trade conflicts to political corruption, also became increasingly obvious as the decade progressed. All of the preceding are deserving of the following elaboration as they shaped the macroeconomic policy of Japan of this decade and the developments of the 1980s.

Even though some Japanese economists suggested in July 1971 a "crawling peg" to revalue the yen because of the trade surplus that had been growing steadily during the three preceding years (making a cumulative current surplus of the current balance for 1968–71 just about $10 billion, of which $4.2 billion was against the United States), their suggestion remained unheeded. This was not surprising because Japan's political leaders and monetary authority had shown little reaction to the facts that the Deutschemark had gone to the float in May 1971 and that many influential voices in the American Congress had been since 1969 demanding currency realignment.

Thus, the Nixon policy came as a "shock." The reaction of Japan (motivated in part to minimize the deflationary effects of revaluation on the economy that was just then in a recession) was to increase the money supply and to adopt import liberalization measures (further reductions in tariffs, efforts to reduce non-tariff barriers, and the like).

To explain why Japan demonstrated these reactions instead of revaluing the yen, Yutaka Kosai considered three possible explanations: such reactions were rational (i.e., concern for deflationary effects);[25] the bureaucracy, given its "code of behavior," was unwilling to venture into the new world of a revalued yen; and bureaucratic sectionalism prevented them from taking necessary action (Kosai 1981, 179–81).

None of these answers is satisfactory in that a simple and obvious answer, I argue, is the incentives that both the LDP and the bureaucracy had in keeping the yen undervalued and in responding to the Nixon policy by offering short-run palliatives of increased money supply and opening Japanese markets a little more. For the LDP, the growth maintained by increasing exports was crucial in enabling it to remain in power, and for the bureaucracy, continuing to preserve the bargain could assure its turf and power. Thus, currency adjustment was to be postponed as long as possible even if it meant, as indeed was the case, more "administrative guidance" by the ministries became necessary to scrutinize exports, promote imports, and suppress price increases (Kosai 1981, 182). Seen in this light, Prime Minister Tanaka's plan to Rebuild the Japanese Archipelago, accompanied with a rapid increase in the money supply, too played a part in keeping the bargain as his plan helped to inflate the economy visibly.

From the summer of 1971 on and with Tanaka's desire to expand public works, the budget expanded, interest rates fell, and more government bonds were issued (to cover budget shortfalls and increasing costs of welfare programs as will be discussed below) into 1973. An important part of the justification for this fiscal and monetary expansion was its contribution to a reduction in the trade surplus.

By 1972, the rate of increase in the money supply had reached 24.7 percent (following 24.3 percent in the preceding year), land prices were rising at the rate of 25 percent, and the CPI was rising at 11.8 percent. Such developments in a full-employment economy could not but lead to excess demand. Visible shortages, thus further momentum to price increases, were occurring by the late summer of 1972 in textile products, steel, cement, and chemical products. For Japan, the counterpart of the American stop-go monetary policy (necessitated by an increasing burden of debt) was a periodic "adjustment inflation" to stimulate aggregate demand because for a developmentalist-supporter it was a necessary policy that had to be adopted. Put differently (and restating the preceding criticism of the explanations Kosai offered), Japan, in its effort to continue to benefit from the hegemon-supporter bargain, was finding that it too was bound by the "law" that Hume and Ricardo had found long ago: within a fixed exchange rate regime, if a nation cannot reduce its trade surplus even after expanding aggregate demand and reaching full employment, then inflation is the only way to a balance of payment equilibrium.

A *coup de grace* was administered to Japan in the midst of this discovery. The first oil "shock" of 1973 came, quadrupling oil prices. Prices rose sharply. The rate of increase in the WPI doubled (from 15.9 to 31.3 percent) and the CPI increased even faster (from 11.8 to 24.3 percent) between 1972 and 1973. The government had no choice but to put on price controls and sharply tighten monetary policy.

Though moderated, inflation persisted into 1974. While the WPI now rose only 3.0 percent, the CPI was still climbing at an 11.9 percent rate because of the accumulated excess liquidity and shortages. Then a political development intervened. The LDP was badly upset in May 1974, losing a majority for the first time in the Upper House election.

Because of the declines, in real terms, in investment, housing construction, and government consumption, Japan now faced a post-oil crisis recession (GNP for 1974 recorded the first negative growth in the postwar period of −1.8 percent in 1965 prices). The budget deficit steadily increased because of increasing welfare expenditures (discussed below) and the government's inability to raise public utility fees (which had been planned) because of the political setback and the recession. Thus, inflation continued at the rate of 10.4 percent in 1975, 9.4 percent in 1976, and 8.6 percent in 1977 while the real growth rate remained significantly less than that Japan had become accustomed to before the oil crisis, i.e., 3.4 percent in 1975, 5.7 percent in 1976, and 5.1 percent in 1977.

The stagflation of these years in Japan was mild in comparison to that in the Western industrial economies for two principal reasons. One was firms' efforts to "slim down" by reducing employment and making more efficient uses of productive capacities and energy (especially petroleum) as has been well documented.[26] The other was the increase in exports, as was the case in the recessions of the 1960s. Exports began to expand swiftly from the beginning of 1976 as seen in the fact that the current balance that was a mere $100 million in surplus in 1975 rose rapidly to $4.6 billion in 1976, and escalated to $13.9 billion in 1977 and remained at $11.8 billion in 1978. International, especially American, criticisms were heard again against Japan's exporting recession. This of course was the reason for Japan's obliging response to the "locomotive theory" noted earlier.

In understanding the political-economic development of Japan in this decade and because it plays an important role in the macroeconomic relations between the United States and Japan in the 1980s, this review of the 1970s must also include the following observation on the steady increase in the budget deficit of the decade due to the burgeoning social welfare expenditure unaccompanied by tax increases. That is, mainly for political reasons (the declining trend in the LDP's share of votes and seats in the late 1960s and such developments as the political setback of 1974 noted above), the LDP government increased expenditures on various "safety nets" beginning in 1971; these expenditures continued to rise steadily through the recession of 1974–77 and to the end of the decade.[27] The result was a rapid increase in the dependency ratio—expenditures covered by the issuance of deficit bonds—from 12.4 percent in 1971 to well over 30 percent in several years later in the decade (with a maximum of 39.6 percent in 1979) and an increasingly large total bonds outstanding. As a proportion of GNP, bonds issued in 1971 were only 0.23 percent but rose to 6.55 percent in 1978 and 7.04 percent in 1980. To add perspective, I note here that even in 1983 at the height of the Reagan deficit, the same ratio for the United States was 5.95 percent (for both countries, the proportion is calculated using the 1985 GNP deflator of each country).

Japan had managed to put the 1974–77 recession behind it, thanks to increasing exports, and had begun to show signs of renewed growth performance. However, it then encountered an *endaka* (high yen) recession from mid-1977 to 1980 that caused Japan to record a current account deficit of $8.69 billion in 1979 and $10.75 billion in 1980. The latter figure was larger than that reached in 1974 ($4.72 billion) following the first oil crisis. The yen rose during the 21 months between January 1977 and October 1978 from ¥293 to ¥176 or by 66.5 percent for a combination of interrelated reasons. The primary reason, however, was the sharply decreasing confidence in the dollar, reflecting such economic malaises of the United States of the Carter years as evidenced in the rapid inflation rate in excess of 10 percent, the widely fluctuating prime rate at times exceeding 20 percent, and the rate of increase in consumption that was almost double the rate of increase in the income of households (both in real terms). Also, 1977 was the first year the American trade balance of goods (exclusive of services) recorded a deficit in double digits; it rose from −$9.47 billion in 1976 to −$31.11 billion (and remained in double-digit deficit until the triple-digit deficit era began in 1984).

Among other reasons for the rapid increase in the yen, the following two are noteworthy. One was that there was during these years a demand for yen-denominated assets by foreigners wishing to realize arbitrage gains. The reason for this was that, as Ito has carefully analyzed, the yen had not yet reached a "covered interest parity" because of the various remaining restrictions on flow of capital into and out of Japan (Ito 1986). And, the other was that Japan's monetary authority adopted a half-hearted, thus less than effective, "leaning against the wind policy" of buying dollars (selling yen) from mid-1977 to late 1978 when the yen was appreciating and helped to cause the yen to reach, as noted above, ¥176 in October 1978, the highest ever to that date.[28]

Reflecting on the policies adopted and the developments seen in Japan during the 1970s, one cannot but note that developmentalism is like a huge tanker. Because of its size and momentum, it cannot easily change its direction and stopping it requires a long time. To be sure, developmentalist involvement by the state was being reduced during the decade, but it was proceeding slowly and only to a limited extent prompted in large part by foreign (read American) pressure. While, for example, Japanese markets continued to be liberalized (e.g., tariff reductions), the expenditure patterns of the Fiscal Investment and Loan Program (FILP) administered by the Ministry of Finance (MOF) were allocating more funds for housing and public amenities and fewer to aid industries, and direct subsidies to industries declined significantly, much remained little changed. As evidenced in the administrative guidance issued by the Ministry of International Trade and Industry (MITI) to petroleum refiners and distributors following the oil crisis, the ministry remained involved in "guiding" prices. Financial institutions remained "protected" by numerous regulations issued by MOF. Various ministries continued to require a large number of licenses and permits which in effect protected the interests of producers over those of consumers. And, even when policies were being moderated, there was little change in developmentalism, which had become a dense web of relationships maintained between bureaucracy and industries and between politicians and bureaucracy. Cooperation of many types fostered in the name of developmentalist growth performance often became collusion (e.g., cartels) and at times outright corruption (such as that which ended the political life of Prime Minister Tanaka).[29]

By the end of the decade, Japan had emerged as a super-economic power saddled with a large accumulated budget deficit and the increasing political and economic costs of its developmentalism. During the decade, the benefits of being a supporter seemed to have diminished as the hegemon, now mired in serious inflation—the wage of the overabsorption of the preceding decades— was much less able to maintain the value of the dollar and the buoyancy of Japan's largest export market.

The *endaka* recession lasted well into 1980 but the economy began to recover and was growing, if at a significantly reduced rate of 3.5 percent. The current account turned to a modest surplus of $4.77 billion in 1981 and $6.85 billion in 1982. But as the Reagan deficit began to mount, the dollar continued to be overvalued, thus causing the yen to decline from ¥226 in 1980 to ¥249 in 1982 and to remain in the high 230s well into 1984. The result was rapidly rising exports, thus the trade surplus of Japan rose very rapidly from $20.79 billion in 1983 to $49.17 billion in 1985. In the latter year, it was equal to 3.6 percent of GNP. The American share of Japanese exports rose from 24.2 to 37.2 between 1981 and 1985. The economy that managed to grow 3.5 percent in 1981 was growing at 5.2 percent by 1985 (in real terms). It appeared that the developmentalist-supporter could now be more sanguine of the benefits of the bargain with the hegemon led by a neoliberal president pursuing a Keynesian policy. The major supporters of the LDP—the exporters of manufactured products— had little doubt of the wisdom of the policy courses taken by the LDP and the American president.

The Reagan boom was, however, costly. The U.S. trade deficit was mush-rooming with Japan as its major culprit. Protectionist demands rose as noted in the preceding section. And its denouement was the Plaza Accord for the reasons already discussed. The yen began to appreciate rapidly; for the period of 28 months following the accord (September 1985 to January 1988), the yen rose from 244 to 121 or by 101.7 percent. Since this rapid appreciation began immediately after domestic business cycles had peaked in June 1986, and the sudden *endaka* of such a magnitude was causing a wave of bankruptcies among export-dependent small and medium-sized firms and industrial investment was slowing perceptibly (to reduce the rate of growth from 12.4 percent in 1985 to 3.0 percent in 1986), Japan reacted by rapidly increasing the money supply.

The official discount rate (5 percent in January 1986) was cut steadily, as noted at the outset of this chapter, to reach the lowest ever rate of 2.5 percent in February 1987, and it remained at that level for 27 months until May 1989. Money supply (M2+CD) rose at the rate of 10.4 in 1987 and 11.2 percent in 1988. The Research Committee of the Institute of Fiscal and Monetary Policy of MOF observed that such monetary easing was undertaken "not only to assuage fears over the business downswing, but also to help satisfy international expectation that Japan do something to expand domestic demand" (Inst. of Fiscal Monetary Policy 1993, 8).

The monetary policy caused spiraling asset prices or the "bubble," the major determinant of the magnitude and pace of capital outflow from Japan in the decade.[30] Since much has been written on the "bubble" and Hamada and Noguchi describe and offer insights on its causes and effects in this volume, I present here only Figure 4, which shows the course of the "bubble" in stock prices, and a succinct summary of the process of, and the main reasons for, the "bubble."[31]

The "bubble" occurred because of the following closely linked and mutually reinforcing developments.

(1) As the money supply continued to increase, reducing the cost of capital, non-financial firms issued large and increasing amounts of stocks, bonds, and warrants. The funds so raised amounted to ¥58 trillion (or approximately $480 billion), a significant part of which was used for "financial engineering" (*zai-tech*) and the remainder for capital investment (causing a rapid increase in gross private capital formation in plant and equipment, i.e., the rate of increase from the level of the preceding year was 14.3, 15.5, and 13.6 percent in 1988, 1989, and 1990 respectively as against 3.0 and 4.8 in 1986 and 1987) (Min. of Finance 1992). "Financial engineering" of this magnitude was motivated by the fact that the returns on bank deposits and assets (both financial and land) yielded higher returns than the cost of raising the funds.[32]

(2) Because many of their major borrowers—large non-financial firms—were raising funds as described above, banks competed to lend to real estate

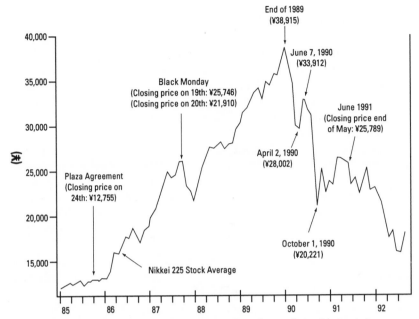

FIG. 4. Trend in stock price (*Source: Tokyo Stock Exchange, "Monthly Statistics Report"*)

firms (and financial institutions specializing in lending to such firms) and small and medium-sized firms. Bank lending to real estate firms, which accounted for only 24 percent (¥16.5 trillion) of the total bank loans in the 1984–85 period, rose to 74 percent (¥40 trillion) by 1990. The same to small and medium-sized firms more than doubled between 1985 and 1990.[33] As Noguchi notes, there is little doubt that a large proportion of the acquisitions of land during this period was made for speculative purposes.[34]

(3) Taking advantage of rapidly rising revenue, "fiscal reconstruction"— reduction in public debt by reducing issuance of deficit bonds and expenditures—was pursued by MOF. The "dependency ratio" dropped from 4.86 percent of GNP in 1985 to 1.58 percent by 1990, reducing the total outstanding government debt by more than 5 points to 38.1 percent of GNP. This of course had the effects of adding liquidity to the economy and reducing the financial instruments available, thus encouraging those engaged in "financial engineering" to compete for other instruments.

(4) The increasing pace of liberalization-internationalization of financial activities which had been accelerated by the enactment of the new Foreign Exchange Control Law in 1980 contributed significantly to the "bubble."[35]

In addition, it is crucial to recall that the super-easy monetary policy was continued (despite the increasing doubt on the desirability of doing so from the domestic perspective) because of the Black Monday of October 1987. The main reason for continuing the easy money policy was that the monetary authority did not wish to tighten the money supply lest it cause a further drop in stock prices in Japan as well as elsewhere. That is, Japan did not wish to cause the value of the dollar to decline further and "trigger a general state of panic worldwide" (Inst. of Fiscal Monetary Policy 1993, 10). That the yen was then rising and hovering at around ¥120 was also a crucial factor contributing to maintaining the low discount rate.

Japan's monetary policy and the "bubble" it created did not, however, meet the international, especially American, expectation in a very important way. Despite the very rapid rise in the yen, Japan's current account balance that was $96.4 billion in 1986 declined only to $76.9 billion in 1989; more than one-third (34 to 38 percent) of this surplus was earned from the United States whose current account deficit was declining steadily during these years ($-$145 billion in 1986 to $-$106 billion in 1989).

This was the reason for renewed public and scholarly interest in the pricing behavior of Japanese firms and the intensified trade friction between Japan and the United States. Many studies by MITI, the Department of Commerce, and the OECD found that the prices of manufactured products were higher, often significantly, in Japan because the "pass-through" ratio was demonstrably lower in Japan than in the United States and elsewhere. And the major reason identified for this was that Japanese firms engaged in "pricing-to-market" significantly more than did firms in the United States and Europe.[36] For example, Marston, in an econometric analysis, was led to conclude that "in general, pricing to market plays a major role in Japanese manufacturing" and "Japanese firms appear to change their prices more than American firms" to maintain their market share (Marston 1991, 136, 40).

The bilateral trade conflict intensified. Article 301 (Super 301) of the Omnibus Trade and Competitiveness Act of 1988 was invoked against Japan, and Market-Oriented Sector-Specific (MOSS) talks were conducted in 1986. These were followed by Structural Impediments Initiative negotiations that began in 1989 (in the American efforts to change Japan's land use patterns, distribution system, pricing, and other business practices, enforcement of the antitrust law, etc.) and by the Miyazawa-Bush framework agreement of 1992 by which Japan consented to negotiate the means to reduce or eliminate what the Americans believed were trade barriers existing in Japanese markets for telecommunications, automobiles, auto parts, and insurance.

Before concluding these observations on the "bubble" and its consequences, let me add the following which I believe is useful in better understanding the significance of the "bubble" both to Japan and to the United States. When an examination of the returns earned on Japanese investment in the United States during the "bubble" years is made, as shown in Table 2, we find that they were appreciably lower than those earned by U.S. direct investment abroad (USDIA) and by all foreign direct investment in the United States (FDIUS). Note that the returns on USDIA and FDIUS by all foreigners that are calculated on current and market value bases are distinctly lower than FDIUS and USDIA calculated based on historical costs. The main reason for this of course is that since these investments, especially USDIA, are older (and higher in value today) the returns calculated on a historical cost basis are most likely to overstate their rate of return. Current value only for Japanese investment, however, is not available.

When the data are analyzed by industry, as in Table 3, the rates of return on investments (measured on a historical cost basis) show that Japanese investment, which had been performing better relative to the investments made by all nations until 1986, earned appreciably lower rates in 1988 and 1991 for all industries and in manufacturing, which accounted for 21.5 percent of the total investment or an amount second only to wholesale trade (including automobile producers) which accounted for 31.1 percent in 1991.[37] Simply put, what we find in these two tables is that Japanese investors in the "bubble" years appear to have overinvested.[38]

It is important also to note that the "bubble" did have significant distributional effects in Japan or, as Tachibanaki (1992) noted based on extensive quantitative studies of the effects of land prices, Japan for the first time in the postwar years began to have an explicit and serious distributional conflict between those who own land and those who do not.

Charged with the task of analyzing the "mechanism and economic effects" of the "bubble," a MOF research committee was unequivocal in concluding that the "bubble" was the principal cause for the severity of the post-"bubble" recession and for "income and wealth distortions" and various other economic consequences. But, as for the "mechanism" of the "bubble," the committee, interpreting it narrowly, offered only the following:

(1) Following the Plaza Accord, "the money policy was relaxed significantly to mitigate for the deflationary effects of the sharp rise in the value of the yen" and an "easy monetary policy was maintained" after Black Monday "to deal with the repercussions stemming" from it and "in response to the ensuing gentle uptrend in the yen's exchange value" (Inst. of Fiscal Monetary Policy 1993, 7).

(2) The United States eased its monetary policy because of Black Monday and this "quashed an opportunity for Japan to alter its monetary stance" and Japan had its own reasons why it was unable to raise interest rates as did the United States and Germany. The reasons were (a) the yen was growing stronger and the further strengthening of the yen that would follow a tightening of monetary policy could bring about a "spiralling downward" of the dollar "and trigger a general state of panic worldwide"; (b) Japan was under international

42 KOZO YAMAMURA

TABLE 2
Rates of Return of Foreign and Japanese Investment in the U.S.,
U.S. Direct Investment Abroad and All U.S. Businesses, 1982–91 (%)

Year	Returns Based on Market Value			Returns Based on Current Value		Returns Based on Historical Cost		
	FDIUS	USDIA	All US	FDIUS	USDIA	FDIUS	USDIA	Japanese
1982	n.a.	n.a.	11.0	1.2	6.0	2.7	11.4	4.6
1983	4.0	11.4	9.9	2.3	7.0	3.9	12.9	9.6
1984	5.7	11.6	11.1	4.4	8.3	6.3	14.4	13.8
1985	3.2	9.1	8.7	3.3	7.9	4.3	12.6	8.8
1986	2.2	7.2	7.2	2.8	7.6	3.7	12.2	4.4
1987	2.5	7.7	8.1	2.6	8.3	3.6	13.4	1.9
1988	3.9	8.4	9.0	3.4	10.0	4.4	15.5	3.4
1989	2.2	7.9	7.6	1.6	10.2	2.2	15.2	1.1
1990	−0.3	7.6	7.7	0.2	9.4	0.4	13.8	−1.7
1991	−0.2	6.9	6.0	−0.8	7.7	−0.7	11.2	−1.8

NOTE: n.a.=not available; FDIUS=Foreign direct investment in the United States; USDIA=U.S. direct investment abroad; All US=All U.S. businesses.
SOURCE: U.S. Department of Commerce, *Survey of Current Business*, various issues.

pressure to reduce its burgeoning current account surplus; and (c) price levels in Japan were stable (Inst. of Fiscal Monetary Policy 1993, 9–10).

(3) "There is a question as to whether or not the deflationary impact of the surging yen has been overestimated" because "one effect of the stronger yen is to damage the earnings of export industries." This concern tended to be "more emphasized" than consumers' gains, i.e., "higher income and consumption," by "both the public and private sector" because the Japanese economy "at that time had already entered a slowdown" (Inst. of Fiscal Monetary Policy, 11).

(4) In "the recent process of asset price inflation, exchange rate considerations kept interest rates low, resulting in an increase in the money supply" (Inst. of Fiscal Monetary Policy 1993, 65).

As evident in the above, this report by a committee composed of leading economists is consistent with the central argument of this chapter. That is, had these economists chosen not to circumscribe their task so narrowly, their findings would support the argument that Japan's monetary policy which created the "bubble" was shaped by a desire to remain a supporter who wished not to "damage the earnings of the export industries" but who was eager to be cooperative with the hegemon's efforts to limit what are in effect the consequences (including Black Monday) of its past and ongoing overabsorption. The committee concluded that Japan pursued an easy money policy because it placed

TABLE 3
Rates of Return by Industries in Selected Years, Japan and All Nations (%)

Year	1982		1984		1986		1988		1991	
	All Na-tions	Japan	All Na-tions	Japan	All Na-tions	Japan	All Na-tions	Japan	All Na-tions	Japan
All industries	2.7	4.6	6.1	13.8	2.7	4.4	4.7	3.4	−0.7	−1.8
Manufacturing	0.1	−4.6	4.9	−1.6	0.1	−6.8	6.9	−2.8	0.6	−9.1
Wholesale trade	0.1	3.8	11.6	17.3	4.7	4.8	6.0	6.4	−1.0	0.3
Retail trade	7.3	−6.4	13.6	−2.5	10.4	−5.9	2.2	3.1	−18.4	−9.2
Banking	8.3	19.0	7.9	24.5	12.2	25.3	9.5	13.0	−1.5	10.6
Finance (exc Bank)	−4.3	D	1.7	D	1.3	−5.1	−2.3	2.2	−4.2	1.6
Insurance	4.5	D	−7.0	−3.8	12.5	D	0.8	13.2	1.3	6.9
Real estate	−1.6	*	4.6	2.1	0.4	*	0.5	1.9	−5.3	−0.5
Others	−0.3	4.4	−3.1	5.8	−3.9	6.4	−2.1	−5.6	−1.9	−7.2

NOTE: D=Suppressed to avoid disclosure of private information; *=Less than 0.05% in magnitude.

SOURCE: U.S. Department of Commerce, *Survey of Current Business*, various issues.

emphasis on "exchange rate considerations" and because it wished to prevent a "general state of panic worldwide." But the fact remains that the policy was even more strongly motivated to benefit its exporters—the LDP's major political supporters whose international performance continued to be critical in maintaining the "political fortune" of the LDP and the economic health of Japan.

The easy money policy that created the "bubble," however, could not but be the last hurrah of Japan as a supporter-developmentalist because the "bubble" had to burst, plunging Japan, as the committee described persuasively, into a long-lasting and serious recession. Thus, it was the last hurrah of the LDP, too. Both the hegemon and the supporter hoped that their bargain could withstand more of their respective self-serving political and economic needs a little longer. But the hope was dashed in the disappearing "electoral fortune" of Bush and in the aftermath of the "bubble."

IV. REFLECTIONS ON THE LEGACIES

The obvious but important fact I wish to stress in concluding this chapter is that what we observe today and into the first decade of the next century are substantially determined by the following: the demise of the hegemon-supporter bargain, the legacies of "overabsorption" in the United States and "developmentalism" in Japan, and the fact that the advanced industrial economies are now undergoing a "climacteric," i.e., a period of change in the technological paradigm during which sustaining high economic performance in all industries is difficult and trade conflicts are inevitable.

Because of the bargain and especially Reaganomics, the United States today is burdened with a huge debt that is rapidly approaching $4.5 trillion. Despite the attempts to reduce the burden by substantial tax increases and reductions in military and other expenditures, the federal deficit still stood at $254.7 billion in 1993 and is estimated to be $243.8 in 1994 and $176.1 in 1995, assuming the projected growth scenarios of the administration hold. What should not be forgotten also is the fact that the true deficit is significantly larger than these numbers indicate because the trust account for social security—$45.3 billion in 1993, $55.3 billion in 1994, and $59.9 billion in 1995—consists exclusively of U.S. treasury bills, the government debt to future recipients of social security payments. And, few knowledgeable observers dispute that the federal debt will rise again after mid-decade for various reasons.[39]

Above all else, this debt burden is the principal factor accounting for the increases in the federal discount rate in the spring of 1994. As Alan Blinder, the vice chair of the Fed, observed, if "growth persists for longer than two years at the annual rate of three percent, a fairly moderate rate, then inflation could resume" (Bradsher 1994). This is to say that the performance of the economy now must be sacrificed because of the debt even when the economy is growing at three percent. The debt is also the principal reason for the continuing American trade deficit and the seemingly continuing erosion of the value of the dollar.

Although the trade deficit and the weakness of the dollar are due substantively to the legacies of the bargain—the debt and also the declined competitiveness of American manufacturing firms in many industries—the Clinton administration chose to adopt a trade policy that is "result-oriented" to reduce the continuing large trade deficit with Japan. The policy, most objective observers acknowledge, is qualitatively different from one pursued by a diminished hegemon compromising its liberal trade policy in the face of intense domestic economic and political needs. Various other policies (which can only be characterized as industrial policy) that have been adopted by the Clinton administration to increase the competitiveness, thus exports, of American firms, too are reflections of American efforts to undo the legacy of the bargain and decades of overabsorption.

Japan too is today paying the price of the bargain and its developmentalism. Along with political instability and the prolonged and serious post-"bubble" recession of the past few years, the legacies of having been a supporter-developmentalist take other forms as well. Most evident among them is, as many have observed, the dense and entrenched webs of institutions and practices favoring producers and exports at the expense of consumers and public amenities. The large trade surplus, earned directly and indirectly because of sacrifices made by consumers, increases the value of the yen, the export of capital, and conflicts with the United States and other trade partners. Concerns are being increasingly expressed in Japan that the continuing export of capital is retarding improvement in long-neglected housing and public amenities and is increasing the risks of "hollowing" the economy.

However, despite the demonstrated desire and attempts to change on the part of many in Japan, the entrenched institutions and practices of "developmentalism" are extremely difficult to change. In many ways that are by now fully documented, savers and producers, especially the exporters of manufactured products and capital, continue to be favored. For ordinary citizens, the days of living in a "*seikatsu taikoku*"—a "superpower in living standard" commensurate to Japan's export prowess and to the high value of the yen—remain in the future. It should be stressed that, among the many legacies of "developmentalism," the power and turf of the central bureaucracy which grew and became entrenched in the postwar decades, as typified by those of MOF, continue to be a principal obstacle to Japan becoming a living standard super-.power.[40]

Put differently, both the United States and Japan will be faced in the coming decade if not longer with the difficult tasks of coping with the legacies of the recent past and with the changing technological praradigm and of finding ways to sustain economic growth while reducing or at least not worsening the disparity in income distribution at home and trade conflicts with each other. As already noted and as we are reminded daily, the difficulties faced by each of the two nations are evident. And, the impasse reached in the bilateral trade negotiations in 1993 between Clinton and Hosokawa still remains unresolved even after the Napoli summit of July 1994. This is because the Clinton trade policy, as noted, differs qualitatively from that pursued by the preceding Republican administrations and more importantly because the hegemon-supporter bargain ceased to exist between Clinton's United States and the post-LDP and post-developmentalism Japan of today.

If the perspective offered in this chapter and the analysis supporting it are correct, the economic relations between the United States and Japan will undergo a prolonged period of adjustment, trials, and even conflict. This is because both nations have their respective legacies of the past 40 years which must be overcome before a new bargain, a modus vivendi between two more equal trade partners, can be struck. As typified by the American debt and the Japanese institutions and practices of developmentalism, what grew over time can only be eliminated over time. Perhaps what is most needed today on the part of both Americans and Japanese is the wisdom to recognize this fact.

NOTES

1. The term "absorption," defined as in the text (thus the trade balance is equal to income minus absorption), was first used in Alexander (1952) and has been used by many economists since then.

2. Chapters 7 to 11 in Volume 2 of Murakami (1992) offer economic analytical and political-economic analyses of developmentalism which Murakami sees as a version of capitalist economy not specific either to Japan or East Asia. Murakami's analyses that include economic analyses and implications to the world economic and political regimes of developmentalism differ in very significant ways from the developmentalism that Johnson (1982) discussed. My translation of Murakami's book is forthcoming from Stanford University Press in 1996: *An Anticlassical Political-Economic Analysis: A Vision for the Next Century.*

3. For the following discussion on technological paradigm, I owe a great deal to Yasusuke Murakami, since it is a freely adapted version of his study (1983). In addition, the following studies provided the analytic bases for, and are useful in better understanding, the discussion presented in this section: Abernathy (1978); Abernathy and Abernathy (1975); Chandler (1977); Dosi (1983); Kurth (1979); Modelski (1978); Rosenberg (1976); and Touraine (1969).

4. This is defined as the total capital flow from Japan to the United States minus Japanese portfolio investment in the United States, the amount of which was more directly affected by the exchange rate, the "bubble," and other reasons discussed in other chapters of this volume.

5. The series was also drawn from Bureau of Labor Statistics data.

6. Technology balance of payment refers to money paid for the use of patents, licenses, trademarks, designs, know-how, and closely related technical services and for industrial R&D carried out abroad. The data used were compiled by OECD (1993) and made available on disk, entitled "Main Science and Technology Indicators." For the regression, the ratio of the net payments was used.

7. The power of the tests for endogeneity of the real exchange rate and technology balance of payments was 0.12 and 0.1, respectively. The results should be interpreted with this in mind. For more information on the Hausman specification test, see Hausman (1978).

8. The Durbin-Watson probability is 0.190053, thus the null hypothesis of no positive autocorrelation cannot be rejected at a 10 percent significance level. A graph of the residual revealed that negative autocorrelation is highly unlikely.

9. A likelihood ratio test was performed to test the joint significance of these three variables. The null of the three coefficients jointly equal to zero is rejected at .01 significance level with a test statistic of 24.8. The likelihood ratio statistic associated with the test of joint significance of the output and productivity ratio is 21.1, thus these two variables are jointly significant.

10. The insignificance of the coefficient may be due to multicolinearity with the unit

labor cost variable. A likelihood ratio test of the joint significance of the real exchange rate and the unit labor cost coefficients yields a test statistic of 7.91. Thus the null is rejected at a .025 significance level.

11. Net military transactions rose from -$2.75 billion in 1960 to -$3.35 billion in 1969 and were below the surplus earned in current balance by 1968 (current balance in 1968 was $621 million and in 1970 $2.36 billion). The sources of these data are: U.S. Government (1990, 410); and OECD (1990, 10–11).

12. The general, of course, was expressing his frustration against what is well known as the fundamental dilemma of the Bretton Woods system that had been articulated five years earlier by Triffin (1960).

13. The rate of inflation which hovered around 2.3–2.4 percent during the first half of the decade was heading toward 5 percent in the last years of the decade.

14. The data are from Bureau of Labor Statistics, U.S. Department of Labor (1989).

15. The source of budget and other data cited in this section is, unless noted otherwise, U.S. Government (1990) and OECD (1990).

16. The rate is the difference between the nominal rate and the expected inflation rate as calculated by Blanchard (1987, 20).

17. See the contribution by Slemrod in this volume for descriptions of the Reagan tax policy and its effects on capital flow.

18. Real median family income in 1989 dollars declined from $33,656 in 1973 to $31,637 by 1980. U.S. Government (1991, 320).

19. The federal tax burden which stood at 22.5 percent of net national product (NNP) in 1980 came down to 21.2 percent by 1984.

20. For a full discussion of the Report and the bilateral trade tension of these years, see Yamamura (1987).

21. For further data relating to the economic performance during these years, see Branson (1987, 48–52).

22. For an excellent description and analyses of the changes in the dollar-yen rate following the Plaza Accord, see Ito (1992, 341–57).

23. Useful sources offering descriptions of Japan's developmentalist policies include: Patrick and Rosovsky (1976); Okimoto (1989); Johnson (1982); Pempel (1977); Johnson, Tyson, and Zysman (1989); and Yamamura and Yasuba (1987).

24. As Murakami stressed, competition in many industries tended to be "excessive" in the decade because firms rapidly adopting new technology could reduce unit costs by producing more. Murakami and Yamamura (1982).

25. As this was just before the reversion of Okinawa to Japan, there also were various political incentives not to revalue the yen.

26. See, for example, Kosai (1981, 193–95) for data demonstrating how the "slim down" was achieved.

27. For analyses and further descriptions of the increases in the deficit, see: Noguchi (1987), and Yamamura (1985, 467–508).

28. For further discussion of the monetary policy and political economic analyses of the period, see Hamada (1985).

29. The sources cited in note 23 above contain many descriptions of these developmentalist policies, their changes, and consequences. Murakami (1992, Vol. 2, 367–430) distinguishes developmentalism of the state and of firms with the latter referring to various developmentalist firm behavior such as maintaining *keiretsu* relationships. Given the goal of this chapter, I do not discuss the developmentalism of firms.

30. I am using the term "bubble" in the technical sense Noguchi uses; see p. 56.

31. For the data, specific policies, and effects of the rapid increase in land price that occurred as an important part of this "bubble," see Haley and Yamamura (1992).

32. For those who wish to obtain data and analyses relating to this development, an additional useful source is: Noguchi (1993).

33. For the annual data of this period, see Noguchi (1993, 114).

34. Noguchi, pp. 59–60.

35. See Hamada's contribution in this volume, pp. 84–85, and Hamada and Horiuchi (1987). The latter also provides many descriptions and analyses that are valuable in better understanding the policy and institutional changes discussed in this chapter.

36. For a discussion of these studies and examples of the price data themselves, see Yamamura (1990, 39–42).

37. Department of Commerce includes automobile producers in wholesale because Japanese automobile producers first entered the U.S. market as distributors. The third largest industry in 1991 was real estate which accounted for 17.2 percent of total Japanese investment in that year.

38. As Hamada suggests in referring to the work of Froot and Stein, more work is needed to establish whether or not Japanese entrepreneurs, benefiting from the appreciating yen, did raise capital cheaply using their improved collateral value and credibility, i.e., the returns Japanese earned in the United States from their investment did not constitute an overinvestment but can be explained by using information theoretic analysis. Hamada in this volume, pp. 102–4.

39. As of January 1995, the fate of the balanced budget amendment to the constitution is uncertain and, even should it pass the Senate, ratification by the necessary majority of states will be time-consuming. Meanwhile, due to the expected rising costs of so-called "entitlements," political efforts to reduce the deficit will continue to face an uphill battle as demonstrated in the Clinton budget for FY 1995–96.

40. For a fuller discussion of the motivations of and efforts made by many political and business leaders as well as by various ministries to change "developmentalist" institutions and practices and the reasons for their limited success, see Yamamura (1994).

REFERENCES

Abernathy, J. M. and Abernathy, W. J. 1975. A dynamic model of process and product innovation. *Omega: the international journal of management science* 3:639–56.

Abernathy, William J. 1978. *The productivity dilemma: roadblock to innovation in the automobile industry.* Baltimore: Johns Hopkins University Press.

Alexander, Sidney. 1952. The effects of devaluation on a trade balance. IMF Staff papers (April).

Blanchard, Oliver Jean. 1987. Reaganomics. *Economic policy* 5.

Bradsher, Keith. 1994. US shifts stance in effort to slow economic growth. *New York times,* May 8: 1, 18.

Branson, William. 1987. Discussion. *Economic Policy* 5:48–52.

Bureau of Labor Statistics. 1989. U.S. Department of Labor.

Chandler, Alfred D. 1977. *The visible hand: the managerial revolution in American business.* Cambridge, Mass.: Belknap Press.

Chubb, John E. and Peterson, Paul E. 1985. *The new direction in American politics.* Washington: The Brookings Institution.

Cleveland, Harold van Buren. 1990. Europe in the economic crisis of our time: macroeconomic policies and macroeconomic constraints. In *Recasting Europe's economies: national strategies in the 1980s,* ed. David P. Calleo and Claudia Morgenstern. Lanham, Md.: University Press of America.

Dosi, Giovanni. 1983. Technological paradigm and technological trajectories. In *Long waves in the world economy,* ed. Christopher Freeman, 78–101. London: Butterworths.

Gilpin, Robert. 1987. *The political economy of international relations.* Princeton: Princeton University Press.

Gowa, Joanne. 1983. *Closing the gold window: domestic politics and the end of Bretton Woods.* Ithaca: Cornell University Press.

Grieder, William. 1981. The education of David Stockman. *The Atlantic monthly* (December).

Haley, John O. and Yamamura Kozo, eds. 1992. *Land issues in Japan: a policy failure?* Seattle: Society for Japanese Studies.

Hamada Koichi. 1985. *The political economy of international monetary interdependence.* Cambridge, Mass.: MIT Press.

Hamada Koichi and Horiuchi Akiyoshi. 1987. The political economy of the financial market. In *The political economy of Japan, volume 1: the domestic transformation,* ed. Kozo Yamamura and Yasukichi Yasuba, 223–60. Stanford: Stanford University Press.

Hausman, Jerry A. 1978. Specification tests in econometrics. *Econometrica* 46:1251–72.

Inoguchi Takashi. 1986. Japan's images and options: not a challenger, but a supporter. *Journal of Japanese studies* 12:95–119.

Institute of Fiscal Monetary Policy, Ministry of Finance. 1993. *The mechanism and economic effects of asset price fluctuations.* Tokyo: Ministry of Finance.

Ito Takatoshi. 1986. Capital controls and covered interest rate parity between the yen and the dollar. *Economic studies quarterly* 37:223–41.

———. 1992. *The Japanese economy.* Cambridge, Mass.: MIT Press.

Johnson, Chalmers. 1982. *MITI and the Japanese miracle.* Stanford: Stanford University Press.

Johnson, Chalmers; Tyson, Laura D'Andrea; and Zysman, John, eds. 1989. *Politics and productivity: the real story of why Japan works.* Cambridge, Mass.: Ballinger.

Keohane, Robert O. 1984. *After hegemony: cooperation and discord in the world political economy.* Princeton: Princeton University Press.

Kindleberger, Charles. 1975. *The world in depression.* Berkeley: University of California Press.

————. 1981. Dominance and leadership in the international economy: exploitation, public goods and free-rides. *International studies quarterly* 25:242–54.

Kosai Yutaka. 1981. *The era of high-speed growth.* Tokyo: University of Tokyo Press.

Kurth, James R. 1979. The political consequences of the product cycle: industrial history and political outcomes. *International organization* 33:1–34.

Lake, David A. 1991. International economic structure and American foreign economic policy, 1887–1934. In *International political economy,* ed. Jeffrey A. Frieden and D.A. Lake. New York: St. Martin's Press.

Lipson, Charles. 1983. The transformation of trade: the sources and effects of regime change. In *International regimes,* ed. S.D. Krasner, 233–71. Ithaca: Cornell University Press.

Markus, Gregory. 1982. Political attitudes during an election year: a report on the 1980 NES panel study. *American political science review* 76:538–60.

Marston, Richard C. 1991. Price behavior in Japan and U.S. manufacturing. In *Trade with Japan,* ed. Paul Krugman. Chicago: Chicago University Press.

Miller, Warren E. and Shanks, J. Merrill. 1982. Policy direction and presidential leadership: alternative interpretations of the 1980 presidential election. *British journal of political science* 3:351–52.

Ministry of Finance. 1992. *Main economic indicators of Japan.* Tokyo: MOF Printing Office.

Modelski, George. 1978. The long cycle of global politics and nation states. *Comparative studies in society and history* 20:214–35.

Murakami Yasusuke. 1983. Henkansuru sangyō bunmei to nijūisseiki e no tenbo. *Ekonomisuto,* April 5.

————. 1992. *Han-koten no seiji keizai-gaku,* 2 vols. Tokyo: Chūōkōronsha.

Murakami Yasusuke and Yamamura Kozo. 1982. A technical note on Japanese firm behavior. In *Policy and trade issues of the Japanese economy: American and Japanese perspectives,* ed. Kozo Yamamura. Seattle: University of Washington Press.

Noguchi Yukio. 1987. Public finance. In *The political economy of Japan, volume 1: the domestic transformation,* ed. Kozo Yamamura and Yasukichi Yasuba. Stanford: Stanford University Press.

————. 1993. Asset price inflation and economic policies. *Hitotsubashi journal of economics* 34 (December): 111–46.

OECD. 1990. *Historical statistics, 1960–1988.* Paris: OECD.

————. 1993. *Main science and technology indicators.* Paris: OECD.

Okimoto, Daniel I. 1989. *Between MITI and the market: Japanese industrial policy for high technology.* Stanford: Stanford University Press.

Patrick, Hugh T. and Rosovsky, Henry, eds. 1976. *Asia's new giant.* Washington: The Brookings Institution.

Pempel, T.J. ed. 1977. *Policymaking in contemporary Japan.* Ithaca: Cornell University Press.

Rosenberg, Nathan. 1976. *Perspective on technology.* New York: Cambridge University Press.

Tachibanaki Toshiaki. 1992. Higher land prices as a cause of increasing inequality: changes in wealth distribution and socio-economic effects. In *Land issues in Japan: a policy failure?* ed. John O. Haley and Kozo Yamamura. Seattle: Society for Japanese Studies.

Tax Foundation. 1990. *Facts and figures on government finance.* Baltimore: Johns Hopkins University Press.

Tobin, James. 1988. Reaganomics in retrospect. In *The Reagan revolution?* ed. B.B. Kymlicka and J.V. Mathews. Chicago: Dorsey Press.

Touraine, Alain. 1969. *La société post-industrielle.* Paris: Gonthier.

Triffin, Robert. 1960. *The gold and the dollar crisis: the future of convertability.* New Haven: Yale University Press.

Tufte, Edward R. 1978. *Political control of the economy.* Princeton: Princeton University Press.

U.S. Department of Commerce. Annual. *Survey of Current Business.*

U.S. Government. 1990. *Historical tables: budget of the U.S. government, fiscal year 1990.* Washington: Government Printing Office.

U.S. Government. 1991. *Economic report of the president.* Washington: U.S. Government Printing Office.

U.S. Government. 1992. *Budget of the United States,* fiscal 1992. Washington: U.S. Government Printing Office.

Webb, Michael C. and Krasner, Stephen D. 1989. Hegemonic stability theory: an empirical assessment. *Review of international studies* 15:183–98.

Yamamura Kozo. 1985. The cost of rapid growth and capitalist democracy in Japan. In *The politics of inflation and economic stagflation,* ed. Leon N. Lindberg and Charles S. Maier, 467–508. Washington: The Brookings Institution.

———. 1987. Shedding the shackles of success: saving less for Japan's future. In *The trade crisis: how will Japan respond?* ed. Kenneth B. Pyle, 33–60. Seattle: Society for Japanese Studies.

———. 1990. Will Japan's economic structure change? In *Japan's economic structure: should it change?* ed. Kozo Yamamura, 39–42. Seattle: Society for Japanese Studies.

———. 1994. The deliberate emergence of a free-trader: the Japanese political economy in transition. In *Japan: a new kind of superpower?* ed. Craig Garby and Mary Bullock, 35–52. Washington: Woodrow Wilson Center Press.

Yamamura Kozo and Yasuba Yasukichi, eds. 1987. *The political economy of Japan, volume 1: the domestic transformation.* Stanford: Stanford University Press.

Macroeconomic Policies and

Asset Price Inflation

A Political-Economic Analysis

of the "Bubble" Economy

YUKIO NOGUCHI

THE PURPOSE OF this chapter is to review economic events and policies in Japan during the 1980s and to analyze changes in underlying economic structures. I place particular emphasis on the latter half of the 1980s because this was an exceptional period in the postwar economic history of Japan. The extraordinary increase in stock and land prices was especially noteworthy. In this paper, I argue that asset price inflation was mostly due to policy failures: excessively loose monetary policy and excessively stringent fiscal policy.

My main interest is to analyze why this particular combination of policies was chosen in Japan, and I argue that the fundamental cause can be found in the bias in the Japanese economy in which producers' interests are regarded as utmost and consumers' interests tend to be neglected. In this sense, the view expressed in this paper is in line with Yamamura's paper in this volume: events in Japan of the 1980s can be interpreted as an outcome of the macroeconomic policy that was followed by a "developmentalist-supporter" of the American-led international economic regime. The view presented in this paper is different from Yamamura's, however, in that it argues that the basic structure still remains.

In the first section, the Japanese economy in the 1980s is briefly reviewed. The latter part of the decade was an unusual period in terms of both real economic activity and the movement of asset prices. On the real side, the Japanese economy enjoyed a remarkable investment boom. Unlike booms in the past, this was accompanied by a spectacular rise in asset prices; both stock and land prices showed unprecedented increases. On the international front, the external surplus in the current account continued to increase during the early half of the 1980s.

In the latter half of the 1980s, there was a significant change in the method used by corporations to raise funds and hence in the flow of funds in the economy. This is analyzed in the second section. Thanks to the rise in stock prices, corporations were able to raise huge amounts of funds from the capital market, which were then invested in financial assets. Banks were thus forced to allocate funds to real estate companies, who used the money for speculative purchases of land. This was the mechanism underlying asset price inflation.

The third section is a discussion of macroeconomic policies during this period. As is often pointed out, the easy money policy regarded as necessary to cope with the appreciation of the yen was the fundamental cause of the change in the flow of funds and hence of asset price inflation. We must also note that the government sector was the biggest beneficiary of the bubble economy in the sense that tax revenues increased substantially. Since fiscal authorities succeeded in restraining expenditures, the budget deficit decreased dramatically and this increased surplus in the external current account. The main factor that caused the mismanagement of macroeconomic policy was the aforementioned bias in the Japanese economy, i.e., overemphasis on producers' interests.

The fourth section reviews the situation after the bubble. I argue that the role of Japan as a capital-exporting country will not be diminished by the collapse of the bubble. The last section is a conclusion. The main message here is that in order not to repeat the policy failures of the 1980s, it is necessary to reform the economic structure to a more consumer-oriented one. The change in the financial system in this period is very important in explaining asset price inflation. However, this topic is not discussed in this chapter because it is dealt with in Yoshino's chapter.

THE JAPANESE ECONOMY IN THE 1980S

Economic Boom of the 1980s

The Japanese economy experienced spectacular growth in the latter half of the 1980s. Overcoming the recession caused by the sharp appreciation of the yen, it started to expand in December 1986 and went on to record the second-longest boom since World War II. The first demand category that showed remarkable growth was residential investment, which grew substantially in 1986 and 1987 (see Table 1). The number of housing starts, which until 1984 had

TABLE 1

Annual Growth Rate of Real GNP and Its Components (%)

FY	GDP	Business Investment	Housing Investment	Public Investment
1986	2.9	3.0	10.6	6.2
87	4.9	8.6	26.3	9.3
88	6.0	16.8	4.9	0.4
89	4.5	14.3	1.0	−0.1
90	5.1	11.4	4.9	4.3
91	3.6	3.5	−12.1	6.7
92	0.7	−5.7	−3.6	13.3
93	0.2	−7.2	8.5	...
94	2.4	0.1	5.2	...

NOTE: Figures for FY 1994 are government outlook.
SOURCE: Economic Planning Agency, *Yearbook on National Account*, each year.

been about 1.2 million a year, maintained a level in excess of 1.6 million a year from 1987 through 1990 (see Table 2).

Next to post strong growth was business fixed investment, which grew in real terms at double-digit rates annually from 1988 through 1990, a pace comparable to that of the rapid growth era in the 1960s. The ratio of business fixed investment to GDP, which had averaged around 15 percent from fiscal year 1980 to 1986, started to rise in 1987 and was pushed up sharply by the investment boom, reaching 21.7 percent in FY 1990. The cumulative ratio of investment to GDP for the FY 1987–90 period was 17.5 percent higher than that for the preceding six years. As a result, the capital-output ratio (the ratio of private capital stock to GDP) also went up. This ratio shows a general tendency to rise, but in the late 1980s it increased faster than normal. As of 1991 it had reached a level about 10 percent higher than the trend line. This suggests that the investment boom had resulted in an over-capacity condition. Production of consumer durables also increased. Annual domestic sales of passenger cars, which had previously stood at around 3 million, went over the 5 million mark in 1990 (Table 2).

The expansion of the economy resulted in a tightening of demand-supply conditions in the labor market. The ratio of job openings to job seekers went above 1.0 in 1988, and by 1990 it reached the extremely high level of 1.4 (Table 2). The shortage of labor became a very serious problem for employers, particularly in the construction industry.

There was also a marked increase in corporate profits during the late 1980s. According to the Corporate Statistics (*Hōjin kigyō tōkei*) compiled by the Min-

TABLE 2

Trends in Various Indicators

FY	Housing Starts 10,000 Units	Automobile Sales 10,000 Cars	Job Openings Ratio
1980	126	285	0.75
1981	115	286	0.68
1982	114	303	0.61
1983	113	313	0.60
1984	118	309	0.65
1985	123	310	0.68
1986	136	314	0.62
1987	167	327	0.70
1988	168	371	1.01
1989	166	440	1.25
1990	170	510	1.40
1991	137	487	1.40
1992	140	445	1.08
1993	149	420	0.76

SOURCE: Monthly Statistics, *Tōyō keizai,* each issue.

istry of Finance, current profits for all industries rose 31.7 percent over the previous year in FY 1987 and rose another 29.6 percent in 1988. By 1989, profits had reached a level 1.87 times higher than in 1985.

Advances in information technology and the internationalization of financial business led to a further concentration of business activities in the Tokyo metropolitan region. The influx of population into this region increased significantly in the latter half of the 1980s. This was reflected in the rise in rent for office space. Until the mid-1980s, rents increased virtually in line with GDP. But in the latter part of the decade, the situation in Tokyo changed sharply. The annual rate of increase in rents, which had been around 6 percent, became 10 percent in 1986; the following year the figure reached 27.6 percent, and double-digit increases continued in subsequent years.

Asset Price Inflation

Economic growth during this period was accompanied by an extraordinary increase in asset prices. The Nikkei average of 225 issues on the Tokyo Stock Exchange practically doubled from ¥8,800 in 1983 to ¥16,401 in 1986 (annual averages). The surge, which took the index to a peak of ¥26,646 on October 14, 1987, was temporarily halted by the "Black Monday" crash that hit the New

York stock market at that point. But the slump in Tokyo was short-lived. By April 1988 the market had climbed past the previous October's record high, and prices continued to climb up to the closing session of 1989, when the Nikkei average hit ¥38,915. Stock prices were by this time more than four times the level they had been in 1983.

The 1980s also saw an extraordinary surge in land prices. In 1986 land prices shot up throughout the Tokyo metropolitan area, and the sharp rise continued in 1987. In fact, Tokyo land approximately tripled in price during these two years. In the following years prices in the Tokyo area more or less leveled off, but meanwhile they had started rising in other regions of the country. Land in the Osaka area appreciated sharply in 1988 and 1989 and, though it started a bit later, the Nagoya area experienced a similar rise. The escalation subsequently spread to resort areas and to major regional cities.

Under normal circumstances, stock and land prices rise in line with growth in returns—dividends or corporate profits in the case of stocks and rentals in the case of land—and with declines in interest rates. As we have seen, corporate profits increased significantly and the rental value of real estate in the Tokyo area increased due to the concentration of economic activities. Moreover, interest rates fell dramatically during this period (see Table 3). These factors would push up the "fundamental prices" of assets. Thus, in order to see whether there were "bubble" elements in asset prices, further analysis is needed.

If the price of assets such as stocks and land is based on economic fundamentals, it should be equal to net return divided by the interest rate in the case when return is a constant and there is no risk. Let us assume here that returns (such as stock dividends) can be expressed as a fixed percentage of GDP. In that case, the total value of assets should be equal to a fixed (or perhaps slowly changing) percentage of the value of GDP divided by the interest rate.

The actual figures for this percentage are shown in the last two columns of Table 4. In the first half of the 1980s, the figures were fairly steady for both stocks and land (though the stock figures show something of a rising trend and the land figures a falling trend). In other words, during this period both stock and land prices can be regarded to have moved in keeping with the economic fundamentals. In the latter part of the decade, however, the figures for both stocks and land deviated greatly from the trend. This may be seen as evidence of the formation of a speculative bubble in the asset market.[1]

Current Account Surplus

Japan's current account registered massive surpluses in the 1980s, and there was a striking increase in the level of overseas investment. The current account surplus started to expand around the middle of the decade, and in 1986 it reached $85.8 billion, or 4.2 percent of GDP. The long-term capital deficit,

TABLE 3
Trends in Official Discount Rates

Date of Change		New Rate (%)	Date of Change		New Rate (%)
Jan. 30	1986	4.50	Aug. 30	1990	6.00
Mar. 10	1986	4.00	Jul. 1	1991	5.50
Apr. 21	1986	3.50	Nov. 14	1991	5.00
Nov. 1	1986	3.00	Dec. 30	1991	4.50
Feb. 23	1987	2.50	Apr. 1	1992	3.75
May 31	1989	3.25	Jul. 27	1992	3.25
Oct. 11	1989	3.75	Feb. 4	1993	2.50
Dec. 25	1989	4.25	Sep. 21	1993	1.75
Mar. 20	1990	5.25			

SOURCE: Monthly Statistics, *Tōyō keizai*, each issue.

representing Japanese investment in other countries, exceeded the $130 billion level for three years from 1986 to 1988. The long-term outflow of Japanese capital alone reached $192.1 billion in 1989.

What is worth noting here is the fact that the long-term capital outflow during this period substantially exceeded the current account surplus. Viewed over the long term, the two ought to be equal, since the surplus on the current account supplies the funds for this outflow. What this excess indicates is that Japanese financial institutions were not only steadily recycling the current account surplus (equal to the domestic surplus of saving over investment) but were also functioning as financial intermediaries, converting short-term funds procured overseas into long-term funds and investing them abroad.

As a result of this increase in overseas investment, Japan overtook Britain in 1985 to become the world's largest creditor, with net foreign assets of $129.8 billion. It held on to the top place through the end of 1989, at which point the figure had reached $293.2 billion (Japan was overtaken by Germany in 1990 but subsequently regained the number one spot).

CHANGES IN THE FLOW OF FUNDS AND LAND SPECULATION

Changes in Corporate Fundraising Methods

A remarkable change occurred in the fundraising method of corporations in the latter part of the 1980s. Thanks to the booming stock market, major corporations found it very cheap to raise money through the issuance of stocks and bonds. They could also sell convertible bonds or bonds with warrants,

TABLE 4

Stock and Land Values

FY	GDP (Trillion yen)	Value (Trillion yen)		Value X Interest Rate/GDP	
		Stock	Land	Stock	Land
1981	261	81	128	2.572	4.089
1982	273	91	135	2.747	4.082
1983	286	107	139	2.885	3.760
1984	305	138	149	3.232	3.494
1985	324	169	176	3.177	3.308
1986	338	230	280	3.498	4.260
1987	354	301	449	4.166	6.217
1988	377	394	529	5.184	6.961
1989	403	527	521	7.362	7.272
1990	434	478	517	7.611	8.235
1991	457	373	504	4.475	6.058
1992	465	297	428	3.400	4.900
1993	472	352	373	3.527	3.740

NOTE: (1) Interest rate is the yield on long-term national bond. (2) Value of stock is the total value of stocks listed in the Tokyo Stock Exchange. Value of land is that in Tokyo-to (the metropolitan area) (National Account Statistics).

which investors bought at low interest rates in the hopes of realizing capital gains. In the three years from 1987 to 1989, corporations raised over ¥58 trillion in this manner.

Not all the funds that were raised were channeled into plant and equipment investment; quite a large proportion was used for what was called *zai*-tech, or financial engineering, i.e., investment in bank deposits and trust accounts and purchase of other financial assets offering high yields. In this way, corporations increased both their liabilities and financial assets.

The tendency to rely more on equity and equity-linked financing was particularly pronounced among large manufacturing companies. For incorporated businesses as a whole, borrowing from financial institutions accounted for roughly 80 percent of the outstanding volume of funds raised as of the end of fiscal 1984, and this level was not substantially different six years later. In the manufacturing sector, however, the share of borrowing fell from 70 percent to less than 56 percent over this period. Among the largest manufacturing corporations (capitalized at over ¥1 billion), the proportion of loans fell even more sharply, from 59 percent to 34 percent. There was also a net decrease in the volume of borrowing.

By contrast, businesses other than large manufacturing corporations basically remained dependent on borrowing. More than ¥181 trillion was procured in this way during this six-year period, of which 70 percent consisted of borrowing by small and medium-sized corporations. Approximately 26 percent of the total amount (¥48 trillion) was borrowed by the real estate industry.

Channeling Funds to the Real Estate Industry

Because large corporations reduced their borrowing, banks faced difficulties in finding takers for their funds. They therefore shifted their lending from large corporations and the manufacturing sector, the traditional targets of their loans, to smaller companies and the real estate industry. Also, an increasing number of loans were channeled through nonbank intermediaries instead of being made directly from banks. This is how the funds for land speculation were supplied.

If we look at changes in the balance of outstanding loans for different industries, we find a steady decline for manufacturing in the years from 1986 to 1989, reflecting the decreased reliance on banks by large manufacturing corporations. For real estate, by contrast, we find a remarkable increase. In 1984 outstanding loans to the real estate industry amounted to ¥16.5 trillion, only 27 percent of the figure for the manufacturing sector, but by the end of 1991 the balance had risen to ¥40 trillion, approximately 74 percent of the size of loans to the manufacturing industry. Financial institutions also supplied funds to real estate companies indirectly through nonbank finance companies. If this indirect financing is included, approximately ¥44 trillion was loaned to real estate companies in the FY 1985–90 period.

The unprecedented land speculation of the latter part of the 1980s was thus supported by an enormous volume of lending by financial institutions to the real estate industry. Behind this lending was the *zai*-tech activity of businesses raising low-cost capital and using much of the proceeds to make bank deposits and buy other financial assets. This flow of funds was problematic. The basic problem was the emergence of an environment that made this sort of financial transaction enormously profitable. To take a broader view, we can say that the problem ultimately lay in the macroeconomic policies, in particular, an excessively loose monetary policy. I discuss this issue in the next section.

Speculative Purchase of Land by Real Estate Companies

According to the National Account Statistics compiled by the Economic Planning Agency, the household sector has consistently been a net seller of land; the main net purchasers have been nonfinancial corporations and the public sector. Total net sales by the household sector over the five-year period from FY 1985 to 1990 amounted to approximately ¥64 trillion. Net purchases by nonfinancial corporations had ranged from several hundred million to a trillion yen annually until the mid-1980s, but the pace then picked up dramatically; total purchases for the FY 1985–90 period came to about ¥40 trillion. If we consider the level of purchases up to the early 1980s, it is difficult to believe that the actual need for sites could have risen so suddenly during the latter part of the decade. Most of the increase must have represented purchases made for speculative purposes.

According to the Corporate Statistics compiled by the Ministry of Finance, which allow us to examine industry-by-industry figures for land ownership, the value of land owned by corporations in all industries was approximately ¥51 trillion at the end of 1984 and rose to around ¥119 trillion by the end of 1990.[2] Hence, the net purchases of land in this period came to about ¥68 trillion. Of this amount, large companies accounted for just under 30 percent and smaller firms for something over 70 percent.

By sector, the real estate industry was by far the largest purchaser of land in this period, with total net acquisitions of approximately ¥28 trillion, or 38 percent of the total. The peak year for purchases was FY 1987, when real estate companies' holdings of land shot up by ¥15.5 trillion. The balance of the industry's holdings at the end of fiscal 1990 came to ¥38 trillion, approximately four times the level of six years earlier. Small and medium-sized real estate companies accounted for 76 percent of the industry's holdings of land as fixed assets and over 80 percent of the holdings in inventory. The manufacturing sector, meanwhile, acquired land on a relatively minor scale during this period.

To sum up the real estate industry's borrowing and investment performance in the FY 1984–90 period, it received loans of approximately ¥44 trillion (including amounts borrowed through nonbank organizations); purchases of land during this six-year period came to about ¥28.5 trillion, while other investment totaled around ¥19 trillion, including ¥10.7 trillion for buildings and other fixed assets and ¥8.6 trillion for net purchases of securities.

MACROECONOMIC POLICIES

Japan's macroeconomic policy during the latter half of the 1980s can be characterized as an "easy money, tight budget" position. This can be regarded as the main cause of asset price inflation and the increase in the current account surplus during this period. An unprecedented easy money policy made stock and land prices soar. Excessive reduction in the budget deficit caused a serious misallocation of economic resources.

Monetary Policy

The major factor behind the leap in asset prices was monetary relaxation. The official discount rate, which had been 5 percent since October 1983, was lowered in a series of steps starting in January 1986, and in February 1987 it became 2.5 percent, the lowest level ever (Table 3). This loosening of monetary policy was seen as necessary to cope with the sudden appreciation of the yen in the wake of the Plaza Accord of September 1985. Japan was also under strong pressure from the United States to lower its interest rates. In 1987, the United States began to tighten monetary policy in September, and the Bank of Japan tried to follow suit. But the move toward monetary restraint was put on hold because of the "Black Monday" stock market crash in October, and the record low 2.5 percent rate remained in place until May 1989.

It was thought that if Japan raised its interest rates there would be a reduction in the outflow of capital, which would cause difficulties in capital-importing countries such as the United States and possibly trigger another stock market crash. Another factor was the value of the yen, which continued to rise even after Black Monday, going from around ¥140 to the dollar in October 1987 to around ¥120 to the dollar the following autumn. These external considerations delayed monetary tightening and allowed asset prices to spiral even higher.

Another policy that indirectly contributed to the asset price spiral was financial liberalization, which made possible the *zai*-tech maneuvering that became popular among business corporations in the latter part of the 1980s. This issue is discussed in detail in Yoshino's paper in this volume.

Fiscal Policy

Economic Boom and Increases in Tax Revenue. After the oil shocks of the 1970s, Japan found itself running large annual budget deficits, and fiscal reconstruction became the supreme objective for the policymakers of the Ministry of Finance in the 1980s.[3] At first, the target was to end the government's reliance on deficit-financing bond issues by FY 1984. Because of the large revenue shortfalls of FY 1981 and FY 1982, however, the target had to be put off to FY 1990.

The latter half of the decade brought spectacular growth in tax revenue. Corporate taxes showed a particularly high rate of increase, rising 20.8 percent in fiscal 1987 and 12.0 percent in fiscal 1988. The surge in asset prices was one of the main factors behind this increase. According to the government's 1989 economic white paper, normal economic activities accounted for only about five percentage points of the increase in each of the two years; most of the 1987 increase is seen as attributable to asset-related factors, such as higher property income and capital gains, and to profits resulting from inventory revaluation. Income tax also increased remarkably due to bracket creep. Reflecting the sharp increase in revenues, the ratio of national and local taxes to national income rose from 22.2 percent in FY 1980 to 28.1 percent in FY 1990 (see Table 5).

TABLE 5

Ratio of Tax Revenue to National Income (%)

FY	National Tax	National and Local Tax	FY	National Tax	National and Local Tax
1950	16.9	22.4	1986	15.9	25.0
1955	13.4	18.9	1987	17.0	26.6
1960	13.3	18.9	1988	17.4	27.5
1965	12.2	18.0	1989	17.8	27.8
1970	12.7	18.9	1990	18.3	28.1
1975	11.7	18.3	1991	17.6	27.4
1980	14.2	22.2	1992	16.5	26.1
1985	15.1	24.1	1993	16.9	26.1

SOURCE: Ministry of Finance, *Fiscal and Monetary Statistics,* each issue.

During this period, tax revenues increased at a significantly higher rate than the long-term trend.

Fuji Sōgō Kenkyūjo (1994) estimates that actual tax revenue during the latter half of the 1980s was significantly greater than the trend value. It calculates "normal" tax revenue assuming a real economic growth rate of 4.1 percent and tax revenue elasticity of 1.1. (The actual growth rate was 4.3 percent and elasticity was 1.3. The same deflator as the actual value was used.) It finds that the cumulative difference throughout this period amounted to about ¥3 trillion, which is about 10 percent of the actual tax revenue (see Table 6).

Suppressed Expenditures. On the expenditure side, however, there was no substantial increase during this period. In fact, the 1980s saw a sharp fall in the ratio of public investment to GDP. This was because the government clamped down hard on spending, particularly on public works. In all the initial budgets from FY 1982 through 1988, public-works-related expenditures were held below the previous year's level. Reflecting this stringency, these expenditures, which had accounted for 15.6 percent of the general account in FY 1980, fell to a 9.4 percent share as of FY 1991. The total general account, meanwhile, fell as a percentage of national income during the first half of the 1980s and then stabilized at a more or less fixed level in the second half of the decade.

In terms of the general government (national and local governments) expenditure, the ratio of investment expenditures to GDP which was about 6.3 percent in 1979 fell continuously throughout the 1980s to 4.7 percent in FY 1985 (Table 6). It rose a little in the late 1980s (especially in FY 1987), reflecting the government economic package to increase domestic demand. It remained, however, at a level of about 5 percent until FY 1990.

TABLE 6

Actual and Estimated Tax Revenue

(100 million yen)

FY	Actual Tax Revenue (a)	Growth Rate	Estimate (b)	Growth Rate	Difference (a−b)
1980	260,278	13.7	260,278	13.7	0
1981	277,792	6.7	279,747	7.5	−1,955
1982	292,484	5.3	296,671	6.0	−4,187
1983	310,641	6.2	314,620	6.1	−3,979
1984	335,733	8.1	336,426	6.9	−690
1985	367,862	9.6	356,777	6.0	11,085
1986	403,010	9.6	378,362	6.1	24,648
1987	449,757	11.6	394,594	4.3	55,163
1988	488,943	8.7	414,126	4.9	74,817
1989	529,617	8.3	443,280	7.0	86,337
1990	582,114	9.9	473,025	6.7	109,089
1991	580,716	−0.2	503,724	6.5	76,992

NOTE: (1) Figures in column b are calculated assuming real economic growth rate of 4 percent and tax elasticity of 1.1. (2) Settlement base.

SOURCE: Fuji Sōgō Kenkyūjo (1994).

Two major factors contributed to this outcome.[4] One was the change in the role of the LDP politicians. Until the 1970s, their role in the budgetary process was mainly to put pressure on the Ministry of Finance to realize the demands of interest groups. Starting in the 1980s, some of the leading politicians began to assume a role of coordination. In many important policy issues, they were successful in meeting the demands of interest groups. This change occurred because the politicians gradually accumulated knowledge on policies. The second factor was the across-the-board ceiling imposed on budget demand. This was particularly effective in reducing current expenditures and public works expenditures.

Reduction in Deficit. The increase in tax revenue combined with the belt-tightening in expenditures produced a significant reduction in the budget deficit. The general government balance (including local government balances) was in deficit up to fiscal 1986, but it went into the black in the following year, and in both 1990 and 1991 it registered a large surplus in excess of 3 percent of GDP (see Table 7). Since the deficit stood at 4.4 percent in 1979, this was a significant improvement.

In terms of the deficit in the general account of the national budget, the bond

TABLE 7

Components of General Government Expenditure and Revenue
(Ratio to GDP, %)

	Gc	SS	Ti	Td	Sc	Gi	D
1978	9.66	7.48	7.13	10.38	7.00	6.25	−4.19
1979	9.74	7.65	7.41	10.37	7.13	6.28	−4.45
1980	9.82	7.97	7.38	11.12	7.40	6.08	−4.04
1981	9.97	8.42	7.53	11.31	7.85	5.96	−3.71
1982	9.86	8.82	7.50	11.56	8.03	5.74	−3.41
1983	9.91	9.22	7.58	11.86	8.11	5.37	−2.94
1984	9.77	9.11	7.60	11.97	8.05	4.94	−1.83
1985	9.57	9.18	7.52	12.25	8.37	4.74	−0.77
1986	9.62	9.64	7.70	12.45	8.78	4.80	−0.32
1987	9.39	9.79	8.11	13.02	8.48	5.21	0.68
1988	9.17	9.63	8.39	13.41	8.47	4.96	2.18
1989	9.13	9.60	8.24	13.79	8.64	5.03	2.66
1990	9.14	9.47	8.10	14.08	9.09	5.05	3.54
1991	9.15	9.56	8.08	13.64	9.28	5.21	3.48

NOTE: Gc=Government consumption, SS=Social security payment, Ti=Indirect tax, Td=Direct tax, Sc=Social security contribution, Gi=Government investment, D=Deficit.

SOURCE: Economic Planning Agency, *Yearbook on National Account,* each year.

dependence ratio (the ratio of bond revenues to total revenue) fell from 33.5 percent in 1980 to 7.6 percent in FY 1991 (see Table 8). Issuance of deficit-financing bonds was terminated in this year and fiscal reconstruction was achieved. The balance of the national debt stood at a record 42.7 percent of GDP in FY 1986, but this percentage fell continuously in subsequent years, reaching 35.9 percent at the end of FY 1992.

If we compare the ratios of the general account budget items to GDP between 1980 and 1991, we find that the ratio for expenditures fell by about 2.3 percentage points, whereas that for tax revenue increased by about 2.0. Thus, it seems that fiscal reconstruction was achieved by both increased revenue and suppressed expenditure. This is true as far as the general account is concerned. The view, however, is not correct for the general government. This is because some of the reductions in the general account budget were superficial, particularly for social security expenditures. Although the outlay from the general account was reduced, social security payments continued to increase as shown in Table 7, because the reductions were compensated by increased social security contributions. Hence, we must say that the essential factor that brought about fiscal reconstruction was the increase in tax revenues. If we recall the mechanism

TABLE 8

Trends in National Bonds

	Total National Bond (A)	Deficit Financing Bond (B)	Bond Dependence Ratio (%)	Ratio of A to GDP (%)
1975	20,000		9.4	9.8
1976	72,750	37,500	29.9	12.9
1977	84,800	40,500	29.7	16.8
1978	109,850	49,350	32.0	20.4
1979	152,700	80,550	39.6	25.0
1980	142,700	74,850	33.5	28.7
1981	122,700	54,850	26.2	31.6
1982	104,400	54,850	21.0	35.3
1983	133,450	39,240	23.5	38.4
1984	126,800	69,800	25.0	39.8
1985	116,800	64,550	22.2	41.3
1986	109,460	57,300	20.2	42.7
1987	105,010	52,460	19.4	42.6
1988	88,410	49,810	15.6	41.3
1989	71,110	31,510	11.8	39.6
1990	55,932	13,310	8.4	38.1
1991	53,430	0	7.6	37.2
1992	72,800	0	10.0	35.9

NOTE: A and B are in 100 million yen.

SOURCE: Ministry of Finance, *Finance and Monetary Statistics*, each issue.

behind this increase, we must conclude that fiscal reconstruction was achieved by the bubble economy of the 1980s.

Macroeconomic Balance

Saving-Investment Balance and External Surplus. As mentioned before, the external surplus, which was almost zero in FY 1981, increased to above 4 percent of GDP in FY 1986. Table 9 shows this trend in relation to the change in the domestic saving-investment balance in terms of the ratio to GDP (since saving in this table is net saving while investment is gross, the difference is not equal to the external surplus).

Needless to say, this relation does not tell causality. Yet, the following observation can be made. As shown in Table 9, government and private investments

TABLE 9
Trends in Saving-Investment Balance
(Ratio to GDP)

	I/Y	GI/Y	PI/Y	S/Y	F/Y
1978	0.307	0.063	0.244	0.205	0.012
1979	0.318	0.063	0.255	0.180	−0.014
1980	0.314	0.061	0.253	0.188	−0.006
1981	0.302	0.060	0.243	0.180	0.005
1982	0.292	0.057	0.235	0.166	0.008
1983	0.278	0.054	0.224	0.168	0.020
1984	0.276	0.049	0.227	0.171	0.030
1985	0.275	0.047	0.228	0.180	0.037
1986	0.273	0.048	0.225	0.181	0.044
1987	0.290	0.052	0.238	0.188	0.033
1988	0.302	0.050	0.252	0.198	0.026
1989	0.313	0.050	0.263	0.198	0.019
1990	0.324	0.050	0.273	0.204	0.011
1991	0.313	0.052	0.261	0.202	0.026

NOTE: Y:GDP, I:Domestic capital formation, GI:Government investment, PI: Private investment, S:Net national saving, F:External surplus.

SOURCE: Economic Planning Agency, *Yearbook on National Account,* each year.

fell by roughly the same magnitude during this period, the former by about 1.2 percent of GDP and the latter by about 1.7 percent of GDP. That is, changes in both private and government investments were the major factors behind the increase in the current account surplus.

During the latter half of the 1980s, on the other hand, domestic investment (the sum of private and government investment) increased dramatically (its ratio to GDP increased from 27.3 percent in FY 1986 to 32.4 percent in FY 1990, as shown in Table 9). As a result, external surplus shrank in spite of the (slight) increase in net domestic saving. Note that although government investment increased during this period, the magnitude was quite small compared to the change in private investment. Namely, the reduction in external surplus during this period was mainly accompanied by an increase in private investment.

The surplus in around FY 1986 was greater than the trend level probably because it was partly brought about by the cyclical low level of private investment. Also, the reduction in external surplus during the latter half of the 1980s was cyclical because it was mainly brought about by a cyclical increase in private investment.

Breakdown of the Saving-Investment Balance by Sectors. Table 10 shows a breakdown of domestic saving. There was a very distinct trend throughout the 1980s: in terms of the ratio to GDP, government saving increased substantially, reflecting the increase in tax revenue and suppressed expenditures. On the other hand, household saving continued to fall. Corporate saving, on the other hand, stayed at almost the same level until FY 1986, increased during 1986–89, and fell dramatically thereafter, reflecting the boom and recession, respectively.

It is interesting that the decrease in household saving was to a large extent offset by the increase in government saving until about FY 1986 as shown in column (b+c) of Table 10; hence, the national saving rate during this period stayed at almost the same level in terms of its ratio to GDP. In the latter half of the 1980s, however, this relation broke down due to a remarkable increase in government saving and the national saving rate increased as mentioned above.

The above trend in saving and investment produces very different patterns of saving-investment balance in different sectors, which are shown in Table 11. The balance of households did not show a remarkable trend throughout this period; investment in this sector fluctuated roughly in accordance with the change in saving. The balance of the government sector showed spectacular improvement throughout the 1980s. Also, the deficit of the corporate sector shrank until the mid-1980s. As mentioned before, these factors caused an increase in the external surplus. During the latter half of the 1980s, the balance of the corporate sector deteriorated considerably, and this caused a reduction in the external surplus in spite of the increase in the government saving-investment gap.

Was "Japan Money" Due to the Bubble? The following arguments are often made concerning the increase in external surplus in the 1980s. First, it has been argued that because the collateral value of land increased due to the rise in land prices, landholders were able to borrow from financial institutions utilizing land as collateral and used the money for investments, including foreign investment. Second, it has been claimed that the increase in foreign investment can be explained as an effort to attain a balance between domestic and foreign assets in investors' portfolios.

The first argument cannot be accepted. As mentioned earlier, large corporations holding huge amounts of land reduced rather than increased their borrowing from financial institutions. Moreover, the rise in the collateral value of land itself cannot affect the total amount of investment in Japan and hence the macroeconomic saving-investment balance. It might have increased borrowing and hence investment by landholders, but on the other hand those by non-landholders must have been suppressed. The second view is also unpersuasive. If portfolios of domestic and foreign assets are already in equilibrium conditions, such balancing action may become necessary as the value of domestic assets increases. However, Japan is currently in the process of increasing

TABLE 10

Trends in Saving

(Ratio to GDP)

	Corporations	Households		Government	
	a	b	a+b	c	b+c
1978	0.030	0.140	0.170	0.029	0.168
1979	0.021	0.123	0.144	0.026	0.150
1980	0.025	0.126	0.151	0.029	0.156
1981	0.022	0.126	0.148	0.030	0.156
1982	0.019	0.113	0.132	0.029	0.142
1983	0.027	0.111	0.138	0.028	0.139
1984	0.028	0.110	0.137	0.034	0.144
1985	0.030	0.109	0.139	0.043	0.152
1986	0.034	0.106	0.140	0.047	0.153
1987	0.039	0.101	0.140	0.061	0.161
1988	0.038	0.095	0.133	0.075	0.170
1989	0.040	0.091	0.131	0.079	0.171
1990	0.028	0.088	0.116	0.094	0.182
1991	0.021	0.096	0.116	0.093	0.189

SOURCE: Economic Planning Agency, *Yearbook on National Account*, each year.

its domestic and foreign assets in the long term (the ratio of Japan's net foreign assets to GDP is around 11 percent; it is still quite low compared to those of other countries—22 percent in the United Kingdom and 21 percent in Germany, for example).

Indeed, these hypotheses do not explain the actual trends, because the surplus of the current account fell after 1988 when land and stock prices continued to increase. The main reason behind the change in the current account was the increase in domestic investment, as mentioned before. Thus, the increase in asset prices in the latter half of the 1980s did not raise foreign investment, but decreased it.

The major cause of the increase in the current surplus can be found in the aforementioned macroeconomic policies during this period. The effect of the asset price increase existed only in the sense that it made foreign investments greater than the current account surplus during this period. As mentioned earlier, this is the result of short-term fundraising-cum-long-term investment activities of Japanese financial institutions. In particular, Japanese banks took in funds through Euro-markets, and passed them on to real estate finance abroad.

TABLE 11
Trends in Saving-Investment Balance by Sectors
(Ratio to GDP)

	Corporations	Households	Government
1978	−0.033	0.084	−0.042
1979	−0.059	0.074	−0.044
1980	−0.061	0.091	−0.040
1981	−0.058	0.096	−0.037
1982	−0.051	0.080	−0.034
1983	−0.040	0.091	−0.029
1984	−0.048	0.088	−0.018
1985	−0.057	0.097	−0.008
1986	−0.042	0.094	−0.003
1987	−0.049	0.076	0.009
1988	−0.068	0.082	0.028
1989	−0.071	0.086	0.027
1990	−0.098	0.091	0.035
1991	−0.080	0.091	0.035

SOURCE: Economic Planning Agency, *Yearbook on National Account*, each year.

Assessing the Macroeconomic Policy of the 1980s

The analysis in the preceding section indicates that the way public finance functioned in the 1980s had very important consequences for the macroeconomic performance of the Japanese economy. The very stringent fiscal policy that remained unchanged even in the late 1980s when tax revenue increased dramatically owing to economic boom and the bubbles in asset prices caused a remarkable improvement in the budget deficit. This was no doubt desirable from the point of view of the budget authority. It was, however, not necessarily so from the point of view of the economy as a whole. In fact, we can argue that this caused a considerable distortion in resource allocation in the Japanese economy.

What would have happened if there had been a higher level of public investment? This would have pushed up domestic interest rates, increasing capital inflow from abroad (or decreasing capital outflow), and hence would have led to a stronger yen and a smaller current account surplus. Overseas investment would therefore have remained at a lower level. Thus, there would have been less increase in the level of Japan's foreign assets and a corresponding improvement in domestic social capital.

What actually happened was that domestic savings were directed not into improvement of social infrastructure but into the acquisition of assets abroad. The Japanese, with their low level of social capital, may be compared to a family living in a dilapidated house who have worked hard and scrimped to save money and have then used it not to improve their own home but to lend to others.

The same thing can be said for monetary policy. What would have happened if the authorities had not loosened the reins? Here too the effect would have been to strengthen the yen, reduce the current account surplus, and cut the level of overseas investment. Domestically, it would have decreased the level of lending by financial institutions, thereby preventing the abnormal increase in land purchases by the real estate industry.[5]

To sum up the above discussion, there is a strong possibility that, under different macroeconomic policies, i.e., less loose monetary policy combined with more aggressive fiscal policy, the asset-price inflation of the 1980s would not have happened and living standards would have been raised. It can be argued that a bias in economic mechanisms gave rise to a mismanagement of policies and hence to a distortion of resource allocation. This can be described as follows.

Improvements in productivity gave rise to a stronger yen. In principle, people should have reaped the rewards of their hard work as a stronger yen acted to lower the prices of imported goods. What actually happened, however, was that the profits produced by the appreciation of the yen were not passed on to consumers but absorbed by producers and distributors. This increased corporate profits, and businesses rushed to channel these funds into *zai*-tech investment activities. The rise in corporate profits also pushed up stock prices, making it easier for companies to raise funds cheaply by issuing equity or equity-linked bonds. And these funds were channeled into land speculation via financial institutions. Meanwhile, credit was relaxed to prevent further appreciation of the yen, and this allowed stock and land prices to rise even further.

Asset price inflation increased tax revenue and also increased consumer spending on goods such as automobiles. Businessmen took this increase as a permanent increase and expanded production capacities. This brought about an economic boom and a further increase in tax revenue. In this sense, it can be said that the government was the biggest gainer from the bubble economy. But, since expenditures were suppressed, the government deficit decreased, and this increased the external current account surplus.

The main reason the easy money policy was adopted was that the government was anxious about the effect of the appreciation of the yen on domestic industry. While a stronger yen should benefit consumers by lowering the cost of imported goods and thus raising their real incomes, it tends to hurt producers, particularly those who depend heavily on exports. In the actual economy, however, the benefits of the yen's sharp rise were not passed on to consumers because of numerous regulations and the imperfections of the market. As a result, people were conscious only of the negative effects of the stronger yen, and a consensus emerged in favor of curbing the rise. Japan would have done better if it had adopted an economic policy that balanced the interests of producers with those of consumers.

AFTER THE BUBBLE

A Battle with the "Bubble"

The Bank of Japan changed its policy in May 1989, when the official discount rate was raised from 2.5 to 3.25 percent. It was raised further in several subsequent steps, and by the fifth step in August 1990, it became 6.0 percent (Table 3). Long-term interest rates (yield of government bonds) rose from a low of 4.7 percent during April-June 1988 to 7.8 percent in August 1990.

It must be noted, however, that the real interest rate did not rise as much as the nominal rate, since the rate of inflation rose during this period. (The annual rate of increase in the CPI, which was 0.1 percent in 1987, rose to 2.3 percent in 1989.) In fact, the movement of land prices was not the same as that in nominal interest rates: land prices in Osaka continued to rise during 1989.

In addition to the general tightening of monetary conditions, the Ministry of Finance imposed a special restriction on bank lending to real estate companies in April 1990. This was to restrict the growth rate in the lending of individual banks to real estate companies to less than that of the total lending of the bank. As a result of this restriction, loans to real estate companies declined during 1990. This had a strong impact on land transactions and land prices.

Also, it has come to be recognized, correctly, that the low cost of landholding in Japan was one of the major causes that enabled land speculation. Increasing the property tax would be the most powerful method to discourage speculative land transactions. There are, however, strong oppositions to this policy. Since more than half of all households possess land in some form or other, the anti-property-tax sentiment is strong.

In spite of this, the government significantly changed its attitude toward land taxes. The Basic Land Law, which passed the Diet in December 1989, recognized the importance of a land tax, though in an abstract expression. The Subcommittee on Land Tax, which was established in the Tax Council in April 1990, released a report in October 1990, recommending the introduction of a new landholding tax. The new tax, called *chika-zei* (land price tax), was introduced in 1991.[6]

Collapse of the Bubble and Recession

At the beginning of 1990, stock prices started to fall. After recording an all-time high of ¥38,915 at the end of 1989, the Nikkei average turned down sharply, dropping to about ¥28,000 in April 1990. In August, following Iraq's invasion of Kuwait, the downward trend picked up speed again. The total market value of shares listed on the Tokyo Stock Exchange fell from ¥850 trillion in December 1989 to ¥365 trillion in December 1990. Stock prices stabilized somewhat in 1991 but started to fall again in 1992.

Land prices also started to fall in the second half of 1990 and dropped sharply in 1991. According to the National Land Agency's 1992 appraisals, the rate of decline in residential land prices over the period from July 1991 to July 1992 was 14.7 percent in Tokyo, 23.8 percent in Osaka Prefecture, and 33.2 percent in the city of Kyoto. Given the fact that land prices had risen every year since World War II with the sole exception of 1975, when the country was reeling from the first oil shock, the precipitous fall in 1991 may fairly be described as an utterly new experience for the Japanese economy. Land prices have continued to fall until the present.

The continued plunge in asset prices was particularly unusual in that it occurred against a background of monetary relaxation. This is further evidence that there were considerable bubble elements in asset prices.

The real economy entered into recession in the middle of 1991. Housing investment started to fall in FY 1991 (Table 1). Business investment followed. It recorded a negative growth rate in FY 1992–93. Demand for consumer durables declined too. As shown in Table 2, the number of automobiles sold in the domestic market continued to fall after a peak in 1990. The labor demand-supply condition also slackened considerably.

It must be noted, however, that the present level is not so low from a long-run viewpoint. For example, even automobiles, which are usually regarded as the "symbol" of the recession, had recent sales figures that are not low compared to the trend during the early 1980s (Table 2). This implies that the activity level in the late 1980s was abnormally high. This is also confirmed from the labor demand-supply condition (Table 2). The level until 1990 was abnormally high and this brought an illegal inflow of labor forces from abroad. It is apparent that the economic activities of the late 1980s were above the full employment level, and the Japanese economy could not have sustained them.

Macroeconomic Policy in the 1990s

Confronted with the recession, the Bank of Japan began to ease monetary policy in July 1991. Some people argued that the change was late, i.e., monetary policy should have been relaxed earlier. It must be noted, however, that the cautious attitude of the monetary authority was not without reason, because the bubble elements in asset prices, especially land prices, still remained at that time. In other words, there were two conflicting objectives for the monetary authority. It can be argued that if monetary policy had been relaxed earlier, the bubble would have continued longer, making the problems resulting from the bubble more serious. Since the recession continued, the official discount rate was further lowered by several steps, and it reached the historic low level of 1.75 percent in September 1993 (Table 3).

As a result of the recession, tax revenue fell significantly, and the budget deficit began to increase again. The issuance of deficit-financing bonds was revitalized in FY 1994 due to the shortfall in tax revenue. The bond dependency ratio has been raised to 18.7 percent and the ratio of national debt outstanding to GDP is expected to become 41 percent at the end of FY 1994.[7]

With a growing external surplus and prolonged recession as background, some say Japan should adopt stimulative macroeconomic policies. In the international discussion, there is pressure from abroad, especially from the United States, for Japan to adopt a stimulative package such as an income tax reduction in order to reduce surplus in the external current account. In the domestic scene, businessmen call for a stimulative package for the recovery of the economy and to prevent further appreciation of the yen. The Ministry of Finance, on the other hand, strongly resists these ideas, arguing that any further increase in the budget deficit is impermissible.

The above arguments, however, cannot be accepted because of the following reasons. First, with regard to the claim of the businessmen that a stimulative package is necessary, it is important to recall that in a world where there are free movements of international capital flow, fiscal policy would normally lead to an appreciation of the currency and hence would be neutral to the aggregate demand. Second, with regard to the American argument for an income tax reduction, it is necessary to note that under the situation where the household consumption attitude is timid due to uncertain expectations for the future, an income tax cut could only lead to an increase in saving.

This argument, however, does not imply that an increase in public spending is unnecessary. On the contrary, an increase in public expenditure, especially that in investment for infrastructure in urban areas, is a very urgent task for Japan today. It is important to note, however, that this policy is primarily necessary in order to raise the living standard of Japanese citizens and not for the short-run pumping-up effect. A reduction in external surplus would follow, but this should be regarded a result of the policy and not an objective.

Japan's Role in the World Economy

Some people suggest that Japan is currently experiencing a new type of recession, claiming that the aftereffects of the bubble, weighing heavily on both households and businesses, will cause the economy to continue to stagnate.

Others argue that Japan's apparent economic strength in the 1980s was no more than a temporary illusion created by the bubble; the bursting of the bubble, they say, signals the end of the brief "age of Japan." They point out that Japanese financial investors facing difficulty with funds due to the bubble collapse pulled out of foreign assets, thereby disrupting international capital markets.

It is true that, in 1991, an unprecedented case of a long-term capital balance turning into a surplus (excess inflow) despite the increase in the current balance surplus occurred. Yet, its main cause lay in the increase of investment in Japanese stocks by foreign institutional investors and the resulting increase in the inflow of funds to Japan. On the other hand, Japanese banks returned short-term funds through the Euro-market. Thus, the supply of funds in such forms continued. In other words, the cause of the extraordinary results in 1991 was the reversal of the forms of special fundraising in the latter half of the 1980s.

As stated previously, long-term capital supply surpassing the current balance surplus through short-term fundraising was a special case in the second half of the 1980s; it may not occur in the future. Nevertheless, even in such cases, capital supply from Japan will not disappear. From a long-term perspective, capital outflow financed by a current balance surplus will continue in the future.

The surplus of the current balance has increased compared to the latter half of the 1980s. This is because the gap in saving and investment was enlarged due to reduced domestic investment. And, the outflow of long-term capital has increased along with it. This effect will surpass the decrease in the aforementioned financial intermediary mechanism.

Whether Japan continues to be a capital-exporting country in the longer-term depends on how the domestic saving-investment balance changes in the future. Since the saving rate is expected to decrease due to the future aging of the population, the difference in domestic saving and investment, or the surplus in the current balance, will gradually decrease. Yet, at least during this century, Japan's position as a capital-exporting country will not change.

To relate the decline in asset prices and the sudden decrease in long-term capital outflow in 1991, and to think that "Japan has sunk," is a myopic view.

CONCLUDING REMARKS

A Shift to a Consumer-Oriented Economy?

I have argued above that because consumers could not reap the benefits of the appreciation of the yen and because the employment of many workers depended on the performance of exporting industries, preventing the appreciation of the yen came to be regarded as the most important objective of macroeconomic policy. This became the major cause of the bubble. Also, since the demand by urbanites for social infrastructure was not sufficiently reflected in the budget-making process, public investment continued to be suppressed despite the increase in tax revenues, and this brought the increase in external surplus. In this sense, policy errors and distortions in resource allocation during the 1980s were caused by a fundamental bias in Japan's economic structure in which consumers' interests were neglected.

This situation has gradually changed in the 1990s. First, the difference between domestic and international prices has been reduced. As a result, many people have come to recognize that an appreciation of the yen is desirable for consumers and, along with it, public opinions on exchange rate issues have gradually changed.

Second, the government policy for public investment changed. Partly influenced by the Structural Impediments Initiative with the United States, the government formulated a plan to spend ¥430 trillion on public investment during the decade starting FY 1991. Not only the volume but also the composition of investments was altered. The new emphasis is on consumer-oriented social infrastructure such as sewers, streets, and parks, and this may illustrate a shift from producer-centered aims to consumer-centered aims.

In general, many people have come to feel that Japan's economic structure should be reformed to one that is more consumer-oriented. The present economic plan, formulated by the Miyazawa administration, declared *seikatsu taikoku* (a superpower in people's lives) as its goal. The Hosokawa administration also emphasized consumers' interests in economic policies and designated "deregulation" as one of the top priorities of its economic policy. It must be noted, however, that these changes are not quite sufficient to reform the basic structure of the Japanese economy.

First, with regard to the exchange rate policy, the majority of public opinions still support the prevention of a stronger yen. This reflects the fact that the benefit of the appreciation of the currency is not sufficiently channeled to consumers. It also reflects many people's beliefs that the present export-oriented industrial structure must be maintained in order to secure employment.

Second, with respect to budget policy, the Ministry of Finance still opposes any increase in the budget deficit. This became quite visible in the case of the Hiraiwa Committee, established by then Prime Minister Hosokawa and chaired by Chairman Hiraiwa of Keidanren (Japan Federation of Corporations). Although the purpose of the committee was to advise on means for fundamental change of the economic structure, it was forced to mention in its final report that if public investment were to be increased, it must be financed by "measures that do not leave a burden for the future," meaning that it must be financed by a tax increase rather than by increased deficit.

The 1940 Regime

The above observation suggests that the basic structure of the Japanese economy which caused problems in the late 1980s still remains. In a very simplified form, this may be described as follows.[8]

The basic feature of the corporate sector is the employee-oriented structure. This is represented by the lifetime employment practice, the seniority wage system, and the custom that the top managers consist of in-house workers rather than representatives of stockholders. This system has given strong incentives for workers to work hard for the sake of "their company" and has raised the productivity of leading manufacturing industries.

On the other hand, there are sectors whose productivity growth lags behind the manufacturing industries. They consist of agriculture, retail, and small service businesses such as small restaurants and barbers. In order to prevent the social tension that could arise from the productivity differentials, the government has intervened heavily in this sector, by giving protection in the form of import restrictions and entry restrictions. It also provided heavy financial aid to this sector through budget subsidies, tax concessions, and government financial programs.

It is important to note that this system has a long history; its origins can be traced back to the economic reforms introduced around 1940. The employee-oriented form of corporations was brought about by the restriction of stockholders' rights by the Total Mobilization Act of 1938. The Foodstuff Control Act was introduced in 1942. Many business organizations that are the vehicles of administrative guidance were also introduced during this period. In this sense, the Japanese economic system may be called the "1940 regime."

This system, originally introduced in order to fight the "total war" (the Pacific War), remained almost intact despite the defeat in the war and functioned quite well to fight another total war, namely, the war for rapid economic growth. It is also important to note that the basic characteristic of the 1940 regime is the emphasis on producers' interests.

This system, which functioned so well in the past, has gradually become an obstacle for the future development of the Japanese economy. With "employee-oriented" corporations, it would be difficult to realize substantial changes in industrial structure, because workers are reluctant to move to other firms. With heavily protected sectors such as agriculture and retail, it would be difficult for consumers to obtain the benefits of the appreciation of the currency.

The view presented here concerning the basic structure of the Japanese economy is similar to Yamamura's "developmentalism-supporter" thesis, in particular, the "developmentalism" part. Both recognize a bias in policy formation in which consumers' interests tend to be neglected. Unlike Yamamura, however, this paper emphasizes the continuity from the prewar period. As

Yamamura correctly points out, developmentalism is like a huge tanker and it is very difficult to change its course. Whether or not the Japanese economy will be able to transform itself into a truly consumer-oriented economy depends on whether a fundamental change can be made to the "1940 regime."

NOTES

1. Needless to say, a rigorous analysis of the bubble is more complicated. The difficulty lies in that future rentals or future dividends in the formula of the "fundamental" prices are those of expected values conditional upon available information. Since we cannot directly observe these variables, we cannot calculate fundamental prices in a direct fashion. Although this is an important issue, I do not enter into a detailed discussion in this paper.

2. The figures in the Ministry of Finance's Corporate Statistics for the value of land owned are significantly lower than the figures from the EPA's national accounts. While the latter values land at current prices, the former are based on acquisition prices. The figures for the value of land purchased, by contrast, are higher in the Corporate Statistics.

3. This issue is discussed in Noguchi (1987).

4. For details, see Noguchi (1991).

5. It can also be argued that the overemphasis on fiscal reconstruction was a major cause of the "bubble economy." The reduction in the deficit meant there were fewer national bonds available for financial institutions to invest in, forcing them to place more of their funds in loans and thereby indirectly fueling speculative activity, namely, the cut in the volume of government bonds aggravated the portfolio-management difficulties of financial institutions. If the supply of government bonds had gone on increasing during this period, banks and other institutions would not have had to compete so intensively to make loans.

If, for example, the national debt had continued to be the same percentage of GDP from 1986 on, it would have been about ¥20 trillion more at the end of fiscal 1990 than it actually was. And ¥20 trillion is approximately the amount by which loans to the real estate industry increased during the second half of the 1980s. This is no mere coincidence. If there had been no reduction in government bond issues, there is a strong possibility that the abnormal increase in the volume of loans to the real estate industry would not have occurred.

6. For details, see Noguchi (1992).

7. Another important change was that in politics. The Liberal Democratic Party, which had been the ruling party since 1955, was forced to become the non-government party in 1993, and the new coalition government took power.

8. For details, see Noguchi (1993) and Okazaki and Okuno (1993).

REFERENCES

Economic Planning Agency. 1989. *Keizai hakusho.* Tokyo: Government Printing Office.
Economic Research Institute, Economic Planning Agency. Annual. *Kokumin keizai keisan nenpō.* Tokyo: Government Printing Office.
Fuji Sōgō Kenkyūjo. 1994. *Nihon keizai kaikaku no senryaku.* Tokyo: Tōyō Keizai Shinpōsha.
Ministry of Finance. Annual. *Zaisei kinyū tōkei geppō, hojin kigyō tōkei tokushū-gō.* Tokyo: Government Printing Office.
Noguchi Yukio. 1987. Public finance. In *The political economy of Japan, Vol. 1: The domestic transformation,* ed. Kozo Yamamura and Yasukichi Yasuba. Stanford: Stanford University Press.
————. 1991. Budget policy-making in Japan. In *Parallel politics: economic policy making in Japan and the United States,* ed. Samuel Kernell. Washington: Brookings Institution.
————. 1992. Land problems and policies in Japan: structural aspects. In *Land issues in Japan: a policy failure?* ed. John O. Haley and Kozo Yamamura. Seattle: Society for Japanese Studies.
————. 1993. Nihongata shisutemu kaikaku no mokuhyō wa 1940 nen taisei no daha. *Gekkan asahi* 5(9).
Okazaki Tetsuji and Okuno Masahiro, eds. 1993. *Gendai Nihon keizai no genryū.* Tokyo: Nihon Keizai Shinbun.

Capital Movements Between
the United States and Japan in
the Context of Yen-Dollar Politics

KOICHI HAMADA

THE CURRENT ACCOUNT of Japan has recorded an almost continuous surplus since the late 1970s. Replacing the United Kingdom and, in particular, the United States, Japan has emerged as a main supplier of capital to the world market in the last two decades. At the end of 1992, the net foreign assets of Japan were estimated to be $513 billion, and the net liability of the United States to be $611 billion. Since 1981, a substantial portion of Japan's current account surplus has been vis-a-vis the United States. This implies that Japan has been lending directly or indirectly to the United States.

The main direction of foreign direct investment is rather one-sided. Flows of direct investment have been predominantly from Japan to the United States. The relative scarcity of U.S. direct investment into Japan is an issue of academic discussion (Lawrence 1993, Mason 1992) as well as a topic in trade negotiations where the American representative emphasizes the closedness of the Japanese market. On the other hand, flows of portfolio investment and acquisition of long-term and short-term securities have moved substantially in both directions and fluctuated according to economic conditions in the United States and in Japan. In a highly developed financial market, exogenous shocks often cause instantaneous reshuffling of portfolio investment which leads to volatile movements in exchange rates, and exchange rate movements or changes in their expectations in turn cause reshuffling of the portfolio.

On an intuitive level, motivations for international capital movements can be analyzed from supply or "push" factors and demand or "pull" factors. The surplus of the current account of Japan, namely, the difference between domestic savings and domestic investment, creates the accumulation of net wealth abroad of Japan in general, which is an important push factor for capital outflow from Japan to the United States. By the national income identity, the current account surplus of a country is to be matched by the net increase of its foreign assets, whatever form—direct investment, direct lending, short or long-term portfolio investment—they take. The appreciation of the yen increases the national wealth of Japan from which capital outflows take place and often seems to work as a push factor for Japanese investment abroad. In the case of direct investment, the accumulation of entrepreneurial and organizational capacities works as a push factor. A decline in the rate of prospective return to domestic investment or in the rate of interest is also a push factor. However, when the rate of prospective return to investment in Japan is low, the attitude of entrepreneurs becomes pessimistic and generally the magnitude of foreign direct investment outflow is not large.

On the other hand, there are demand or pull factors in the recipient country. A deficit in the current account is again a fundamental determinant of capital inflows in various forms. A low level of exchange rates makes it easier for foreign investors to buy firms, real estate, and securities. A boom and good prospects for future returns in the host country are certainly pull factors as well.

We have noticed the effect of the level of exchange rates as push or pull factors. The same applies to the level of prices for equities and land. Moreover, expectations for future exchange rates and stock prices are crucially important. A rising stock market or real estate market in a country gives incentives for direct investment into the country. Expectations for the appreciation of the future value of U.S. stock, for example, invite in particular portfolio investment into the United States from Japan.

Of course, we are not living in a two-country world. In the two-country world, if Japan accumulates current account surplus vis-a-vis the United States then, automatically, the same amount of capital moves from Japan to the United States. However, in a multi-country world it does not necessarily follow that course. Japan can lend to Europe and Europe can in turn lend to the United States, even if Japan's current account surplus with respect to the United States is large. During the early part of the 1980s, this was indeed the case, as Kuroyanagi, Hamada, and Sakurai (1991) documented. Therefore, in addition to push factors, we have to consider the role of international financial intermediaries and the role of financial centers in our global picture. Thus, "channeling" factors are important to the direction and magnitude of capital flows as well.

Those economic factors have been, at the same time, influenced by macroeconomic policies and the process of deregulation in the financial markets in both countries. These policy changes have been sometimes motivated by deliberate considerations of economic objectives, but were often generated by the interaction of political forces that represent interests of various industrial groups, the central bank, and ministries of the government. Capital movements have been affected by international policy coordination and the yen-dollar politics on both sides of the Pacific. One emphasis of this paper is on the political economy aspects of the factors that have affected flows of funds between the two countries.

In Section I, I briefly trace the development of capital flow between Japan and the United States, distinguishing various types of capital flows. In Section II, I introduce a coherent framework to understand the relationship between current account imbalance and the role of each component of capital movements. A completely general equilibrium framework is indeed difficult to use for operational hypothesis testing, but the understanding of the overall picture is useful as a frame of reference.

In Section III, I describe the institutional development of the Japanese economy and the United States in such a way as to highlight the institutional development that would have worked as the push or pull factor on the flows of capital between the two countries. In Section IV, I discuss the political economy aspect behind capital flows and changes in the balance of payments as well as institutional development in the two countries. The success of the Ministry of Finance to reduce the budget deficit by introduction of the consumption (or national sales) tax certainly reinforced the saving-investment discrepancy in Japan, just as the supply-side policy of tax reduction in the Reagan administration worked in the opposite direction. The leadership of James Baker as a synthesizer of international monetary coordination kept the value of the dollar from depreciating after the Louvre Accord, and the merit of policy coordination during 1987–89 was doubtful because it created a basis for the easy money policy that triggered asset bubbles in Japan, and also because the resulting depreciated dollar most likely slowed down the adjustment of the U.S. current account. Section V gives a brief sketch of foreign direct investment between the two countries.

In my opinion, the fact that monetary contraction policy was too late and too abrupt was an important factor that triggered the current stagnation in the Japanese economy. The present recession has contributed to the current account surplus through the lack of effective demand in Japan. It has affected the composition of capital flows by reducing outward foreign direct investment from Japan through a discouraging effect on the entrepreneurship of Japan's foreign investors and through disrupting credit conditions.

I. AN OVERVIEW OF TIME-SERIES DATA

Let us begin by reviewing the trend and pattern of capital movements between Japan and the United States. Though some discrepancies exist between
Japanese and U.S. statistics, they are not large. Thus, except where noted, I trace
primarily the Japanese statistics.

Figure 1 depicts Japan's current and trade balance accounts (Bank of Japan).[1]
In the last two decades, the service account of Japan has always been in deficit
and Japan's current account was accordingly less than its trade account. After
1981, both accounts show a consistent upward trend until 1987. The downward
trend between 1987 and 1990 corresponded to the domestic economic boom
of Japan. However, even in the domestic boom period, the level of Japan's
current account surplus was substantial. This created a "push" factor for the
accumulation of foreign assets.

Figure 2 indicates the relationship between the yen/dollar exchange rate and
the balance of the current account. Figure 3 shows the relationship between
the long-term capital balance and the exchange rate. When the dollar was
depreciating after the Plaza Accord in 1985, the outflow of long-term capital
increased.

In 1991, Japan experienced a substantial surplus in long-term capital; the
inflow of long-term capital exceeded outflow. The net inflow of long-term
capital was about $40 billion during fiscal year (FY) 1991. Since the current
account of Japan was in surplus by $90 billion in FY 1991, this implies that
offsetting transactions of about $130 billion took place in terms of the surplus
in the short-term capital account, increase in official reserves, and the improvement of the credit-liability position of the banking sector. Since the private
(non-banking) short-term capital surplus and the increase in official reserves
were about $16 billion and $2 billion respectively, this means that the credit-
liability position of the banking sector was greatly improved.

As Kindleberger argues, a country—in his case the example was the United
States in the 1960s—serves as an international financial intermediary if it
borrows short and lends long. In the 1980s, as regulations on outward portfolio
investment by Japan's institutional investors were gradually relaxed, long-term
outward investment increased. Thus Japan appeared to be following on the
path to be a global financial intermediary (Kawai 1993). Yet the phenomenon
in 1991 indicates that the pace with which Japan became an international
financial intermediary slowed down for a while. Japanese firms became more
cautious about foreign direct investment (FDI) abroad, and institutional investors were less eager to invest in foreign securities. Banks reduced lending
abroad and repaid short-term borrowing. Since 1992, long-term capital outflow
has started to revive. However, the short-term private capital balance is still in
net deficit, i.e., outflows exceeding inflows.

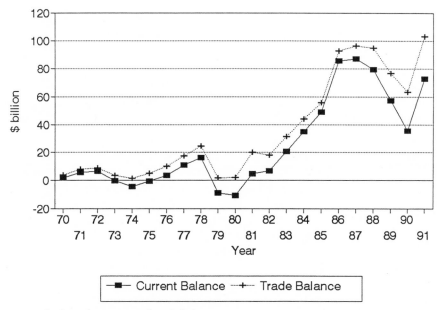

FIG. 1. Japan's current and trade balance

In my opinion, this slowing down in the progress of financial intermediation, or disintermediation from Japan, can be explained by several factors. First, there was a wealth effect thanks to the bubble in Japan's asset markets. Higher stock prices and land prices had a wealth effect. In other words, Japan's investors had higher net wealth from which they could invest at home or abroad. The crash of the bubble worked to reduce long-term investment through this wealth effect. Moreover, the high net asset value of a borrower may have reduced the cost of borrowing under asymmetric information because the risk of bankruptcy involved in the loan to such a borrower was small. Thus, as indicated by Froot and Stein (1991), it might have increased the FDI of an entrepreneur who borrowed money and invested abroad. (In fact, the high value turned out to be illusionary after the bursting of the bubble. During the bubble, people believed that the inflated net worth was correct.) This could be one of the reasons the long-term capital outflow from Japan was discouraged in 1991 after the collapse of the asset and land bubble.

The second reason is closely connected with, or a dynamic aspect of, the first reason just mentioned. During the period of the asset price bubble, loans were extended on the collateral of inflated land and stocks without sufficient scrutiny of the ongoing project. Once expectations on increasing asset values were betrayed, some loans became delinquent. Chain reactions in the credit network occurred in such a way that one bad loan generated another bad loan to a

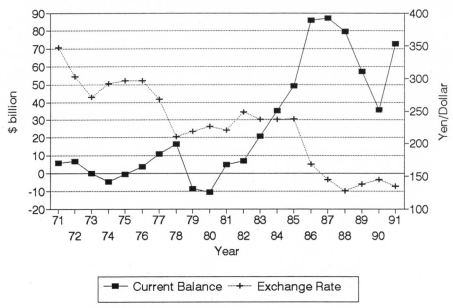

FIG. 2. Current balance vs exchange rate

company that held the first bad loan. In spite of the Bank of Japan's attempt to fix the discount rate at the historical low level of 1.75 percent in 1993, the domestic financial intermediation has not recovered yet (at the time of writing, spring 1994) as is indicated by the decreased growth in commercial lending. These disturbances certainly affected the international role of the Tokyo market as a center of global financial intermediation.

Third, the capital/risky-assets ratio standard agreed upon at the Bank for International Settlements (BIS) also raised concern about future possible constraints for Japanese banks. Banks became conservative in their lending to satisfy the requirement. For these reasons Japan had to suspend, or at least slow down for a while, its movement toward becoming a global financial intermediary.

Figure 4 relates the movement of the exchange rate to the movement of direct investment and to securities investment abroad. During 1985 to 1988, there was a strong negative correlation, which was explained in an information theoretic model of capital cost by Froot and Stein (1991). The recent decline in dollar exchange rates has been accompanied by a decline in FDI into the United States, which is contrary to their regression on the relationship between the exchange rate and FDI in the United States.

After Japan's new Foreign Exchange and Foreign Trade Control Law went into effect in December 1980, the upward trend of portfolio investment was

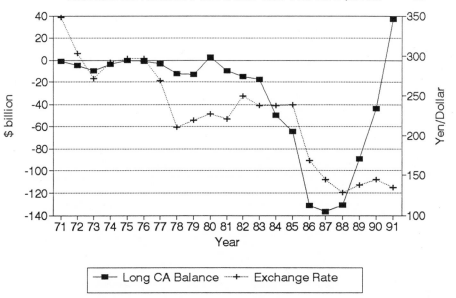

FIG. 3. Japan's long-term CA balance vs exchange rate

prominent until 1986. After the post-Plaza decline of the dollar, portfolio investment abroad reached a plateau and decreased in 1990.

Figure 5 shows the U.S. current account balance.[2] From the beginning of the Reagan era—of military build-up and tax reduction—the current account recorded a truly large deficit. Although the current account has been improving since 1987, the current account deficit with Japan has been more persistent than the overall deficit. Figure 5 shows the outflow of U.S. assets to foreign countries. There was a trough around 1984–85, approximately coinciding with the worsening of the current account. This imbalance was more than offset by the inflow of capital to the United States, which allowed some outflow of capital from the United States.

A sharp contrast is depicted in Figures 6 and 7, which compare the relative importance of U.S. investment in Japan with the relative importance of Japan's investment in the United States. The relationship has been amazingly one-sided since the beginning of the 1980s. The fact that U.S. direct investment to Japan remained extremely small became a subject of complaints from the United States in trade negotiations. The sharp contrast of magnitudes between U.S. investment in Japan and Japanese investment in the United States is taken as a symptom of the closedness of the Japanese market (Mason 1992).

Security investment in Japan, however, has shown large fluctuations since 1984. Japan is only a marginal recipient of U.S. FDI, but Japan began to play a substantial role in 1991 as a host for U.S. securities investment. There is a clear

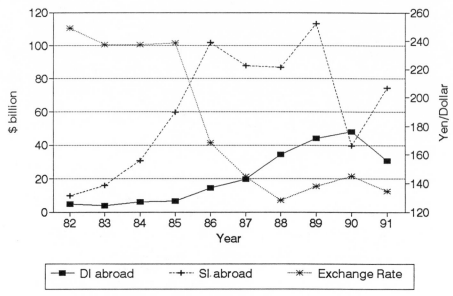

FIG. 4. Japan's DI and SI abroad vs exchange rate

asymmetry in capital flows between the United States and Japan. Nearly half of Japanese FDI goes to the United States. Although the importance of the United States for Japan's security investment has decreased in recent years, the United States is still a large recipient of Japan's security investment abroad. U.S. direct investment is minimal.

The variation of U.S. securities investment in Japan became substantial after 1986. American investors probably sold too much and too soon after Black Monday, because the Japanese stock market enjoyed an overheated boom until 1989. In contrast, the Americans were not affected much by the precipitous decline of the Japanese stock market that started from the beginning of the new decade. From 1990 to 1991, investment was increasing. There was a decrease in Japan's securities investment to the United States in 1990.

II. A THEORETICAL FRAMEWORK

Let me present here a simple accounting framework from which to view various components of capital accounts. From the national income identity, the following accounting identities approximately hold:

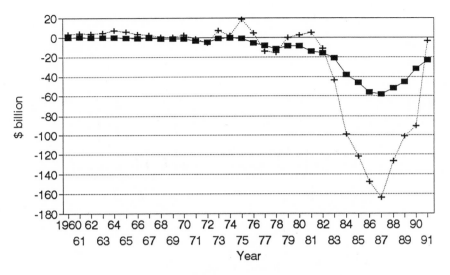

FIG. 5. U.S. balance on current account (*Source: Survey of Current Business, 92*)

The Trade Account of the Balance of Payments = Export − Import

= The Current Account of the Balance of Payments

$$= \text{National Product} - \left(\text{Consumption} + \frac{\text{Domestic}}{\text{Investment}} + \frac{\text{Government}}{\text{Expenditures}} \right)$$

= (minus) Net National Absorption

= National Savings − Domestic Investment

= The Net Increase in International Assets

= (minus) Capital Accounts

= Various Components of Net Capital Outflow

= Net Foreign Direct Investment

+ Net Long-term Portfolio Investment

+ Net Short-term Portfolio Investment

+ Increase in Foreign Reserves

This series of identities holds only approximately because we neglect the effect of investment income and transfers, the effect of change in valuation of assets due to asset price, as well as exchange-rate fluctuations, the distribution of special drawing rights (SDRs), and so forth. But these relationships clarify the overall picture of the economy and relate various approaches to the balance of payments.

The elasticity approach to the balance of payments concentrates on the first

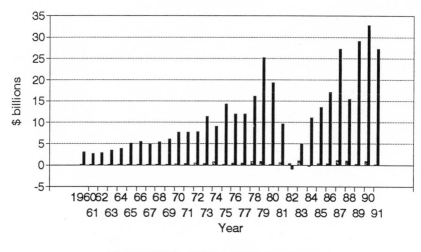

FIG. 6. US DI abroad vs US DI in Japan (*Source: Survey of Current Business, 92*)

and second identity, and emphasizes the effect of the relative price of exports and imports, i.e., the terms of trade on exports and imports. The absorption approach focuses on the income identity and emphasizes the role of aggregate income on components expenditures. The role of non-traded goods can be taken into account as well. Also, the role of time preference comes into the picture. According to the absorption approach, if a nation spends for current consumption and domestic investment for future consumption less than it earns, then the difference will be accumulated as a current-account surplus and must be automatically invested in foreign assets. In this sense, the current account surplus is a form of savings that a nation can make as a whole. If a nation cares more about the future generation, in other words, and if the rate of time preference is low, then it tends to generate a current account surplus.

Incidentally, national income identities can also be used to interpret the monetary approach to the balance of payments that claim the overall balance of payments. That is, the official reserve transactions (ORTs) balance equals the net excess demand for money of the public unsatisfied by the supply of money from domestic credit expansion.

The capital account consists of FDI and long-term as well as short-term portfolio investment. For portfolio investment, the rate of interest and the rates of return to equities as well as their variance, and expectations on the future asset price and exchange rates become important factors. A part of portfolio investment is the purchase of treasury bills (TB) by the United States. Accordingly, government deficits are an important factor because they determine the

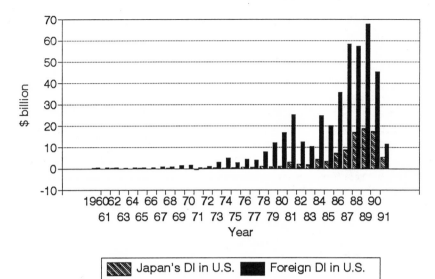

FIG. 7. Foreign direct investment in U.S. (*Source: Survey of Current Business, 92*)

issue of U.S. treasury bills, and the TBs purchased by Japanese financial investors affect the exchange rate and various components of capital accounts.

The identity remains regardless of what kind of economic theory one has—classical, Keynesian, monetarist, new classical, or new Keynesian. Any good economic theory should be able to tell the relationship between these variables consistently. Often one phenomenon is called a macroeconomic phenomenon, micro phenomenon, monetary phenomenon, or real phenomenon, but all the phenomena are related. Thus, all the possible approaches to the balance of payment account surplus, or capital account, should explain the same phenomenon if they are genuinely good systematic theories.

It is important to know what components are relatively more autonomous than others, in other words, to know what items on the list of components of the balance of payments trigger the movement of other items and the movement of the exchange rate. In the current world economy, with continuous and highly developed financial markets that trade outstanding stocks of financial assets, such as the stock and bond markets and the foreign exchange market, prices adjust instantaneously.

On the other hand, prices in the markets of goods and services only adjust gradually. Thus, the following would be a reasonable picture of the functioning world economy. First, exogenous shocks on current or expected interest rates and on the expected future exchange rate affect instantaneous market adjustment on the foreign exchange and other asset markets. Then changes in the exchange rates and interest rates in related countries lead to slow adjustments in the market of goods and services. The adjustment in the trade or current account will take time. The change in monetary policy can easily work as current and (if expected) future exogenous changes in the asset market equilibrium in the foreign exchange market.

Of course, some changes in future exchange markets are related to changes in expectations related primarily to flow markets such as the discovery of a new product or of oil fields and the future course of deficit spending. Thus, the interaction between the markets of flows and of stocks is mutual. However, the simplest and most probable linkage is that instantaneous changes in valuations in the markets of stocks trigger gradual movements in flow variables. Therefore, the study of components of a capital account has become all the more important in this highly developed world economy.

The closest attempt to the suggested research here[3] was done by Komura (1990). He developed a VAR model for 1974–87 of the variables that are pertinent for the determination of the Japanese exports to the United States and U.S. exports to Japan. He found the length of the J-curve by the impulse response faction of the export and the import to an innovation in the exchange rate, and the lagged response of Japan's exports or imports to GNP on both sides of the Pacific. According to him, in order to solve Japan's trade surplus phenomenon, Japan can either rely on exogenous import-promoting policies, increase its income, or rely on the appreciation of the yen.

III. FACTORS AFFECTING CAPITAL FLOWS:
ECONOMIC FACTORS, INSTITUTIONAL DEVELOPMENT,
AND MACROECONOMIC POLICIES

Among the many factors that affect the "push" and "pull" factors, some are technically and exogenously given from the environment. Others, however, are affected by governmental policies and institutional developments in Japan and the United States and possibly in third countries that channel financial inter-mediation. I will review some important factors including macroeconomic policies and institutional development. (For comprehensive studies of capital flows from Japan, see Kawai 1991, 1993.)

Since 1970, the progress of financial innovation in the world has been re-markable. There was a technological element because of the advance in com-munication technology. Information can be transmitted immediately, account-ing can be recorded quickly and efficiently. Also, the internationalization of financial markets proceeded very rapidly. Because of these factors, that is, technical innovations in communication and globalization, a regulated finan-cial system cannot sustain itself well. One country cannot easily contain finan-cial transactions within its borders in this "borderless" economy. Otherwise, regulations would generate disintermediation from, say, a banking sector within a country, as well as disintermediation out of the financial market of a regulating country.

Japan

Before 1971, Japan was under the fixed-exchange rate system of the Bretton Woods regime. Before 1974 most Japanese short-term capital flows were regulated and as Ito (1986) indicates, the degree (shadow price) of regulation constraints can be measured by the discrepancy from the covered interest parity. So before the exchange rate was floated, Japanese foreign investments were under strict control. From 1974 through 1980 the degree of capital control varied—sometimes tight, sometimes loose, and sometimes imposed in different directions depending on the balance of payment circumstances. Fukuda (1993) finds that the degree of control was decided in response to the current account deficit. When the balance of payments deficit grew, outflows of capital were discouraged; when the balance of payments surplus grew, more restrictions on the inflow of capital were imposed.

In December 1980, the new Foreign Exchange Control Law was put into effect. Curiously, it is still called a "control" law. After December 1980, Japanese portfolio investment and direct investment were almost completely liberated with a few exceptions. There was a strong trend of outward capital flow from Japan corresponding to this easing of foreign capital control.

Let us turn to the quantitative aspect. The large surplus of savings in Japan is certainly a strong push factor and should be explained by a theory of intertemporal choice. Japanese individuals may save for their long-lived family tree or dynasty rather than just planning for their own individual life cycles. The Japanese may also save more for their old age because the population is aging so fast; in order to enjoy a given standard of living during old age, you have to save a larger portion of income because you cannot be supported by younger people. Or, people may expect the price level to go down because of the further liberalization of trade, so that they save much right now. Whatever the correct explanation may be, the Japanese have accumulated a large amount of wealth that serves as a source for the outflow of capital.

An important development in Japan that worked as a push factor was the tremendous land and stock price boom after 1985. The Nikkei index of the Tokyo stock market grew about three times during the five years between January 1985 and December 1989. Postwar land prices soared almost continuously until 1990 except for the period after the first oil crisis. During 1987 and 1989, the index of residential land in Japan increased more than 30 percent and commercial land increased 46.8 per cent during 1987. Indeed, the average land price in the six largest cities increased almost 200 percent during the five years between March 1985 and March 1990 (Bank of Japan 1993). It was once said that the total land of Japan, which is about 4 percent of the area of the United States, was about four times as valuable as that of the United States.

The Tokyo stock market started a precipitous decline with the change of the decade, namely January 1990. By August 1992, in the recent trough of the market it lost about 63 percent of its value. One could say that those earlier stock price increases had been bubbles. Probably myopic expectations on arbitrage conditions were satisfied. There was no assurance, however, that those prices satisfied the long-run transversality conditions. In this sense, I believe there were bubbles and they were burst in Japan.

Those fluctuations of wealth certainly affected fluctuations in Japanese investment abroad both in the form of direct investment and in the form of portfolio investment. Japan's foreign assets in the United States were in fact reduced in 1990 as well as in 1991. There was net disinvestment in 1990. The amount of Japan's direct investment was still positive in 1991, but the amount was about one fourth the level of 1989 and 1990. Also, when the Japanese economy is in a boom, firms have more entrepreneurial optimism or incentive. Accordingly, the outflow of direct investment, which is interpreted as the outflow of entrepreneurship, is encouraged. Probably, we may attribute this phenomenon to the increase in risk aversion that takes place during recessions at home. In other words, in booms entrepreneurs get less discouraged and try to invest abroad in spite of uncertainties. Figure 8 shows the Nikkei stock index and FDI of Japan from the Ministry of Finance (MOF) (notification basis) as well as the balance of payment data. The substantial correlation between the stock index and foreign investment abroad seems to imply the wealth effect and/or the effect of entrepreneurial spirit.

The main reason for these bubbles was the policy of a low rate of interest after the Baker-Miyazawa meeting in autumn 1986 and the Louvre Accord in February 1987. Japanese monetary policy was assigned not so much to stabilize the domestic economy as to sustain the value of the dollar. The Bank of Japan pursued an extremely low interest policy. The discount rate was fixed at the historically low rate of 2.5 percent for more than two years, which certainly triggered the speculative boom. Since the consumer price index was stable and the wholesale price index was declining, the Bank of Japan (BOJ) might not have realized the need for monetary contraction. Also, international policy coordination affected the subtle political balance between the Bank of Japan that would aim at stable monetary policy and the Ministry of Finance that would put priority on recovery from the government budget deficit. As we will see in the next section, international policy coordination seems to have strengthened the influence of MOF relative to that of the BOJ.

The Bank of Japan, which was influenced by monetarism at least to the extent that it publishes the forecast of money supply, increased money supply (M2 plus CD) around 10 to 11 percent through 1987 to 1990, while the real GNP

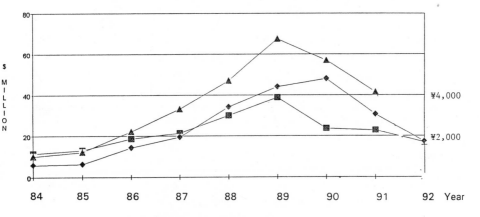

FIG. 8. Nikkei and outward FDI

of Japan was growing around 4.4 to 6.6 percent. The Bank of Japan might have recognized the effect of money on the price level through the channel of goods transactions, but did not though recognize the liquidity effect of high asset prices triggered by a large rate of money growth as well as by the low interest rate policy. What was neglected was the channel through which high asset prices such as stock price and land price are transmitted to investment demand by making the value of Tobin's q much above unity.

In October 1987, the New York Stock Exchange had a record decline on Black Monday. Japanese business circles also worried about the deflationary effect of the appreciation of the yen. Hence, the easy money policy during 1987 may have been justified, but the Bank of Japan was responsible for keeping the discount rate low even after Germany as well as the United States started to raise their discount rates in 1988. It continued to keep the rate low even after the speculative spiral of land and stock prices became apparent and the job offers/applicants ratio exceeded the value of 1.25 in the labor market in 1989. This policy of preventing the yen exchange rate from appreciating apparently reduced Japan's current account surplus by the J-curve phenomenon, but eventually must have worked to widen the current surplus imbalance between the two sides of the Pacific.

The enormous growth of the stock market continued until the end of 1989. After Mieno became governor of the Bank of Japan at the end of 1989, he tightened monetary policy by raising the discount rate several times in order to recover the role of an independent and traditional central bank. Until this tightening, Japanese monetary policy was assigned to defend the value of the dollar rather than the stability of the Japanese aggregate demand level.

In this sense the Japanese monetary authorities noticed a yellow light, and even a red light, but still kept pumping the accelerator. Suddenly they pushed the brake. The Japanese economy at present is resisting the instability created by the sudden stop, that is, the instability due to financial chain reactions that are now hurting the economic health of industrial sectors.

United States

The U.S. financial sector changed rapidly along with the worldwide trend of the development of new financial instruments, and it became the most advanced financial market in the world. The efficiency of the U.S. financial market has played an instrumental role in facilitating both inflows and outflows of capital from the United States. However, the process of deregulation did not take place in a vacuum or without problems. The savings and loan associations (S&L) disaster implied that if you deregulated a part of the system without considering the systemic stability, then there would be a loss of efficiency in the adjustment process and a loss of fairness in income distribution. The S&Ls used to extend long-term loans with relatively low interest rates to housing and real estate transactions. Because of the high rate of inflation and abolishment of the interest rate ceiling, short-term interest rates went up rapidly after the early 1970s. Accordingly, there was a huge loss on the part of S&Ls. Since 1980 regulators have shut down almost 1,200 insolvent S&Ls with assets of over $500 billion, and they expect additional S&L failures will continue in the next few years. Taxpayers will be burdened with $100 billion to $160 billion (Council of Economic Advisers 1993). Since the U.S. population is about 260 million, this implies that the cost is about $400 to $600 per person. Whether problems with respect to S&Ls and associated real estate troubles affected Japanese investment is not well known. It would be interesting to test the relationship between regional and industrial distribution of direct investment from Japan and the failure of financial institutions.

Intermediating Countries

As Kuroyanagi, Hamada, and Sakurai (1991) showed, during the years of 1980 to 1987, Japan's net credit position to the United States due to the accumulation of bilateral current account surplus was $254 billion, but only $82 billion of it was not realized by the direct outflow of capital from Japan to the United States. Even though the flow of funds accumulated large amounts of current surplus vis-a-vis the United States, Japan extended credit to the United

States indirectly through Europe. In a multi-country world, country A can settle the increased current account with country B either directly by lending to A or lending to C which extends credit to B. In a frictionless world, transaction costs do not mean much, so the composition of the portfolio investment is chosen solely by the returns and risks of assets, and the channel of capital movements to the final destination does not seem to matter. However, in a world with transaction costs, friction exists and one can develop in principle a theory to explain through which financial center funds are moved. The Big-Bang of Great Britain in October 1986, for example, transformed the city of London as the most efficient intermediary. All commissions were basically left to negotiations between clients and banks and the market mechanism. Self-regulation was tightened again in a few years. It would be interesting to investigate how much financial innovation in intermediary markets affects the flow of funds from Japan to the United States.

IV. POLITICAL ECONOMY ASPECTS OF MACROECONOMIC POLICY AND DEREGULATION

Behind the policy development in the two countries described above were hidden many political dramas that led to particular policy choices.

Macroeconomic Policies

Macroeconomic policy has two distinct policy instruments: fiscal policy and monetary policy. In fiscal policy, the most important event for Japan was the passage of the consumption tax. After FY1975, the Japanese government budget ran a substantial deficit for many years. The reasons were that it overestimated the revenue from the economy that experienced a slow-down in growth after the oil crisis, and that the social security system installed by the Tanaka cabinet was too generous and benefits were indexed to inflation. MOF made desperate efforts to balance the budget, and the instrument chosen was a consumption tax similar to the value-added tax in European countries.

Premier Masayoshi Ohira lost the general election in 1979 by advocating the consumption tax too "honestly," and in 1987 even Premier Yasuhiro Nakasone could not pass the consumption tax bill through the Diet, because resistance from consumer groups, small and medium-sized businesses, and opposition parties was very strong. The regressive nature of the consumption tax was of course a main reason for the opposition, but another political reason for resistance was that the sales and profits of medium, small, or household enterprises, which were not taxed under the income tax system at the time, would be captured by the Tax Bureau under the consumption tax. It was Premier

Noboru Takeshita who finally succeeded in passing the legislation through the Diet to the relief of MOF (Ito 1992, p. 154).

There is a controversy whether public officials or politicians take leadership in reforming regulations and the tax system and building institutions in Japan. Rosenbluth (1989) takes the view that despite conventional wisdom to the contrary, private interests represented by politicians had important influence. Kato (1993), on the other hand, emphasizes the intermediating and entrepreneurial role of bureaucrats. She claims that because of their technocratic expertise and well-planned strategic maneuvering, Japan's bureaucrats had a strong influence in the consumption tax issue. Indeed, the opinion campaign mounted by MOF toward the general public, academics, and politicians was thorough. Prime Minister Noboru Takeshita was regarded by MOF officials as the most effective politician. Because political support was weak, it took a very long time to implement the consumption tax. However, as far as the case of the introduction of the consumption tax is concerned, the ministry took the leadership.

The consumption tax was set to three percent of the (approximate) value added. Because of the new tax as well as the recovery of the economy, the government budget started gradually to recover its balance. This betrayed the real intention of MOF. MOF had maintained that the introduction of the general consumption tax was "revenue neutral" because a reduction in the income tax was combined with the introduction of the consumption tax. Even though the general account of the national budget still runs a small deficit, the saving-investment balance of the national and local governments which includes the social security account has shown a surplus since 1988.

In early 1994, Prime Minister Morihiro Hosokawa proposed an income tax reduction combined with a future consumption tax increase, to seven percent three years later. This proposal presumably reflected MOF's policy position, but was not accepted by members of the coalition that supported Hosokawa and was withdrawn. Thus, bureaucrats exercised power in initiating the consumption tax, but they were blocked, as far as the attempt of 1994 shows, by political power. It appeared that politicians could keep control. However, according to the plan announced February 1994, the reduction in the income tax will be limited to one year—showing the strength of the will of MOF.

Between the Japanese saving rate and the U.S. saving rate exists a striking difference that can by itself create the current account surplus of Japan and the deficit in the United States. Superimposed on this difference, the difference in the budget discipline in the public sector reinforced the current account imbalances. As already mentioned, it is the accounting identity that the sum of the private saving-investment balance and the public saving-investment balance equals the current account surplus.

On the other hand, monetary policy was kept expansionary since 1987, and it was an important factor for the asset inflation as well as the long recession after asset inflation. Here the political economy factor was important as well. The BOJ was severely criticized for its undisciplined money supply in the early 1970s prior to the first oil crisis (e.g., Komiya 1988). The BOJ was under the pressure of the government (or MOF) which tried hard to avoid further appreciation of the yen. The result was "frenzied" inflation. Therefore BOJ should have known the danger of using monetary policy for stabilizing the exchange rate. Nevertheless, BOJ was apparently not able to resist the pressure from the government that wanted to have expansionary monetary policy using international coordination as a pretext or pressure from MOF which was reluctant to use fiscal policy for demand management because of its priority for achieving a balanced budget.

Moreover, asset inflation in Japan in the late 1980s can be attributed to the wrong policy assignment due to the international coordination of monetary policy. In several attempts at policy coordination in the 1980s, the intentions of the U.S. and Japanese governments were often delicately different. The United States was worried about the depreciation of the yen, and Japan was worried about its appreciation. The Japanese government was strongly concerned about the deflationary impact of the appreciated yen. Thus, international coordination was often used as a pretext, because the United States used to welcome the appreciation of the yen.

After the Louvre Accord, however, the U.S. attitude changed. Baker stopped "talking down the dollar" and the United States intervened substantially in the exchange market to support the dollar. Also, U.S. interest rates were gradually raised (Frankel 1993, p. 307). Accordingly, the need for supporting the dollar then sounded like genuine ground for the government and MOF to persuade the Bank of Japan to continue the low interest policy.

In spite of Japan's adoption of the flexible exchange-rate regime, which in principle allows it to block monetary shocks from abroad, the Japanese monetary authorities used monetary policy toward the stability of the dollar-yen exchange rate rather than toward the stability of the domestic economy. With the reason or the excuse of international monetary coordination, Japan assigned to its monetary policy the objective of halting the appreciation of the yen. I regard this policy error and the following abrupt adjustment as the basic causes of the present recession.

As pointed out elsewhere (Hamada 1985), monetary coordination is helpful and often indispensable under the fixed exchange rate. The advantage of flexible exchange rates is, however, that each nation can pursue its monetary policy more or less independently and autonomously in order to achieve different macroeconomic objectives. In fact, empirical analysis on the effectiveness of policy coordination by Oudiz and Sachs (1984) and many others did not find a large gain from policy coordination under the flexible exchange rate.

Also, if reduction of the current account were the policy objective, the coordination of fiscal policies would have been much more effective than the coordination of monetary policies. It is true in the new classical framework where money is essentially neutral, in the open economy version of a Keynesian framework (Mundell 1968), or in the open economy version of an eclectic framework (Dornbusch 1976). Moreover, in these frameworks, monetary expansion may have a beggar-thy-neighbor effect and increase rather than decrease the current account surplus.

This policy experience provides an interesting situation where one can apply the concept of the two-level game (Putnam 1988). One layer of the game is the diplomatic negotiation between the two national representatives. Behind a representative, there is another layer of conflict. International negotiation is influenced by domestic conflicts, and vice versa. Putnam analyzed the policy conflict between the German Fiscal Authority and the Bundes Bank around the Bonn Summit. Because of international policy coordination, a more expansionary policy was followed.

During 1987 to 1989, the logic of international policy coordination seems to have influenced the political balance between the Ministry of Finance and the Bank of Japan. As a result the easy money policy was continued too long. The Ministry of Finance, which was making every effort to balance the budget, was reluctant to use fiscal policy for reducing the current account surplus, and shifted all the burden onto the monetary policy. Thus, Japan's experience in the late 1980s presents a typical example of the unfavorable effect of policy coordination when there is a conflict of interest within a country (e.g., Rogoff 1984), and the case where the domestic political balance is influenced by the existence of international coordination.

The policy coordination by monetary policies to avoid further appreciation of the yen created, on one side of the Pacific, a speculative bubble in asset prices that was followed by a severe recession in Japan, and, on the other side, a lack of export demand and recession owing to the higher value of the dollar in the United States. The choice of instruments was mistaken if the objective was to reduce the imbalance of the current account.

The governor of the BOJ at that time, Sumita, conceded later (November 1991) in a newspaper interview (*Nihon keizai shinbun*) that the BOJ should have requested more disciplined loan attitudes at that time, but still maintained that the easy money policy was inevitable because of the recessionary pressure owing to the yen appreciation and expanding current account surpluses. The former governor did not seem to understand, even afterward, that the primary responsibility as well as policy instrument of the central bank lies in quantitative control of money and credit conditions and not in its power of moral suasion.

The policy mix of the United States during the 1980s was very different from—almost the mirror image of—Japan's policy mix. Under the Reagan administration, by supply-side economics and military build-up preparing for "star wars," the government deficit developed. As Poterba (1993) says, the decade of the 1980s taught us that it is harder to cut spending and raise taxes than to do the opposite. The U.S. saving rate in the private sector was quite low. From the same reason that generated the current account surplus in Japan, the current account in the United States went into deficit. The prediction by Buchanan and Wagner (1977) on the growth of deficits under democratic processes and the Keynesian ideology was ironically realized not by the administration with Keynesian economists but by supply-siders.

On the other hand, monetary policy in the United States during 1980–82 was assigned to fight inflation or the stagflation left as a legacy of the 1970s. Interest rates soared, and Latin American countries with international borrowing were hit by the debt crisis caused by high interest rates. In 1983 it was eased a while, tightened again in 1984, and turned to a moderately easy monetary policy during 1985–86. From 1987 to 1990, U.S. monetary policy was tighter than Japanese monetary policy. The integrity and reputation of the chairmen of the Federal Reserve Board, Paul Volcker and Alan Greenspan, might have helped the relative independence of the Federal Reserve.

The "political economy" balance between the Treasury and the Federal Reserve in the United States is a curious one. Volcker (1994) states that the exchange rate policy is under the Treasury's discretion. At the same time, he recognizes that sterilized interventions have only limited impact on the exchange rate except for the announcement effect, and, more generally, that effective interventions should be accompanied by consistent monetary policy. International policy coordination certainly played up the role of the Treasury and its secretary, James Baker. Can we say, in a framework of two-level games, that the balance between the Treasury and the Federal Reserve was tipped slightly in favor of the Treasury? The direction of influence of policy coordination on the institutional balance was the same in the two countries, but its effect on the macro-policy mix was different during 1987–89. The policy mix in the United States was a combination of continuing budget deficit and tight monetary policy.[4]

Thus, in contrast to Japan, the situation in the United States was a lack of discipline in fiscal policy combined with the presence of discipline in monetary policy. In both countries, the policy mix was supported by political process. It is interesting but difficult to answer the question of why it was so. A tentative answer is that in Japan bureaucrats, MOF officials in particular, still have strong authority, and that the Bank of Japan is not completely independent of the Ministry of Finance. The Governor of the central bank is under the legal, if not practical, authority of the Minister of Finance.[5]

Because of the asymmetry of the policy mix in the two countries, the difference in the saving-investment balance in the private sector between the two countries was widened. This is the macroeconomic picture behind the substantial current account imbalance.[6]

The Process of Deregulation

Deregulation and the opening of Japan's capital market were, of course, partly motivated by the interests of innovative bankers and financial managers. They were at the same time hastened by demands from foreign businesses and governments, that is, "foreign pressure." Whenever newspapers report that the United States or another government demands that Japan deregulate certain government controls, that interest rates on certain deposits be liberalized, or that new credit instruments or new insurance contracts be authorized by MOF, we realize how many complicated regulations have been effective.

In idealistic terms, it is better that Japan takes its own initiatives to deregulate the capital market. However, the vested interest on the part of regulated sectors as well as on the part of the regulating bureau is so strong that deregulation would take almost forever without foreign pressure. In this sense, foreign businesses and governments are providing valuable services to Japanese consumers.

Generally, government officials in supervising bureaus of specific sectors (*genkyoku*), for example, the Banking Division and Securities Division of MOF, tend to protect the interests of protected sectors and the interest of inefficient (small and medium-sized) financial institutions. However, in the same ministry, there are other bureaus that represent different interests. For example, the Division of International Finance in MOF usually tends to embrace more international views. Thus, the balance of opinions is influenced by foreign pressures.

One of the characteristics of Japanese financial deregulation is that it has been done rather gradually (Cargill and Royama 1988). For example, the liberalization of the interest rate on saving and time deposits started with large-denomination time deposits in 1986. It started, though, with large units of deposits. It was finally in 1993 that virtually all the interest rates on deposits of any scale were liberalized. Deregulation of controls on the establishment of branches also took a long time. This slowness frustrates foreigners and even some Japanese. The road to a really free, efficient global financial market for Tokyo or Osaka still appears to be long.

On the other hand, the process of financial market deregulation in the United States was piecemeal and often without coherent plans. In contrast to the appeal to administrative guidance in Japan, legal changes in regulations played important roles in the United States (Cargill and Royama 1988). Indeed, for the United States, inflationary shocks at the beginning of the 1980s were more severe, and the disintermediation of the flow of funds from the banking sector was more serious than for Japan. But one could not help wondering if more careful deregulation might not have prevented the incidence of substantial economic losses in the financial sector. The disruption due to failures of S&Ls seems to tell all about this.

There were a few waves of crises in the S&L industry. The high rate of interest as a result of the tight monetary policy combating inflation caused the first wave of insolvency among thrift institutions, which was engendered by deposit interest deregulation. But the modest deregulation lagged behind the very high market rate, and thrift institutions continued to lose. Because of the lack of a sufficient incentive mechanism to weed out inefficient thrifts, many of them continued to operate and added to the deadweight loss to be borne by depositors and taxpayers later. In 1985, the industry was hit again by the second crisis. In Maryland and Ohio, thrifts insured by state-sponsored funds were under attack by bank runs, which were appeased by limits on deposit withdrawals and Federal Reserve lending. In the late 1980s the insolvency problem of thrifts became a serious political problem. The Resolution Trust Corporation (RTC) was established and the Financial Institutions Reform, Recovery and Enforcement Act (FIRREA) was legislated in 1989 (Litan 1994, pp. 526–34).

As documented by Litan, the Treasury Department's estimate of the (discounted) costs for FIRREA's future operation amounts to $90 to $130 billion, and estimates of other institutions went even further. There is a question of the unfairness that gains went to only those who took advantage of the subtlety of the existing law, who acted promptly during the upheaval of the S&L crisis, and who had connections to local politicians, and that losses were borne by uninformed depositors and taxpayers. If we set aside this issue of fairness, the magnitude of loss mentioned indicates that the cost from disturbances to financial intermediation was really substantial, and that timing, coherence, and incentive mechanisms in financial crises were crucially important. In my opinion it shows that the U.S. reforms proceeded too abruptly and too hastily, in spite of the remark by U.S. economists (e.g., Joskow and Noll 1994) that partial instead of universal deregulation and lags in responses to crises were factors for the S&L difficulties. Whether or not these financial disturbances affected the inflow or outflow of capital to the United States is a question for further research.

V. DIRECT INVESTMENT

Since the flow of direct investment is treated in Ito's chapter in this volume, I will mention only briefly the following characteristics.

Japan's overall FDI as well as that to the United States grew rapidly until 1990, but started declining in 1991. Until the early 1980s a major part of the direct investment was to Asia and developing countries. Since 1986, the role of the United States and Europe became important. The main motivation of Japan's direct investment to developing countries has been to utilize ample, inexpensive labor, but that for investment to developed countries has been to overcome trade barriers such as quotas, tariffs, and voluntary export restraints, and to develop the marketing network for exports. Direct investment in the United States is typical of the latter.

Usually, FDI is considered to transplant the technology, know-how, and managerial capacities of the investing country to the host country. Recently, however, Japanese firms have invested in advanced countries, in particular, in the United States, in order to absorb technology, know-how, and managerial resources from the host country rather than to transmit. Sony's investment in Columbia Pictures and Matsushita's acquisition of MCA were examples. Those parent companies intended to benefit from the information that would be provided by owning a subsidiary.

As already mentioned, there has been distinct asymmetry between the direct investment from Japan to the United States and that from the United States to Japan. Japan's policy for incoming foreign investment after the war was very limiting by a combination of foreign exchange control and strict authorization procedures (Mason 1990). Even though MITI now gives some advantages to foreign direct investors, the large discrepancy between inward and outward investment by foreigners often gives foreigners a sense of unfairness on the part of Japan. Froot and Stein (1991) have an innovative approach about why the appreciation of the dollar accompanied FDI to the United States. Because of the improved collateral or creditability of entrepreneurs in foreign countries, they can borrow with lower capital costs. This approach is an interesting example of using an information-theoretic apparatus to explain capital movements. After 1990, Japanese land values and stock values went into collapse, and there was a sudden decrease in the outflow of Japanese capital in the form of direct investment. Figure 8 indicates the relationship between the Nikkei stock index and the outward direct investment of Japan. This is consistent with their basic theoretical approach, because a high, even fiducially high by bubble phenomena, net asset value of an investor will be an encouraging factor for outward direct investment. Their particular regressions that relate the weakness of the dollar exchange rate to inward foreign investment to the United States, however, did not seem to fit the data well because the decline of the dollar after 1991 was accompanied by the decline of inward foreign investment into the United States.

VI. TOWARD AN INFORMATION-ORIENTED
THEORY OF PORTFOLIO INVESTMENT

Kawai (1991, 1993) gives a systematic account of capital flows and, in particular, portfolio investment from and into Japan. In spite of rich documentation like his work, however, the theoretical and empirical analysis of portfolio investment is not as well developed as that of direct investment.

There are puzzles in explaining the amount of portfolio investment in the world. First, there is the Feldstein-Horioka (1984) paradox. According to conventional economic wisdom, if investment opportunities are randomly distributed, then the difference in savings would predict the direction of capital outflows. In reality, however, we observe a strong correlation between savings and domestic investment. Second, another puzzle is that the portfolio of international investors is more home-biased compared with the portfolio component than the usual portfolio selection theory or Capital Asset Pricing Market (CAPM) theory would predict.

One can apply the framework by Williamson (1986) of the financial market with costly state verification to international capital movements. The costly state verification model assumes that when a borrower claims to be bankrupt, lenders cannot necessarily observe whether that is true. As long as there is asymmetric information between lenders and borrowers, there should be a cost involved in case a firm is in bankruptcy. The debt contract pattern should reflect this additional cost of ex-post monitoring. Townsend (1979), Diamond (1984), Gale and Hellwig (1985), and Williamson (1987) have proven that a debt contract should be written as a standard debt contract.

In light of these models, international capital flows depend on the rate of returns on microeconomic diversifiable risks, macroeconomic undiversifiable risks, and cost of monitoring (Hamada and Sakuragawa 1993). The level of interest payment on the standard debt contract should reflect the possibility of bankruptcy and additional monitoring costs. Also if there are undiversifiable macroeconomic risks, then they will increase the possibility of additional bankruptcy costs. Further research is needed to test this framework fully.

VII. CONCLUDING REMARKS

In place of summarizing the above, let me speculate a little on the future of capital flows and the saving-investment balance between the United States and Japan.

In Japan, the recovery from recession will take time, because the trough of this recession is quite deep and because political instability will make it difficult to take prompt action against recession. Even if such policies were adopted, they would need quite a while to be credible to the public. The persuading power of bureaucrats, in particular MOF, will continue to be strong, and the government budget will not be in a large deficit in the near future. These factors will work toward maintaining or increasing the current account surplus.

Japan's population is aging rather rapidly and in a decade or two will reach the stage where a smaller proportion of people work and save. This will tend to reduce the national saving rate. Foreign pressures may promote the transformation of the production-oriented Japanese economy into a consummatory one, and the traditional protection-oriented bureaucracy into a more transparent one. These factors will work toward reducing the current account surplus. The problem here is that such a transformation will take a long time.

Further deregulation in the Japanese economy will increase imports and help increase the national expenditure. Further deregulation in the financial market will certainly facilitate direct investment into Japan, and increase gross (i.e., in and out) flows of capital in Japan. It is not clear if this inflow of direct investment will increase or decrease the saving-investment balance between the two countries.

On the side of the United States, the monetary policy of the Federal Reserve seems to remain quite independent. Recent preventive interest rate increases will keep the value of the dollar from falling even lower. The establishment of the North American Free Trade Agreement (NAFTA) will in the short run work against imports from Japan. If the Clinton, or any future, administration were to resolve the government deficit problem, it would certainly work toward reducing the current account deficit. What is still needed for the recovery in the current account balance is a set of policies to encourage private saving, for example, modifying the tax advantage for mortgage loans. Labor productivity in the United States has been improving in recent years. If it could solve safety and education problems in urban areas, the United States would enjoy an improvement in human capital, which would result in a further increase in productivity.

All these changes on the American side will take time as well. Therefore, the present pattern of current account imbalances will probably continue in a more or less similar fashion.

The regional pattern of direct and portfolio investment, however, may change rather drastically. Asia—East Asia, Southeast Asia, China, and even West Asia and Vietnam—are growing vigorously. In trade and in direct investment, the United States, European countries, and Japan are all rushing into the Asian region; NIEs are following the paths of developed countries into ASEAN countries; finally, NIEs and ASEAN countries are investing in China and Vietnam. Portfolio investment will also flow into this region in the future. Thus, the United States and Japan will interact, in terms of capital flows, centering on the fastest-growing Asian region.

APPENDIX:
VAR ANALYSIS OF CAPITAL MOVEMENT

In order to extend the analysis of Komura (1990) and to know the causality between variables that are related to the exchange rate and capital account of the balance of payments, I conducted VAR analysis.

TABLE 1

The Estimated Results of ADF Tests

(Significance Level)

Variable Name	Code	Significance Level of Random Walk	Significance Level of Random Walk with Trend
Current account	CU	0.125	0.099
Export	X	0.000	0.026
Import	M	0.030	0.098
Service balance	SB	0.001	0.000
Capital account	CA	0.489	0.312
Short-term capital balance	SC	0.003	0.001
Foreign direct investment balance	FD	0.427	0.321
Portfolio investment balance	LC	0.457	0.295
Exchange rate	EX	0.044	0.036
Discount rate	DR	0.014	0.005
Call rate	CR	0.006	0.002
Bill rate	BR	0.004	0.001
M1	M1	0.000	0.018
M2+CD	M2C	0.000	0.073
General account of government	GG	0.000	0.000
Special account of government	SG	0.000	0.000

Unit Root Test

Prior to undertaking the regression analysis, I tested the existence of the unit root concerning 16 variables. I conducted the Augmented Dickey-Fuller (ADF) test. Table 1 shows the result of the unit root test of these time series from the first quarter of 1972 and from the fourth quarter of 1992. We cannot reject the hypothesis that a unit root exists with both current account and capital account. This confirms the findings in other studies that the existence of unit root is not rejected in the case of time series of Japan's current account (for example, Shibata and Shintani 1994). It remains a question why all three components of the current account—exports, imports, and the service account—rejected the existence of unit roots with a 5 percent level of significance. Of course, theoretically, at least one component should have a unit root. All I can say is that this occurred as statistical chance. For the remaining series, except for the direct investment balance and the portfolio investment balance, the existence of unit root can be rejected with a significance level of 10 percent.

TABLE 2

The Estimated Results of Granger Causality Tests
(F-statistics, Marginal significance levels in parentheses)

(a) 1972:1 to 1991:4

Effect		Cause					
		CU	CA	EX	DR	M1	GG
Current account	CU	30.362	1.672	2.496	1.201	2.088	2.200
		(0.000)	(0.171)	(0.054)	(0.322)	(0.096)	(0.082)
Capital account	CA	0.967	2.906	1.001	0.176	1.576	1.730
		(0.434)	(0.031)	(0.416)	(0.950)	(0.195)	(0.158)
Exchange rate	EX	0.955	0.518	52.173	0.993	2.902	0.824
		(0.440)	(0.723)	(0.000)	(0.420)	(0.031)	(0.516)
Discount rate	DR	0.464	0.211	1.343	84.884	1.436	1.154
		(0.762)	(0.931)	(0.267)	(0.000)	(0.235)	(0.342)
M1	M1	5.197	3.249	3.306	2.408	99.851	4.617
		(0.001)	(0.019)	(0.017)	(0.061)	(0.000)	(0.003)
General account	GG	0.518	0.234	0.474	0.366	2.682	15.808
of government		(0.723)	(0.918)	(0.755)	(0.832)	(0.042)	(0.000)

NOTE: Lag length is 4 periods.

CA   DR
    ↘   ↙
     M1
   ⤢ ⇕ ↘
EX → CU ← GG
Significance Level 10%   →
Significance Level 5%   →

VAR Analysis

Representing the interest rate by the discount rate, money supply by M1, the degree of fiscal (dis)stimulus by a balance of general account, and adding the current account, capital account, and exchange rate, I conducted a VAR analysis with six variables. A lag length of four is applied here. The results of the analysis are shown in Table 2. Also, I divided the period into two because of deregulation due to the amendment of the Foreign Exchange Control Act. A drawback is that the degree of freedom is reduced to eight.

The overall results can be summarized as follows:

1971–91 (Total Period). During the total period, the current account was influenced by the exchange rate, fiscal policy, and money supply. These three are interrelated. However, the signs of the coefficients that show the interactions are not stable, i.e.,

TABLE 2
(*continued*)

(b) 1972:1 to 1981:1

Effect		Cause					
		CU	CA	EX	DR	M1	GG
Current account	CU	1.380	1.328	1.296	0.646	1.403	0.805
		(0.323)	(0.339)	(0.349)	(0.645)	(0.316)	(0.555)
Capital account	CA	2.602	0.989	0.423	0.560	0.229	0.838
		(0.116)	(0.466)	(0.788)	(0.698)	(0.914)	(0.538)
Exchange rate	EX	1.346	2.652	5.381	3.942	1.037	1.512
		(0.333)	(0.112)	(0.021)	(0.047)	(0.445)	(0.286)
Discount rate	DR	1.599	1.349	0.279	2.111	0.628	0.423
		(0.265)	(0.332)	(0.883)	(0.171)	(0.656)	(0.788)
M1	M1	0.603	2.090	3.370	1.910	60.913	3.001
		(0.671)	(0.174)	(0.068)	(0.202)	(0.000)	(0.087)
General account	GG	0.441	0.221	0.167	0.240	0.342	7.629
of government		(0.776)	(0.919)	(0.949)	(0.908)	(0.842)	(0.008)

NOTE: Lag length is 4 periods.

DR → EX
↓
GG → M1

Significance Level 10%   →

Significance Level 5%   →

positive and negative influences (or statistical causality) alternate with respect to the maker. The capital account by itself is not influenced by the other variables, and with four periods of lag, it seems to have a positive influence on money supply. (See Table 2(a).)

1971–81 (First Period). Until 1981, the causality relations were generally weak. The only strong relationship is between the discount rate and the exchange rate, but the signs fluctuate period by period. A weaker relationship is found from the exchange rate to the money supply, and the effect of fiscal policy to money supply (Table 2(b)).

1981–91. After 1981, the causality relations became generally stronger. This may reflect the opening of Japan's financial market to the world. The link from the exchange rate to current account is strong and the relationship between the exchange rate to the current account has the expected sign, but the level of significance is low. The effect of the interest rate can be traced in such a way that a low rate of interest stimulates consumption expansion and the current account deficit. Even though the statistical significance of estimated coefficients is high, the signs of the coefficients alternate again.

TABLE 2

(*continued*)

(c) 1981:1 to 1991:4

Effect		Cause					
		CU	CA	EX	DR	M1	GG
Current account	CU	3.648	1.860	3.375	4.862	1.860	0.834
		(0.023)	(0.159)	(0.030)	(0.007)	(0.159)	(0.520)
Capital account	CA	2.324	1.728	0.834	0.281	1.075	2.599
		(0.094)	(0.185)	(0.520)	(0.887)	(0.397)	(0.069)
Exchange rate	EX	0.469	0.408	14.016	1.072	0.540	0.360
		(0.758)	(0.800)	(0.000)	(0.398)	(0.708)	(0.834)
Discount rate	DR	1.624	0.203	1.087	13.571	1.159	1.047
		(0.209)	(0.933)	(0.391)	(0.000)	(0.360)	(0.409)
M1	M1	0.584	0.209	1.997	0.588	10.974	3.459
		(0.678)	(0.930)	(0.136)	(0.675)	(0.000)	(0.028)
General account	GG	0.146	0.188	0.979	0.057	1.603	1.155
of government		(0.962)	(0.942)	(0.442)	(0.993)	(0.215)	(0.362)

NOTE: Lag length is 4 periods.

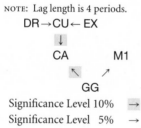

Significance Level 10% →

Significance Level 5% →

The relationship between current account and capital account is always negative except for the first one-period lag. It seems to indicate that the current account is always balanced by the autonomous and capital account with a lag of at least one year (Table 2(c)).

Theoretically, the current account and capital account add up to zero if changes in reserves and banks' short-term positions are neglected. The finding above that the current account is likely to be accommodated by the capital account may suggest that reserves and commercial banks' liquidity position absorbs the current account balance in the immediate time period and, then, the relative autonomous components of capital movements follow it.

In summary, the exchange rate is strongly affected by the tightness of monetary policy and exchange rate affects the current account with about two periods of lag. The comparison of two periods shows that the links between economic variables were statistically strengthened after financial deregulation. This evidence indicates an example of Japanese structural adjustment. The intuitive picture that combines causality tests with economic reasoning can be described as follows. Exogenous shocks (including monetary shocks but not exclusively so) were felt in exchange rates and prices in fast-adjusting asset markets. Exchange rates trigger changes in the balance of payments in the normal (equilibrating) direction with a half-year lag, which induces capital movements with a quarter-year lag. This chain of economic influence seems to be quite plausible. However, the reason for the unilateral causality from the current account still remains a puzzle.

NOTES

I am much indebted to Towa Tachibana for his research assistance and many helpful discussions during the time of preparation. I also thank the participants of the Lanai conference, in particular, the discussants Yukio Noguchi and Joel Slemrod. Ken Togo also provided valuable research assistance.

1. Most data come from the Balance of Payments (Bank of Japan) and Annual Reports of the International Finance Division, Ministry of Finance.

2. Most data on the U.S. side come from the Survey of Current Business.

3. In the appendix, I sketch a causality analysis that clarifies which are the driving factors among the components of the balance of payments identity.

4. Destler and Henning (1989) provide a valuable political economy study of actors of exchange rate policy making. They propose that U.S. exchange rate policy should be designed to be consistent with overall macroeconomic policy by government and the Congress, rather than determined by the treasury and the Federal Reserve. I am not sure if it helps to make exchange rate policy more political than technical by involving more government institutions.

5. Coincidentally, the governor of the Bank of Japan, at the time of easy money policy of 1987–89, Sumita, was an ex-MOF official. But the respected governor who helped the independence of the central bank, Morinaga, was also an ex-MOF official, so we cannot say that the system of sending personnel from MOF to BOJ had by itself impaired the independence of the central bank.

6. Feldstein (1988) develops a negative view on the impact of policy coordination. For a positive view, see Dobson (1991).

REFERENCES

Alesina, Alberto and Carliner, Geoffry, eds. 1991. *Politics and economics in the eighties,*. Chicago: University of Chicago Press.

Bank of Japan. 1993. *Economics statistics annual.* Tokyo: Bank of Japan.

Buchanan, J. M. and Wagner, R. E. 1977. *Democracy in deficits.* New York: Academic Press.

Cargill, Thomas F. and Royama Shoichi. 1988. *The transition of finance in Japan and the United States: a comparative perspective.* Stanford: Hoover Institution Press.

Council of Economic Advisors. 1993. *Economic report of the president.* Washington: Council of Economic Advisors.

Department of Commerce. 1993. *Survey of current business.* Washington: Department of Commerce.

Destler, I. M. and Henning, C. R. 1989. *Dollar politics: exchange rate policy making in the United States.* Washington: Institute for International Economics

Diamond, Douglas. 1984. Financial intermediation and delegated monitoring. *Review of economic studies* 51:393–414.

Dobson, Wendy. 1991. *Economic policy coordination: requiem or prologue?* Policy Analysis in International Economics, No. 30, April. Washington: Institute for International Economics.

Dornbusch, Rudiger. 1976. Expectations and exchange rate dynamics. *Journal of political economy* 84(6).

Feldstein, Martin. 1988. Thinking about international economic coordination. *Perspectives* 2(2).

———. 1994a. American economic policy in the 1980s: a personal view. In *American economic policy in the 1980s.* Chicago: University of Chicago Press.

———, ed. 1994b. *American economic policy in the 1980s.* Chicago: University of Chicago Press.

Feldstein, Martin and Horioka Yuji. 1980. Domestic saving and international capital flows. *Economic journal* 90:314329.

Frankel, Jeffrey A. 1994. Exchange rate policy. In *American economic policy in the 1980s,* ed. Martin Feldstein. Chicago: University of Chicago Press.

French, Kenneth R. and Poterba, James M. 1990. Japanese and U.S. cross-border common stock investments. *Journal of the Japanese and international economies* 4:476–93.

Froot, Kenneth A. 1991. Japanese foreign direct investment. NBER Working Paper, No. 3737.

———, ed. 1993. *Foreign direct investment.* Chicago: University of Chicago Press.

Froot, Kenneth A. and Stein, Jeremy C. 1991. Exchange rate and foreign direct investment: an imperfect capital markets approach. *Quarterly journal of economics* 106(4):1191–1217.

Froot, Kenneth A.; Scharfstein, D. S.; and Stein, J. C. 1992. Risk management: coordinating corporate investment and financing policies. NBER Working Paper, No. 4084.

Fukuda Shinichi. 1993. The determinants of capital controls and their effects on trade balance during the period of capital market liberalization in Japan. The Institute of Economic Research, Hitotsubashi University, Discussion Paper Series A, No. 270.

Funabashi Yoichi. 1989. *Managing the dollar: from the Plaza to the Louvre.* 2d ed. Washington: Institute for International Economics.

Gale, David and Hellwig, Martin. 1985. Incentive-compatible debt contracts: the one-period case. *Review of economic studies* 52:647–63.

Hamada Koichi. 1985. *The political economy of international monetary interdependence.* Cambridge, Mass.: MIT Press.

Hamada Koichi and Sakuragawa Masaya. 1993. Asymmetric information and a theory of international capital movements. Unpublished manuscript, Yale University.

Horaguchi Haruo. 1992. *Nihon kigyō no kaigai chokusetu toshi.* Tokyo: University of Tokyo Press.

Ito Takatoshi. 1986. Capital controls and covered interest parity between the yen and the dollar. *The economic studies quarterly* 37:223–41.

———. 1992. *The Japanese economy.* Cambridge, Mass.: MIT Press.

Joskow, Paul L., and Noll, Roger G. 1994. Economic regulation. In *American economic policy in the 1980s,* ed. Martin Feldstein. Chicago: University of Chicago Press.

Kato Junko. 1992. Tax reform in Japan: the influence and strategy of fiscal bureaucrats in policymaking. Ph.D. diss., Yale University.

Kawai Masahiro. 1991. Japanese investment in foreign securities in the 1980s. Pacific Economic Papers No. 201, November. Australian National University.

———. 1993. Accumulation of net external assets in Japan. In *Japan, Europe, and international financial markets,* ed. R. Sato, R. Levich, and R. Ramachandran. Cambridge: Cambridge University Press.

Kindleberger, Charles P. 1967. The politics of international money and world language. International Financial Section, Princeton University.

Kojima Kiyoshi. 1985. *Nihon no kaigai chokusetu toshi.* Tokyo: Bunshindo.

Komiya Ryutaro. 1988. *The Japanese economy: trade, industry and government.* Tokyo: University of Tokyo Press.

Komura Chikara. 1990. Policy options toward a trade balance: a Japanese case study using the VAR model, 1974–1987. *Journal of Japanese and international economies* 4:24–35.

Kuroyanagi Masaaki, Hamada Koichi, and Sakurai M. 1991. Towards the estimation of the world asset and debt matrix. *NIRA research output* 4(1):6–20.

Lawrence, Robert. 1993. Japan's low levels of inward investment: the role of inhibitions on acquisitions. In *Foreign direct investment,* ed. Kenneth A. Froot. Chicago: University of Chicago Press.

Lipsey, Robert E. 1992. Foreign direct investment in the U.S.: changes over three decades. NBER Working Paper, No. 4124.

Litan, Robert E. 1994. Financial regulation. In *American economic policy in the 1980s,* ed. Martin Feldstein. Chicago: University of Chicago Press.

Mason, Mark. 1990. *Access denied: American multinationals and Japan, 1930–80.* Cambridge, Mass.: Harvard University Press.

———. 1992. United States direct investment in Japan: trends and prospects. *California management review.* 35(1).

Ministry of Finance. 1993. Annual reports of the International Finance Division. Tokyo: Ministry of Finance.

Mundell, Robert A. 1968. *International economics.* New York: Macmillan.

Mussa, Michael. 1994. Monetary policy. In *American economic policy in the 1980s,* ed. Martin Feldstein. Chicago: University of Chicago Press.

Oudiz, Gilles and Sachs, Jeffrey. 1984. Macroeconomic policy coordination among the individual economies, *Brookings Papers on Economic Activities I* 1–64. Washington: Brookings Institution.

Packer, F. and Ryser, M. The governance of failure: an anatomy of corporate bankruptcy in Japan. Working Paper, No. 62, Center on Japanese Economy and Business, Graduate School of Business, Columbia University.

Poterba, James M. 1993. Budget policy. In *American economic policy in the 1980s,* ed. Martin Feldstein. Chicago: University of Chicago Press.

Putnam, Robert. 1988. Diplomacy and domestic politics: the logic of two-level games. *International organization* 42(3).

Rogoff, Kenneth. 1984. Can monetary coordination be counterproductive? *Journal of international economics* 18(3/4).

Rosenbluth, Frances McCall. 1989. *Financial politics in contemporary Japan.* Ithaca: Cornell University Press.

Shibata Akihisa and Mototsuzu Shintani. 1994. Capital mobility in the world economy: an alternative measure. Discussion paper no. 330, Osaka University.

Tobin, James. 1994. Monetary policy. In *American economic policy in the 1980s,* ed. Martin Feldstein. Chicago: University of Chicago Press

Townsend, Robert. 1979. Optimal contracts and competitive markets with costly state verification. *Journal of economic theory* 21:265–93.

Ueda Kazuo. 1990. Japanese capital outflows. *Journal of banking and finance* 14:1079–1101.

Volcker, Paul A. 1994. Monetary policy. In *American economic policy in the 1980s,* ed. Martin Feldstein. Chicago: University of Chicago Press.

Volcker, Paul A. and Gyohten Toyoo. 1992. *Changing fortunes: the world money and the threat to American leadership.* New York: Times Books.

Williamson, S. D. 1987. Financial intermediation, business failures and real business cycles. *Journal of political economy* 95:1196–1216.

On Capital Flows from Japan
to the United States

TAKATOSHI ITO

DURING THE 1970s and 1980s, capital flows in the world financial market increased as various barriers to capital movement were lowered. In particular, capital outflow from Japan increased rapidly in the first half of the 1980s and remained high during the rest of the decade. Gross long-term capital outflow from Japan by Japanese residents increased from $13 billion in 1980 to $191 billion in 1989, an increase of more than 15 fold. The United States was a favorite destination of Japanese capital investment. A dramatic change took place in international asset positions as a result of capital flows, in that Japan became the largest creditor country, while the United States became the largest debtor country.

Although it is not always appropriate to focus on bilateral capital flows, the case of Japan-U.S. capital flows is a subject of interest on several grounds. First, the two largest economies in the world went through a complete reversal in their asset positions. It is important to investigate the economic factors behind this enormous change. Second, given the magnitude of the change, its effects on the capital market are important. In particular, it is interesting to investigate numerically whether massive capital helped keep U.S. interest rates low to support economic expansion.

This paper will examine several aspects of capital flows from Japan to the United States, with an emphasis on the determinants in Japan to push capital abroad and any impact on the U.S. securities market. Conditions in both the Japanese and U.S. capital markets and the relative (pull and push) factors in the two markets are examined to shed some light on capital flows in the 1980s.

This paper is organized as follows. The first section is an overview of the Japanese current and capital accounts from the 1980s to the early 1990s. Then, I focus on two specific questions. First, large Japanese trade surpluses in the second half of the 1980s were often alleged to cause economic slumps in the economies of Japan's trading partners, particularly the United States. Japanese often respond by saying that surpluses were recycled into the world financial market, in particular to the U.S. government bond market. Without the seemingly insatiable demand for U.S. bonds by Japanese investors, the argument goes, the interest rate in the United States would have been higher than the level actually observed, causing economic tightening. The second section of this paper quantitatively investigates this argument. In the following section, I focus on the second specific question: whether the sharp increase in the share of Japanese direct investment in the United States during the 1980s can be explained by the usual determinants of foreign direct investment, in particular exports from Japan. Concluding remarks are given in a closing summary.

JAPANESE CURRENT AND CAPITAL ACCOUNTS

The United States was the largest creditor country at the beginning of the 1980s, but became the largest debtor country in terms of net asset position. In contrast, Japan emerged as one of the largest creditor countries in the world. This trading of places in asset positions is shown in Table 1. The position at the end of 1991 was rather symmetrical: Japan had accumulated more than $383 billion in net external assets, while the United States was indebted to the rest of the world by $381 billion (evaluating direct investment at market value).

The present asset position (in the stock definition) reflects net capital account positions (in the flow definition) in the past. There are two ways to look at changes in capital account positions in the 1980s. First, capital account balances are a reflection of the saving-investment balance; net capital exports are the difference in domestic saving and domestic investment. Japanese saved more than domestic investment could absorb, while Americans as a nation saved too little compared to their investment. Second, capital accounts are the other side of current account (merchandise and service trade balance). Any foreign exchange earned by exports but not used for imports is invested abroad (assuming that official intervention in the foreign exchange market, which changes foreign reserves, is relatively small in magnitude in the floating exchange rate world).[1]

The left panel of Table 2 shows the current and capital accounts of Japan from 1979 to 1992, while the right panel shows the capital account in which long-term flows are broken down into those of Japanese and foreign investors. Asset accumulation takes place mainly through long-term capital net outflows, which is the difference between capital outflow (Japanese capital, column [5]) and capital inflow (foreign capital, column [6]) in Table 2. Long-term capital

TABLE 1

External Asset Positions: Japan and U.S.

Year end	*Net International Asset Position*		
	Japan $bil	*US Current cost,* $bil	*US Market value,* $bil
1975	8.9		
1976	9.6		
1977	22.0	190.5	na
1978	36.2	228.4	na
1979	28.8	342.9	na
1980	11.5	392.5	na
1981	10.9	374.3	na
1982	24.7	378.9	na
1983	37.3	337.4	267.6
1984	74.3	234.2	177.3
1985	129.8	139.1	142.3
1986	180.4	19.2	109.7
1987	240.7	−34.0	46.8
1988	291.7	−140.3	5.4
1989	293.2	−288.5	−128.9
1990	328.1	−291.9	−269.7
1991	383.1	−364.9	−396.4
1992	513.6	−521.3	−611.5

SOURCE: Ministry of Finance, *Zaisei kinyū tōkei geppō,* August 1993, and various years. US, up to 1983: Economic Report to the President, 1993, Table B-99. US, after 1984: Economic Report of the President, 1994, Table B-102. See also June issues of *Current Survey of Business.*

flows usually move parallel to current account surpluses, as was the case during most of the 1980s. However, current account and capital account surpluses do not have to match, as was the case in 1990 and 1991. The discrepancy is the sum of short-term capital movement (borrowing and lending of financial instruments with maturity less than one year), the official and private-sector monetary movement (such as changes in foreign reserves as a result of official intervention, and monetary remittance between headquarters and foreign branches of banks), and the statistical discrepancy.

From fiscal year 1981 to 1990, current account surpluses rose (from $6 billion), peaked (in 1986 at $94 billion), and declined (to $34 billion in 1990). The long-term capital movement follows the same pattern of rise and decline, but during the mid-1980s, the long-term capital net outflow outpaced current

TABLE 2

Japan's International Balance of Payment, Fiscal Year Basis

	Current Account ($bil)				Capital Account ($mil)			
FY	Mer-chan-dise Trade Balance (1)	Service Trade Balance (2)	Transfer (3)	Current Account Balance (4)= (1+2+3)	Long Term, Japa-nese Capital (5)	Long Term, Foreign Capital (6)	Long Term Capital Balance (5)−(6)	Short Term Balance (7)
1979	−2,438	−10,142	−1,273	−13,853	13,851	3,528	10,323	−4,888
1980	6,766	−12,199	−1,579	−7,012	13,123	15,821	−2,698	−4,763
1981	20,358	−12,876	−1,548	5,934	25,727	10,793	14,934	909
1982	20,141	−9,535	−1,471	9,135	27,915	16,039	11,876	3,156
1983	34,546	−8,784	−1,530	24,232	33,930	13,133	20,797	1,338
1984	45,601	−7,064	−1,522	37,015	61,976	7,749	54,227	2,799
1985	61,601	−4,745	−1,837	55,019	92,390	19,213	73,177	1,475
1986	101,648	−5,135	−2,374	94,139	144,461	−219	144,680	−899
1987	94,034	−5,691	−3,869	84,474	121,012	1,547	119,465	−20,502
1988	95,302	−13,521	−4,507	77,274	153,077	31,677	121,400	−31,126
1989	69,999	−12,632	−3,969	53,398	191,573	91,853	99,720	−19,335
1990	69,864	−22,511	−13,637	33,716	122,428	105,635	16,793	−1,333
1991	113,683	−19,386	−4,075	90,222	100,601	140,357	−39,756	15,876
1992	136,109	−5,018	−5,191	125,900	54,575	6,948	47,567	9,726

NOTE: (a) (1) All figures are Fiscal Year (FY) basis: March(t) to April(t+1). (b) Original Source: Ministry of Finance. Reference: Bank of Japan, *Economic Statistics Annual, 1992,* 1993. (c) Gensaki investment (short-term repurchase agreement with long-term securities) by foreigners is classified into "short-term investment," although it used to be classified into the long-term investment before 1979. (d) Definition: The following accounting identity holds: Capital Account Surplus (4) = Long-term Japanese capital outflow (5); − Long-term foreign capital inflow (6); + Short-term capital net outflow (7); + Balance of monetary movement [not shown]; + Errors and omissions [not shown].

account surpluses. Basically, Japan spent more dollars in purchasing securities than it earned by exporting (less importing) from 1984 to 1989. The difference was financed typically by borrowing short-term capital. Short-term borrowing was in excess of $31 billion in 1988. However, the long-term capital inflow exceeded the long-term capital outflow in 1991, despite large current account surpluses ($90 billion).

Some analyses of the behavior of the current account surpluses in 1990 and 1991 are in order. In 1990, current account surpluses declined sharply, and so did long-term capital outflows. Part of this sharp decline was a special payment to the United States for the allied force of the Gulf War. In 1991, however, current account surpluses started to increase again, while long-term capital outflows became negative (that is, net capital inflow). Japan earned foreign exchange in its trade and service accounts and also experienced long-term capital inflow. This apparent paradox can be explained by the massive outflow of short-term capital. This movement may be the "unwinding" of inflows of short-term capital in previous years. Some were just repayments of past short-term borrowing, but others included net outflow resulting from the gold investment account.[2] The outflow of short-term capital continued in 1991, so that the long-term capital outflow remained modest, although current account surpluses reached a record high in 1992. The compositional change in Japanese capital outflow in 1991–92 was significant enough to warrant a closer look.

Table 3 shows bilateral Japanese long-term investment vis-a-vis the United States. The last column of the table shows that about one-third of Japanese investment is directed to the United States. However, this is likely an underestimate. Substantial amounts of investment ended up in U.S. securities and real estate via third countries, mostly tax haven countries. The table shows that a substantial proportion of Japanese investment is directed to the United States. However, the U.S. share seems to have been on the decline since the mid-1980s.

Table 4 shows components of long-term capital outflows of Japanese investors (on a calendar-year basis). This is a breakdown, by types of investment, of column (2) from Table 3. Our main interest is in foreign direct investment (FDI), stock investment, and bond investment since these types of investment reflect relative financial conditions—such as interest rates and growth potentials—of Japan and other nations. The table shows that from 1980 to 1986, securities investment outpaced all other types of investment. In particular, bond investment was favored by Japanese. In the first half of the 1980s, the interest rate differential between the United States and Japan was substantial and Japanese institutional investors were aggressive in buying U.S. government bonds with high coupon yields. In 1987 (compared to 1986), Japanese equity investment in the United States increased despite Black Monday in the New York market, while bond investment declined. This reflected declining interest rates in the United States. FDI increased substantially from 1985 to 1990. All types of long-term investment declined from 1990 to 1992.

Table 5, a companion to Table 4, lists Japanese long-term investment destined to the United States only. This is a breakdown, by types of investment, of column (2) of Table 3. Unfortunately, data before 1986 are not available, nor is a breakdown of securities investment into stocks and bonds.

In sum, during the 1980s, current account surpluses and long-term capital outflows moved in parallel. However, the relationship changed greatly after 1990. We may conclude that fluctuations in the capital account and its components, such as securities investment and direct investment, are not necessarily

TABLE 3

Japan's Long-term Capital Account, Calendar Year Basis

	Long-term Capital Account ($bil)			To the United States only, i.e., Bilateral Flow ($mil)				
Year	Net Total Outflow (1)= (2)−(3)	Japan Capital Outflow (2)	Foreign Capital Inflow (3)	Net Total Ja→US Capital (4)= (5)−(6)	Japan Capital to US (5)	US Capital to Japan (6)	US Share Net (4)/(1) %	US Share Gross (5)/(2) %
1981	6,449	22,809	16,360	2,643	4,109	1,466	40.98	18.01
1982	14,969	27,418	12,449	1,700	3,649	1,949	11.36	13.31
1983	17,700	32,459	14,759	5,541	7,072	1,531	31.31	21.79
1984	49,651	56,775	7,124	14,814	15,429	615	29.84	27.18
1985	64,542	81,815	17,273	33,163	35,384	2,221	51.38	43.25
1986	131,461	132,095	634	65,650	59,186	−6,464	49.94	44.81
1987	136,532	132,830	−3,702	61,030	50,563	−10,467	44.70	38.07
1988	130,930	149,883	18,953	59,260	61,490	2,230	45.26	41.03
1989	89,246	192,118	102,872	53,861	57,145	3,284	60.35	29.74
1990	43,586	120,766	77,180	11,719	16,437	4,718	26.89	13.61
1991	37,057	121,446	158,503	18,358	35,044	16,686	49.54	28.86
1992	28,459	57,692	29,503	27,192	22,842	−4,350	95.55	39.41

NOTE: (a) (1) All figures are calendar-year basis. (b) Original Source: Ministry of Finance. Reference: Bank of Japan, *Economic Statistics Annual, 1992,* 1993.

related to fluctuations in the current account. Among the different types of long-term investment by Japanese investors, bond investment was favored in the first half of the 1980s; stock (equities) investment and then direct investment became increasingly popular after 1986. All types of foreign investment declined in the 1990s. The share of the United States as a destination country has been declining since the mid-1980s.

THE U.S. FINANCIAL MARKETS AND FOREIGN CAPITAL INFLOW

In this section, I will investigate whether inflows of foreign capital into the United States have had an impact. The first column of Table 6 shows the total U.S. public debt securities owned by private investors, including individuals, insurance companies, money market fund corporations, state and local governments, and foreign and international organizations. The second column of

TABLE 4

Long-term Capital Outflow (to the rest of the world) from Japan
by Type of Investment, Calendar Year Basis

| | Long-term Capital Investment (gross) by Japanese Investors to the Rest of the World ($mil) | | | | | | |
| | | | | | Securities | | |
Year	Total	FDI	Credits	Loans	Total	Stock	Bond
1979	16,294	2,898	−1,288	8,102	5,865	575	5,290
1980	10,817	2,385	717	2,553	3,753	−213	3,966
1981	22,809	4,894	2,731	5,083	8,777	240	8,537
1982	27,418	4,540	3,239	7,902	9,743	151	9,592
1983	32,459	3,612	2,589	8,425	16,024	661	15,381
1984	56,775	5,965	4,937	11,922	30,795	51	30,744
1985	81,815	6,452	2,817	10,427	59,773	995	53,479
1986	132,095	14,480	1,836	9,281	101,977	7,048	93,024
1987	132,830	19,519	535	16,190	87,757	16,874	72,885
1988	149,883	34,210	6,939	15,211	86,949	2,993	85,812
1989	192,118	44,130	4,002	22,495	113,178	17,887	94,083
1990	120,766	48,024	−681	22,182	39,681	6,256	28,961
1991	121,446	30,726	−3,928	13,097	74,306	3,630	68,202
1992	57,962	17,222	−5,293	7,623	34,362	−3,012	35,634

NOTE: (a) All figures are Calendar Year basis, reported in IMF format, settlement basis. (b) Original source: Ministry of Finance. (c) Reproduced from Ito (1992, p. 332) and updates by *Zaisei kinyū tōkei geppō*, 1993. (d) Definition: Total = FDI + Credits + Loans + Securities Investment + other [not reported].

Table 6 is the balance held by foreign and international organizations only. (There is no breakdown by country of origin.) It shows that foreign purchases increased in the late 1970s and the second half of the 1980s.

Column (4) in Table 6 shows how much foreign bond holdings increased from December to December. Column (5) shows the amount of Japanese securities made in that calendar year, which is reproduced from the securities investment of Table 5. The two columns cannot be compared directly, because column (4) is only for public bonds, while column (5) includes stocks as well as bonds. However, we should again remember that the number here may be an underestimate due to indirect investment through third countries. The impression from this table is that Japanese securities investment as a proportion of investment by foreigners was significant in the 1980s. The movements of columns (4) and (5) are more or less in parallel. Although the precise share of

TABLE 5

Long-term Bilateral Capital Outflow from Japan to U.S., Calendar Year Basis

Year	Total	FDI	Credits	Loans	Securities Total
			Long-term Capital Investment (gross) by Japanese Investors to the U.S. ($mil)		
1986	59,186	7,973	342	612	49,395
1987	50,563	9,641	488	1,470	37,380
1988	61,490	18,969	1,006	2,818	36,214
1989	57,145	21,238	1,247	4,971	26,660
1990	16,437	25,584	623	3,249	−16,172
1991	35,044	15,213	−317	2,758	15,592
1992	22,842	8,914	−322	4,838	8,490

NOTE: (a) All figures are Calendar Year basis, reported in IMF format, settlement basis. (b) Original source: Ministry of Finance, *Zaisei kinyū tōkei geppō*, 1992, pp. 54–55.

Japanese investment in public bonds is not available, it is not unreasonable to assume that it is a significant portion of bond investment.

I will examine the often-claimed hypothesis that a large foreign capital inflow kept long-term interest rates down. In order to investigate this possibility, I first specify how the long-term interest rate is determined.

The long-term interest rate is determined as an equilibrium of the asset market, where demand and supply of bonds determine the rate. In a sense, a specification is a reduced-form equation, without pretending to specify demand or supply equations. Here we consider the following three specifications:

$$(1) \quad LR(t) = b_1 + b_2 \frac{BOND_t}{GDP_t} + b_3 \frac{M1_t}{GDP_t} + e_t$$

$$(2) \quad LR(t) = b_1 + b_2 \frac{BOND_t}{GDP_t} + b_3 \frac{M1_t}{GDP_t} + b_4 GDPGR_t + e_t$$

$$(3) \quad LR(t) = b_1 + b_2 \frac{BOND_t}{GDP_t} + b_3 \frac{M1_t}{GDP_t} + b_4 GDPGR_t + b_5 SPREAD_t + e_t$$

where LR is the real long-term interest rate, BOND is public debt securities held by domestic private agents, GDP is nominal gross domestic product, M1 is narrow money supply (M1), GDPGR is the growth rate (of real GDP), and SPREAD is the spread between the long-term and short-term interest rates, which is a proxy for future inflation expected in the market. The BOND term and M1 term will not have multicollinearity.

TABLE 6
United States Public Debt Securities by Ownership of Private Investors, 1976–92

Year	Total Debt ($bil.) (1)	Bond Held by Foreigners (2)	Ratio (2)/(1) %	Change in (2), (t−2) → t (4)	J. Securities Investment in U.S. ($bil.) (5)
1976:06	376.4	69.8	18.54		
1976:12	409.5	78.1	19.07		
1977:06	421.0	87.9	20.88		
1977:12	461.3	109.6	23.76	31.5	
1978:06	477.8	119.5	25.01		
1978:12	508.6	133.1	26.17	23.5	
1979:06	516.6	114.9	22.24		
1979:12	540.5	119.0	22.02	−14.1	
1980:06	558.2	118.2	21.18		
1980:12	616.4	129.7	21.04	10.7	
1981:06	651.2	136.6	20.98		
1981:12	694.5	136.6	19.67	6.9	
1982:06	740.9	137.2	18.52		
1982:12	848.4	149.5	17.62	12.9	
1983:06	948.6	160.1	16.88		
1983:12	1,022.6	166.3	16.26	16.8	
1984:06	1,102.2	171.6	15.57		
1984:12	1,212.5	205.9	16.98	39.6	
1985:06	1,292.0	213.8	16.55		
1985:12	1,417.2	224.8	15.86	18.9	
1986:06	1,502.7	250.9	16.70		
1986:12	1,602.0	263.4	16.44	38.6	49.40
1987:06	1,658.1	281.1	16.95		
1987:12	1,731.4	299.7	17.31	36.3	37.38
1988:06	1,786.7	345.4	19.33		
1988:12	1,858.5	362.2	19.49	62.5	36.21
1989:06	1,909.1	369.1	19.33		
1989:12	2,015.8	392.9	19.49	30.7	26.66
1990:06	2,141.8	390.5	18.23		
1990:12	2,288.3	421.7	18.43	28.8	−16.17
1991:06	2,397.9	436.9	18.22		
1991:12	2,563.2	455.0	17.75	33.3	15.60
1992:06	2,712.4	492.9	18.17		
1992:12	2,812.0	457.0	16.25	2.0	8.49

NOTE: In year, month, ":06" means "June" and ":12" means "December."
SOURCES: Columns (1) and (2): Economic Report to President, 1993, Table B-84. Column (5) from Table 5.

One could interpret this regression as a reduced form of the long rate determination in a general equilibrium model of asset markets. One can also interpret it from a more simplistic framework of the IS-LM model: the position of
the LM curve (more relevant to the short-term interest rate) is influenced by
choice between money supply (M1/GDP variable) and long assets (BOND/
GDP), while the IS curve may be shifted by investment fluctuation which is
greatly influenced by the growth rate.

Theory predicts the following sign conditions. When the government borrows more (bond supply increases more than nominal GDP) in the domestic
market, the real interest rate tends to rise ($b_2 > 0$). When monetary conditions
ease, the real interest rate tends to decline ($b_3 < 0$). I assume that the supply
of bonds and the money supply are regarded as exogenous variables.

The inflation rate which is deducted from the nominal long-term rate is the
inflation rate in the preceding six months. It is admittedly a bad proxy for the
expected inflation rate in the following ten years. Any inflation expectation for
the future not captured in the past six months may show up in the estimate of
the spread to be discussed shortly.

First, I will introduce the variable to anticipate overheating of the economy,
namely, the growth rate. When the economy is growing faster, it makes investors
fear inflation so that the rate goes up ($b_4 > 0$). Second, a variable of the term
structure (spread between the long rate and the short [6-month bill] rate is
introduced, assuming the spread represents investors' expectations) is exogenously determined. More expected inflation in the future increases the real
interest rate defined with the spot inflation rate ($b_5 > 0$).

Table 7 shows the estimation results. All estimated coefficients have expected
signs and are statistically significant. According to the estimate, a percentage
point increase in the ratio of bond stock to GDP will increase the long-term
interest rate by about 20 basis points.

Table 8 shows an exercise to consider how much the foreign purchase of
government bonds lowers the long rate. Regression results in Table 7 show that
more bond supply drives up the long rate. Suppose foreigners had not invested
in U.S. securities, and the supply of bonds had remained the same. The difference would have had to have been absorbed by domestic investors. Then the
simulation would show the hypothetical long rate, in the case without foreigners' purchase of U.S. securities. Multiplying the coefficient of the BOND/GDP
variable (b_2) by the amount of foreign buying divided by GDP, the magnitude
of foreign purchase of U.S. bonds reducing the long rate is estimated. This is
shown as the IMPACT column of Table 8.

Depending on the specification, the exact estimates vary. If specification (2)
from Table 7 is employed, the impact amounted to an increase of more than
1.5 percentage points in the mid-1980s, and about two percentage points in
the beginning of the 1990s. This would have had a rather significant effect on

TABLE 7

Long-term Real Interest Rate Determination

Spec	Constant	Bond/GNP	M1/GNP	GDPGR	SP	R bar sq.	D.W.
(1)	17.521	21.424	−124.61			0.183	0.57
	(1.80)*	(2.78)†	(−1.91)*				
(2)	23.46	23.89	−174.47	0.436		0.278	0.69
	(2.46)‡	(3.26)†	(−2.68)‡	(2.25)‡			
(3)	28.54	15.49	−205.17	0.426	1.069	0.400	1.26
	(3.21)†	(2.10)‡	(−3.39)†	(2.41)‡	(2.67)‡		

* significant at 10% level.
† significant at 1% level.
‡ significant at 5% level.

Specifications:

(1) $LR(t) = b_1 + b_2\dfrac{BOND_t}{GDP_t} + b_3\dfrac{M1_t}{GDP_t} + e_t$

(2) $LR(t) = b_1 + b_2\dfrac{BOND_t}{GDP_t} + b_3\dfrac{M1_t}{GDP_t} + b_4 GDPGR_t + e_t$

(3) $LR(t) = b_1 + b_2\dfrac{BOND_t}{GDP_t} + b_3\dfrac{M1_t}{GDP_t} + b_4 GDPGR_t + b_5 SPREAD_t + e_t$

Semi-Annual Data From 76:01 to 92:02; Usable Observations 34

Variables:
LR=US government bond (10-year to maturity) interest rate−inflation rate (CPI inflation annualized rate over the past 6 months). Source: FYGT10 and PUNEW in CITIBASE
BOND=privately held public debt securities (BONDTOTAL)−those held by foreign and international residents. Source: Economic Report to President, p. 446, Table B-84
GDP=nominal GDP. Source: GDP in CITIBASE
M1=money supply M1. Source: FM1 in CITIBASE
GDPGR=real GDP growth rate, real GDP. Source: GDPQ in CITIBASE
SP=SPREAD, 10-year bond rate−6-month bill rate. Source: CITIBASE

SIMULATION:
Define, $IMPACT = b_2 DIFBD_t$
where $DIFBD = BONDTOTAL − BOND$
variable: BONDTOTAL, total (domestic+foreign) privately held public liability

the U.S. economy. Economic expansion, which had its longest spell in peacetime from 1982 to 1990, would likely have been affected adversely. However, if specification (3) is to be believed, then the impact on the interest rate was less than one percentage point throughout the sample period. The withdrawal of foreign investment would not have greatly changed the bond rate in the United States. Hence, the impact was minimal. Comparing the two specifications in Table 7, I believe that specification (3) is more plausible.

TABLE 8
Impact of Foreign Purchases of U.S. Bonds

SIMULATION, Specification (2)		Simulation Specification (3)	SIMULATION, Specification (2)		Simulation Specification (3)
76:01	0.954	0.483	84:02	1.271	0.643
76:02	1.019	0.516	85:01	1.277	0.647
77:01	1.075	0.544	85:02	1.297	0.656
77:02	1.279	0.647	86:01	1.416	0.717
78:01	1.289	0.652	86:02	1.451	0.734
78:02	1.351	0.684	87:01	1.494	0.756
79:01	1.118	0.566	87:02	1.528	0.774
79:02	1.102	0.558	88:01	1.698	0.860
80:01	1.068	0.540	88:02	1.715	0.868
80:02	1.093	0.553	89:01	1.686	0.853
81:01	1.090	0.552	89:02	1.756	0.889
81:02	1.053	0.533	90:01	1.689	0.855
82:01	1.041	0.527	90:02	1.811	0.917
82:02	1.117	0.566	91:01	1.844	0.934
83:01	1.135	0.575	91:02	1.889	0.956
83:02	1.119	0.567	92:01	1.995	1.010
84:01	1.091	0.552	92:02	1.801	0.912

JAPANESE FOREIGN DIRECT INVESTMENT

Literature Survey

Kojima (1978, Ch. 3), Lizondo (1991), and Graham and Krugman (1991, Ch. 2 and App. B) provide convenient overviews on different theories of determinants of FDI. Caves (1993) provides a nice survey of Japanese FDI to the United States. I will comment on some of the hypotheses relevant to the present study. First, several theories suggest the hypothesis that exports and FDI are correlated. Kojima (1978, p. 86) wrote some 25 years ago that "Japan's foreign investment has to date been 'trade-oriented.' It was aimed at complementing Japan's comparative advantage position."[3] The difference between what Kojima observed in 1978 and today is that Japan's investment was mostly into Asian countries in the 1960s and 1970s, while North America, especially the United States, became a favorable investment destination in the 1980s. However, this may still be considered "trade-oriented" in the sense that FDI complements trade by providing distribution networks and by jumping the export ceiling set by "voluntary" export restraints with assembly plants in the customer's country.

In the following, exports are taken to be a candidate for a principal determinant of FDI from Japan. When aggregate FDI is to be explained, aggregate (gross) exports are used; when FDI by region (or by industry) is to be explained, exports by region (or by industry, respectively) are used.

Whether FDI is a substitute for or complement to trade is a debatable point. If investment is "trade-oriented," as Kojima hypothesized for a developmental economy, more trade leads to investment, and gradually sends some comparative disadvantaged industries to other lesser developed countries as a country grows to the next stage. If investment in assembly lines in the destination market replaces exports by jumping over trade protection (such as those among Japanese automobile manufacturers in the United States), then trade and investment may be substitutes, that is, they are negatively correlated.

In a modern theory, investment as a "beachhead" is thought to be necessary to advance exports beyond some threshold level. Building distributors' networks or assembly lines close to customers is sometimes found to be a key to exporting more. In this line of thinking, as emphasized by Embarkation (1992) and Graham (1993), trade and investment are complements, that is, an increase in one is necessary for an increase in the other.[4]

Both trade and investment are driven by other, more fundamental (or exogenous in the econometric sense) factors, such as factor endowments and comparative advantage. Ideally, one can build a model explaining both trade and investment from variables that are exogenous to the system. One such attempt is to apply "gravity" equations, which are popular in the recent trade literature, to foreign direct investment, as done in Eaton and Tamura (1994).[5] They examined the residuals from trade and investment gravity equations. With regard to Japanese exports and investment, they found that "a one-standard-deviation positive shock to outward DFI is associated with a 0.45 standard deviation increase in exports" in an equation with regional dummy variables.

The second strand of this paper is the hypothesis that FDI is determined by cash flows and a "slack" in corporate financing. When firms seek diversification of production facilities and a distribution network, timing for FDI may be chosen on the basis of affordability, namely, firms wait until they have the luxury to do so or they become relatively "wealthy." The role of exchange rates in FDI has been emphasized by Froot and Stein (1991) and Mann (1993) as one of the variables that would affect the relative wealth of corporations. The discrepancy of internal and external financing may be a key cause of FDI. Some proxy variable for the relative wealth (or surplus funds) of Japanese firms should be adopted. One candidate would be stock prices in Tokyo.

FDI from Japan

In the second half of the 1980s, Japanese firms enjoyed relatively cheap funds, raised through new equity issues and convertible bond issues, taking advantage of high and apparently ever-increasing stock prices. Internal funds became so cheap that a large corporation could make money just issuing convertible bonds and then depositing the funds in bank deposits. After the doubling of the value of the yen vis-a-vis the U.S. dollar, assets abroad must have looked inexpensive for Japanese corporations in search of new business horizons. These considerations could be captured by the total value of corporations or cash flows, in the market values of their equities or assets.

In this paper, I use the yen/dollar exchange rate and the stock price (Nikkei 225) index as proxy variables for the cost of capital. Japanese firms are known for their cross-holding of stocks, and changes in stock prices directly affect the balance sheets (or mark-to-market asset values) of many corporations. This in turn affects their ability to raise funds in the capital market. Therefore, the stock price index is a good proxy for testing a hypothesis of internal liquidity as an FDI determinant.[6]

From the host country's view, especially in the United States, these effects—rising stock prices in Tokyo and the appreciation of the yen—are sometimes known as a "fire sale." (See, for example, Graham and Krugman [1991, pp. 80–82].)

Japanese investment into the United States has been the subject of many works, partly because the United States has been a principal destination of Japanese foreign investment in the 1980s, and partly because Japanese capital inflow into the United States caused political repercussions. Kogut and Chang (1991), Drake and Caves (1992), Mann (1993), and Encarnation (1992, Ch. 3) investigated Japanese investment in the United States. All of them emphasized how technological capabilities supported by the research and development of the Japanese firms explained their investment in the United States. In this paper, the United States is identified as one region in the model.

Total outward FDI from Japan as well as major macro and financial variables from 1972 to 1992 are shown in Table 9. According to the table, FDI from Japan had sharply increased during the 1980s, but recorded a decline after 1990. Casual observation shows that the fluctuation of FDI seems to be correlated with stock prices and yen appreciation.

Table 10 (upper panel) disaggregates Japan's outward FDI by region. Investment in the United States, Asian neighbors, and Europe are favored by Japanese investors. These regions are also favorite destinations of Japanese exports, as shown in the same table (lower panel). FDI to the United States accounts for about 40 percent of Japan's FDI.

The pattern of sharp increase in the 1980s and a decline from 1990 to 1992 is common for all destinations, while it is most pronounced for investment into the United States. Japan's FDI into the United States increased six-fold from 1985 to 1989, and then decreased to a level one-third of the peak in three years. While the multiple in the sharp increase was about the same, the decline

TABLE 9

Trade and FDI, Aggregate Time Series

Fiscal Year	FDI Out Report $ mil.	Export Custom $ bil.	Nikkei 225 yen	Nominal GNP tril. yen	Exch Rt Average yen/$
1972	2,338	30.0	4,304	96.5	297.06
1973	3,494	39.7	4,591	116.7	273.88
1974	2,395	58.4	4,177	138.2	292.70
1975	3,280	57.0	4,373	152.2	299.06
1976	3,462	70.6	4,760	171.2	292.35
1977	2,806	84.6	5,061	190.0	256.53
1978	4,598	99.0	5,776	208.8	201.40
1979	4,996	107.0	6,421	225.4	229.66
1980	4,693	138.1	6,999	245.4	217.25
1981	8,931	151.9	7,599	260.3	228.34
1982	7,703	136.6	7,531	273.5	249.68
1983	8,145	152.7	9,323	286.0	236.41
1984	10,155	169.6	11,061	305.7	243.93
1985	12,217	182.6	12,935	325.4	221.68
1986	22,320	215.1	18,032	339.7	159.88
1987	33,364	238.0	24,195	356.3	138.45
1988	47,022	272.9	28,865	379.2	128.27
1989	67,540	273.7	34,968	405.8	142.82
1990	56,911	296.6	26,872	435.3	141.52
1991	41,584	320.6	23,350	458.6	133.31
1992	34,137	344.1	17,189	470.7	124.73

NOTE: Accumulated FDI for 1951–71 is $4,434 million, and accumulated FDI from 1951 to 1992 is $386,529 million.

Definition and Source: Export and import in fiscal year, customs reporting basis: Ministry of Finance. FDI, in fiscal year: Ministry of Finance. Nominal GNP, fiscal year: Economic Planning Agency. Yen/$ exchange rate, daily average for fiscal year: Tōyō Keizai Shinpō. Stock price, Nikkei 225, daily average of fiscal year: Tōyō Keizai Shinpō.

in the 1990s was less for investments toward Asia (one-third off) and toward Europe (one-half off).

Table 11 (upper panel) presents a breakdown of investments in different manufacturing sectors. The difference between "total manufacturing sectors" and "total FDI" is the outward investment in non-manufacturing sectors, such as commerce, banking, and real estate. In fact, 70 to 80 percent of FDI is in non-manufacturing sectors. Among FDI in manufacturing sectors, chemicals (including pharmaceuticals), general machinery, and electronics lead other

TABLE 10
Japanese FDI and Export, by Region

Japan's Foreign Direct Investment by region, unit = $ million

Year	US	Can-ada	C&S America	Asia	Middle East	Europe	Africa	Ocea-nia	Total
1981	2,400	122	1,181	3,338	96	798	573	350	8,931
1982	2,737	167	1,503	1,384	124	876	489	370	7,703
1983	2,565	136	1,878	1,847	175	990	364	166	8,145
1984	3,360	184	2,290	1,628	273	1,937	326	105	10,155
1985	5,395	100	2,616	1,435	45	1,930	172	468	12,217
1986	10,165	276	4,737	2,327	44	3,469	309	881	22,320
1987	14,704	653	4,816	4,868	62	6,576	272	1,222	33,364
1988	21,701	626	6,428	5,569	259	9,116	653	2,413	47,022
1989	32,540	1,362	5,238	8,238	66	14,808	671	4,256	67,540
1990	26,128	1,064	3,628	7,054	27	14,294	551	3,669	56,911
1991	18,026	797	3,337	5,936	90	9,371	748	2,550	41,584
1992	13,819	753	2,726	6,425	709	7,061	238	2,406	34,138

Japan's Exports by region, unit = $ billion

Year	US	Can-ada	C&S America	Asia	Middle East	Europe	Africa	Ocea-nia	Total
1981	38.6	3.4	10.5	34.4	17.7	22.4	5.8	4.8	152.0
1982	36.3	2.9	9.1	31.9	16.9	20.3	4.2	4.6	138.8
1983	42.8	4.6	6.4	34.5	17.1	21.6	2.9	4.3	146.9
1984	59.9	4.3	8.5	36.8	14.2	22.6	3.0	5.2	170.1
1985	65.3	4.5	8.5	33.2	12.2	25.2	2.5	5.4	102.5
1986	80.5	5.5	9.5	41.8	9.8	37.5	2.2	5.2	131.1
1987	83.6	5.6	8.7	53.0	9.2	45.6	2.9	5.1	142.9
1988	89.6	6.4	9.3	67.1	9.4	56.0	2.8	6.7	161.8
1989	93.2	6.8	9.4	73.5	8.6	56.5	2.9	7.8	167.4
1990	90.3	6.7	10.3	82.7	9.9	63.3	3.4	6.9	170.0
1991	91.5	7.3	12.8	96.2	12.3	68.9	3.6	6.5	176.9
1992	95.8	7.1	15.8	104.3	15.2	72.0	4.2	7.0	184.8

NOTE: C&S America=Central and South America, including Mexico. Asia=Asian countries, including China. Europe=EC, EFTA countries, and former Soviet Union.

TABLE 11
Japanese FDI and Exports by Industry ($ million)

FDI by Manufacturing Industry

Year	Food	Tex-tile	Lum-ber	Chem-ical	Steel	Ma-chine	Electro	Auto	Other Manuf	Manuf Total	FDI Total
1981	142	91	65	228	521	207	475	406	169	2,305	8,931
1982	78	67	76	322	468	164	267	439	195	2,076	7,703
1983	77	174	91	450	479	169	502	486	160	2,588	8,145
1984	118	85	115	223	718	185	409	437	215	2,505	10,155
1985	90	28	15	133	385	352	513	627	208	2,352	12,217
1986	127	63	57	355	328	626	987	828	435	3,806	22,320
1987	328	206	317	910	786	687	2,421	1,473	703	7,832	33,364
1988	419	317	604	1,292	1,367	1,432	3,041	1,281	4,051	13,805	47,022
1989	1,300	533	555	2,109	1,597	1,762	4,480	2,053	1,901	16,284	67,540
1990	821	796	314	2,292	1,047	1,454	5,682	1,872	1,207	15,486	56,911
1991	632	616	31	1,602	907	1,284	2,296	1,996	2,666	12,311	41,584
1992	517	428	431	2,015	824	1,014	1,817	1,188	1,732	10,057	34,138

Exports by Industry

Year	Food	Textile	Chem-ical	Steel	Ma-chine	Electro	Auto	Optics	Other	Total
1981	1,739	7,174	6,841	24,578	18,927	31,210	42,498	7,527	11,536	152,030
1982	1,401	6,240	6,365	23,160	17,702	27,599	38,931	6,283	11,152	138,831
1983	1,389	6,613	6,983	20,522	23,103	30,325	39,143	6,989	11,860	146,927
1984	1,440	6,753	7,626	21,437	27,879	38,467	45,556	7,903	13,049	170,114
1985	1,316	6,263	7,698	20,638	29,537	38,931	49,149	8,561	13,544	175,638
1986	1,476	6,874	9,484	20,545	38,381	46,747	59,426	10,473	15,745	209,151
1987	1,546	6,917	11,662	20,541	44,755	50,968	63,925	11,429	17,480	229,221
1988	1,696	6,908	13,964	24,687	56,048	61,975	65,741	13,200	20,697	264,917
1989	1,687	6,862	14,776	24,630	61,085	64,454	66,596	13,337	21,748	275,175
1990	1,646	7,195	15,872	22,766	63,512	65,925	71,814	13,846	24,370	286,948
1991	1,822	7,943	17,475	24,626	69,508	73,724	77,916	15,493	26,020	314,525
1992	1,929	8,590	19,118	25,219	76,270	77,410	87,140	16,008	27,966	339,650

Industry groups, common for both FDI and Exports: "Food": Food processing. "Textile": Textile. "Lumber": Lumber and pulp. "Chemical": Chemical. "Steel": Steel and nonferrous metals. "Machine": General machines. "Electro": Electronics. "Auto": Transportation equipment including automobiles.

For exports, "Optics" means optics and precision industry.

NOTE: Foreign Direct Investment includes investments in non-manufacturing sectors, such as agriculture, forestry, mining, construction, commerce, banking, insurance, and real estate. The non-manufacturing FDI can be derived as the difference between the last two columns of the FDI panel. These numbers are not shown.

categories. Table 3 (lower panel) shows the corresponding export data in manufacturing sectors. They match in most classifications.

Outward FDI is defined as investment that acquires more than 10 percent of stocks issued by a foreign company by sending funds from Japan (including setting up a 100 percent subsidiary, purchasing an existing company, and loans to foreign companies in order to pursue business relationships).

Before December 1980, FDI needed "approval" (*kyoka*). After revision of the foreign trade and investment law in December 1980, most FDI was on a "reporting" (*todokede*) basis. The finance minister still has the authority to "recommend" (*kankoku*) a change in or abandonment of a "reported" plan, if the investment plan is judged to be harmful to the function of the international capital market or contradictory to the objective of the foreign trade and investment law. Investments may have to wait 20 days after reporting, although, in practice, the Ministry of Finance allows investment on the day of reporting except for "restricted areas" (Ministry of Finance 1993). Restricted areas as of 1993 include outward (1) FDI on "fishery, pearl farming, leather and leather products manufacturing, textile manufacturing, weapon manufacturing, illegal drug manufacturing, banking, and securities business"; (2) FDI for businesses in Iraq, Serbia, and Montenegro; and (3) FDI conducted by banks and securities firms.

Cautions on Data

Foreign direct investment data in Japan are subject to the following problems. (1) Japan's FDI data do not include reinvestment of retained profits of past FDI or FDI financed abroad. (2) FDI statistics are on the basis of reported plans. Actual investments may not proceed as planned; simple omissions may be possible (no penalty). (3) Regional statistics may suffer from indirect investment through third countries, especially through tax haven countries, such as the Bahamas and Cayman Islands, or through Hong Kong to the People's Republic of China. And (4) lending from a parent company in Japan to a subsidiary abroad is counted as a part of FDI if lending is for more than a year, but is not counted if less than a year.

Also, export data by region or by industry are subject to some problems. (1) Regional statistics may suffer from indirect trade through third countries, similar to the problem of FDI data. It is also hard to detect discrepancies among countries where goods are actually made, shipped from, and previously owned. (For example, suppose a Japanese citizen bought a century-old French impressionist painting [or a bottle of 50-year-old wine] owned by an American but auctioned in London. Is it an import from France, the United Kingdom, or the United States?) (2) Trade statistics by industry may suffer from inconsistent classification with FDI data or similar data of other countries. For example, the precision products in export statistics do not have a corresponding category in FDI data.

Regressions

Many theories and empirical works have been presented to explain FDI as surveyed above. The usual explanatory variables include exports, imports, and the exchange rate. These variables are chosen in an attempt to explain aggregate outward foreign direct investment from Japan. The following regression was estimated with annual data from 1972 to 1992.

$$\log(\text{FDI}(t)) = a + b1^*\log(\text{StockPrice}(t)) + b2^*\log(\text{Exports}(t))$$
$$+ b3^*\log(\text{GNP}(t)) + b4^*\log\left(\frac{¥}{\$(t)}\right) + e(t)$$

Results are shown in Table 12. We find that Stock Price (Nikkei 225 index) has a significant, positive coefficient. Stock Price here is a proxy for the asset values of corporations, since Japanese corporations hold other corporations' stocks as an asset. This is consistent with the view that Japan's FDI has been mostly motivated by the availability of low-cost funds (such as convertible bonds relying on expectations of increasing stock prices and borrowing with collateral of land and stocks held by corporations).

According to the estimates, (1) a 10 percent rise in stock prices results in a 12–15 percent rise in outward FDI. (2) Exports have an insignificant coefficient. The sign of the coefficient varies depending on the choice of other right-hand-side variables. (3) There is weak evidence that yen appreciation stimulates FDI. This is consistent with the view of FDI as a "fire sale" (from the host country's view), but contradicts Graham and Krugman (1991) on the U.S. case.

A caution on interpreting the results: about three-quarters of FDI is in non-manufacturing sectors, while exports are almost exclusively in manufactured goods. However, FDI by Japan's manufacturing companies is often in the distribution sector (dealerships) in the United States.

FDI disaggregated by destination region was regressed on exports by desti-nation region, with pooled cross-section, time series regressions.

$$\log(\text{FDI}(k,t)) = a + b^*\log(\text{Exports}(k,t)) + c1^*\log(\text{StockPrice}(t))$$
$$+ c2^*\log(\text{GNP}(t)) + c3^*\log\left(\frac{¥}{\$(t)}\right) + e(k,t)$$

where t=1981–92, and k=the United States, Canada, Central and South Amer-

TABLE 12

Determinants of Japan's FDI

Spec #	Constant	Log(stock price)	Log (exports)	Log (GNP)	Log(yen/ $ rate)	R bar sq.	Durbin-Watson
(1)	−5.067	1.551	—	—	—	0.974	1.517
	(−9.73)*	(27.49)*					
(2)	−5.637	1.419	0.155	—	—	0.975	1.627
	(−7.88)*	(10.83)*	(1.154)				
(3)	−8.652	1.407	—	0.253	—	0.975	1.603
	(−3.02)*	(11.15)*		(1.273)			
(4)	−14.375	1.422	−0.334	0.746	—	0.974	1.558
	(−1.12)	(10.69)*	(−0.460)	(0.685)			
(5)	−1.275	1.275	0.104	—	−0.465	0.976	1.752
	(−0.39)	(7.764)*	(0.764)		(−1.354)		
(6)	−17.122	1.233	−0.901	1.503	−0.652	0.977	1.681
	(−1.41)	(7.549)*	(−1.198)	(1.357)	(−1.799)†		

* significant at 1%.
† significant at 10%.
NOTE: All variables are defined in fiscal year (April to March of the next calendar year).
Left-hand-side (dependent) Variable: Log(Foreign Direct Investment)
Sample period: 1972 to 1992
Coefficients and (t-statistics, in parentheses).

ica, Asia, the Middle East, Europe, Africa, and Oceania. Results are shown in Table 13.

We observe the following. (1) Regions where Japan exports more receive Japanese FDI as well. A one percent increase in exports results in about a one percent increase in FDI. (2) Regional differences in FDI can be explained by export differences, while time series differences seem to be explained by stock prices in Tokyo. (3) There is no evidence that GNP or the yen/dollar exchange rate matters for outward FDI from Japan. And (4) there is only weak evidence that FDI to the United States is distinctively higher than to other regions, after controlling for exports and stock prices.

Lastly, FDI disaggregated by industry was regressed on exports by industry, with pooled cross-section, time series regressions.

$$\log(FDI(h,t)) = a + b^*\log(Exports(h,t)) + c1^*\log(StockPrice(t))$$
$$+ c2^*\log(GNP(t)) + c3^*\log\left(\frac{¥}{\$(t)}\right) + e(h,t)$$

where t=1981–92, and h=industries shown in Table 11. The results, shown in

TABLE 13

FDI by Region

Spec No.	Constant	Log (stock price(t))	Log (export (k,t))	Log (GNP(t))	Log (yen/$(t))	US Dummy	Asia Dummy	R bar sq.
(1)	−10.713	0.881	0.963	—				0.546
	(−4.73)*	(3.96)*	(9.493)*					
(2)	−41.932	—	0.956	2.025				0.527
	(−3.56)*		(9.166)*	(3.352)†				
(3)	6.164	—	0.953	—	−1.598			0.540
	(2.43)†		(9.29)*		(−3.77)*			
(4)	−15.700	0.788	0.960	0.301				0.542
	(−0.89)	(2.01)†	(9.36)*	(0.28)				
(5)	−5.333	0.624	0.957	—	−0.550			0.543
	(−0.57)	(1.29)	(9.36)*		(−0.60)			
(6)	−2.247	0.632	0.958	−0.141	−0.627			0.538
	(−0.07)	(1.29)	(9.30)*	(−0.11)	(−0.53)			
(7)	−2.600	0.609	0.841	−0.046	−0.676	0.799	−0.033	0.549
	(−0.09)	(1.25)	(5.49)*	(−0.04)	(−0.58)	(1.74)‡	(−0.07)	

* significant at 1%.
† significant at 5%.
‡ significant at 10%.
NOTE: All variables are defined in fiscal year (April to March of the next calendar year).
Left-hand-side (dependent) Variable: Log(Foreign Direct Investment(k, t))
Sample period: t=1981 to 1992
Sample region: k=US, Canada, Central and South America, Asia, Middle East, Europe, Africa, Oceania.
Coefficients and (t-statistics, in parentheses).

Table 14, strongly suggest that FDI occurs in industries that have been successful in exports. There is also some evidence again that an increase in stock prices will increase FDI, while yen appreciation will also increase FDI. Economic growth (measured by the level of GNP) will also positively influence FDI. These macro effects are robust whether trade and FDI are decomposed by trading partner or by industry.

Evidence from Tables 13 and 14 suggests that FDI from Japan is closely tied to exports, when they are disaggregated by industry or by region.

SUMMARY

In this paper I considered the impact of foreign capital inflows into the United States from abroad and Japanese FDI to the rest of the world. For the

TABLE 14

FDI by Industry

Spec Number	Constant	Log (stock price(t))	Log (export (j,t))	Log (GNP(t))	Log (yen/$(t))	R bar sq.
(1)	−10.597	1.283	0.457	—		0.70
	(−8.88)*	(10.64)*	(8.63)*			
(2)	−62.542	—	0.443	3.279		0.67
	(−9.69)		(7.96)*	(9.77)*		
(3)	14.474	—	0.443	—	−2.426	0.70
	(10.46)*		(8.31)*		(−10.59)*	
(4)	−34.98	0.830	0.441	1.470	—	0.72
	(−3.87)*	(4.09)*	(8.56)*	(2.72)*		
(5)	1.802	0.691	0.443	—	−1.268	0.72
	(0.38)	(2.76)*	(8.61)*		(−2.67)*	
(6)	−18.63	0.641	0.439	0.933	−0.761	0.72
	(−1.18)	(2.54)†	(8.54)*	(1.36)	(−1.26)	

* significant at 1%.
† significant at 5%.
NOTE: All variables are defined in fiscal year (April to March of the next calendar year).
Left-hand-side (dependent) Variable: Log(Foreign Direct Investment(j, t))
Sample period: t=1981 to 1992
Sample region: h=food, textile, chemical, steel and non-ferrous metals, general machines, electronics, automobiles and transport equipment.
Coefficients and (t-statistics, in parentheses).

United States, it was estimated that long-term interest rates would have been higher by 150 to 200 basis points from the mid-1980s to the beginning of the 1990s. It is shown that FDI has been tightly linked to Japanese export behavior. As the United States is the number one destination of Japanese goods, the United States is also the most favored nation for FDI. Recently, however, investment in Asia has increased. These are shown to be closely correlated with trade.

NOTES

Part of this paper was presented at the American Economic Association meeting in Boston, January 1994. Various versions of this paper were discussed in the research group led by Yukio Noguchi and Kozo Yamamura. I thank Professors Koichi Hamada, Yukio Noguchi, Kozo Yamamura, and other participants of this volume for their useful comments. Research for this project was carried out at Harvard University, where I was visiting professor for the 1992–94 academic years. Any opinions expressed or implied in the paper are my own.

1. See Ueda (1988) for earlier years in the 1980s.

2. Gold investment accounts offered by securities firms were popular in 1989 and 1990. Spot and futures transactions on gold and exchange rates (in London) would earn market interest rates for customers above the rates offered by domestic banks for deposits. Spot gold purchase was recorded as capital inflow. The attraction of gold investment accounts faded in 1991 as further deregulations on bank deposits proceeded. Then net decline on accounts was recorded as capital outflow. See Ito (1994) for some details of capital movement idiosyncracies in 1991 and 1992.

3. Kojima writes that the "major part of investment was directed towards natural resource development in which the Japanese economy is comparatively disadvantaged. Even investment in manufacturing has been confined either to such traditional industries as textiles, clothing and processing of steel in which Japan has been losing its comparative advantage, or the assembly of motor vehicles, production of parts and components of radios and other electronic machines in which cheaper labour costs in south-east Asian countries are achieved and the Japanese firms can increase exports" (1978, p. 86) in the 1970s.

It is also noted that foreign investment was restricted before December 1980, so that the government had an influence on what kind of investment would take place, while after 1981, there is no restriction.

4. In the following, I will regress FDI on exports, while Graham (1993) regressed exports on FDI. It is difficult to argue that one way is better than the other for understanding the relationship between trade and investment. Since both exports and FDI are endogenous in a larger system, one way may suffer from a simultaneous equation bias as much as the other.

5. For a trade gravity equation, see Frankel and Wei (1994).

6. See the following statement by Graham and Krugman (1993, pp. 33–34) on Froot and Stein's (1991) argument: "if external sources of finance are more expensive to corporations than are internal sources, negative shocks to relative domestic wealth can raise the cost of capital to domestic bidders for corporate control. . . . Increases in internal liquidity (due, for example, to past profits) or increases in stock market value can also raise relative corporate financial slack and thereby lessen a corporation's reliance on expensive external financing. Unfortunately, there is relatively little systematic testing of this hypothesis outside of that using the exchange rate."

REFERENCES

Caves, Richard E. 1993. Japanese investment in the United States: lessons for the economic analysis of foreign investment. Discussion paper no. 1652, Harvard Institute of Economic Research, Harvard University, September.

Drake, Tracey A. and Caves, Richard E. 1992. Changing determinants of Japanese foreign investment in the United States. *Journal of the Japanese and international economies* 6:228–46.

Eaton, Jonathan and Tamura Akiko. 1994. Bilateralism and regionalism in trade and investment: the U.S. and Japan. *Journal of the Japanese and international economies* 8.

Encarnation, Dennis J. 1992. *Rivals beyond trade: America versus Japan in global competition.* Ithaca: Cornell University Press.

Frankel, Jeffrey A. and Wei Shang-Jin. 1994. Trade blocs and currency blocs. In *Macroeconomic linkage: savings, exchange rates, and capital flows,* ed. Takatoshi Ito and Anne O. Krueger. Chicago: University of Chicago Press. (Earlier version: working paper no. 4335, National Bureau of Economic Research, Cambridge, Mass.)

Froot, Kenneth A. and Stein, Jeremy C. 1991. Exchange rates and foreign direct investment: an imperfect capital markets approach. *Quarterly journal of economics* 196: 1191–1217.

Graham, Edward M. 1993. US outward direct investment and US exports: substitutes or complements—with implications for US-Japan policy. Paper presented at a conference on foreign direct investment, Yale University.

Graham, Edward M. and Krugman, Paul R. 1991. *Foreign direct investment in the United States.* 2d ed. Washington: Institute for International Economics.

———. 1993. The surge in foreign direct investment in the 1980s. In *Foreign direct investment,* ed. Kenneth Froot, pp. 13–36. Chicago: University of Chicago Press.

Ito Takatoshi. 1994. On recent movements of Japanese current accounts and capital flows. In *Macroeconomic linkage: savings, exchange rates, and capital flows,* ed. Takatoshi Ito and Anne O. Krueger, pp. 31–48. Chicago: University of Chicago Press.

Kogut, B. and Chang, S.J. 1991. Technological capabilities and Japanese foreign direct investment in the United States. *Review of economics and statistics* 75: 401–13.

Kojima Kiyoshi. 1978. *Direct foreign investment.* London: Croom Helm.

Lizondo, J. Saul. 1991. Foreign direct investment. In *Readings in international business,* ed. Robert Z. Aliber and Reid W. Click, pp. 85–113. Cambridge, Mass.: MIT Press. (Reprinted from International Monetary Fund. 1991. *Determinants and Systemic Consequences of International Capital Flows,* pp. 68–82.)

Mann, Catherine L. 1993. Determinants of Japanese direct investment in US manufacturing industries. *Journal of international money and finance* 12: 523–41.

Ministry of Finance. 1993. *Annual report of the International Finance Bureau.* Tokyo: Ministry of Finance.

Ueda Kazuo. 1988. Perspectives on the Japanese current account surplus. *NBER Macroeconomic Annual* 3.

Tax Systems and International Capital Flow

Between the United States and Japan

KAZUMASA IWATA

IN THE 1980s major countries, including the United States and Japan, embarked on tax reform aimed at improving the supply side of the economy through a reduction of marginal tax rates on labor and capital income and a broadened tax base. The reduction of the marginal tax rate on capital income in an open economy may affect the domestic investment decision more significantly than in a closed economy; domestic crowding out can be avoided due to an international capital flow in response to the tax incentive for domestic investment, notably under circumstances of both domestic and international financial liberalization. The first tax reform in the United States under the Reagan administration invited a large capital inflow and concomitant sharp appreciation of the dollar. The tax competition to lower the marginal tax rates in an attempt to attract foreign capital became fashionable in the early 1980s.

In the 1990s, notably under the Clinton administration, the focus has shifted to the competition among tax authorities to secure a larger share of tax revenue from multinational companies. For instance, the U.S. tax authority estimated that tax revenue from foreign firms would increase by $4.8 billion over four years, and the estimate of the Congress was $890 million on May 4, 1993; Japanese firms were believed to be the most serious violators of U.S. transfer pricing rules. Yet the recent proposal for stricter taxation of transfer pricing and "thin capitalization" by the United States may not only intensify the tax friction between the United States and other countries, notably Japan, but also risk discouraging foreign direct investment from abroad.

Both transfer pricing and thin capitalization are devices to shift profits within a multinational firm in an attempt to minimize costs. The optimization by firms is constrained by the tax system, regulations, and trade policy. Yet strict implementation of the residence principle to avoid international double taxation renders profit-shifting unprofitable in the absence of trade barriers, regulations, and market imperfections. This is because the same effective tax rate is imposed on all investment by multinational firms, regardless of production location. Both the United States and Japan adopt the residence principle to avoid double taxation of foreign-source income. However, the actual taxation of foreign-source income at the corporate level is closer to the source principle; thus, multinational companies are induced to engage in income-shifting across different tax jurisdictions.

This paper attempts to evaluate the effects of major tax reform in the two countries on international capital movements in the 1980s. It is assumed that capital income earned abroad at the corporate level is taxed based on the source principle, while household capital income is subject to the residence principle. Under this system, multinational firms have an incentive to register profits in a low-tax country. This poses the problem of how to reconcile private incentive with the need for tax collection from globalized firms. I emphasize the need to remove the tax-induced income-shifting in solving the problems of transfer pricing and thin capitalization between the United States and Japan.

The following sections of this paper evaluate the effect of tax reform in the 1980s on international capital movements between the United States and Japan, discuss the problem of transfer pricing and thin capitalization, and summarize the main results and provide a proposal to improve the international taxation system from the standpoint of maintaining nondistortionary international capital movement.

TAX REFORM AND INTERNATIONAL CAPITAL FLOW
BETWEEN THE UNITED STATES AND JAPAN

Tax Reform in the 1980s

Two major tax reforms were implemented in the United States under the Reagan administration in the 1980s. The first, based on the Economic Recovery Act of 1981, reduced marginal tax rates on capital and labor income significantly and provided investment incentives through generous investment credit and a rapid write-off rate of depreciation charges. It aimed at revitalizing the U.S. economy. The investment incentive measures were slightly amended in the Tax Equity and Fiscal Responsibility Act of 1982. Subsequently, the second reform based on the Tax Reform Act of 1986 shifted emphasis from investment incentives to a nondistortionary tax system; it was designed to level the playing field, thereby abolishing investment-promoting measures such as the accelerated depreciation scheme and the investment tax credit.

In Japan, tax reform was implemented under the Nakasone and Takeshita administrations in 1987–88. The reform introduced a consumption tax at the rate of three percent and abolished saving-promotion measures such as the *maruyu* system, while reducing the marginal tax rates on capital and labor income. The capital income tax system came closer to the flat-rate system at the rate of 20 percent.

Table 1 summarizes the differences in tax parameters before and after the 1986 U.S. tax reform and the 1987–88 reforms in Japan. It shows the effective corporate tax to be significantly higher in Japan than the United States both before and after reform. Moreover, the legal depreciation rate on machinery is more generous in the United States, although a lower rate is applied to buildings after 1986. On the other hand, the marginal tax rates on capital income at the personal level are much higher in the United States.

Calculation of Capital Cost

Based on tax and other parameters bearing on the method of financing and the distribution of assets held by the personal sector, we can calculate the combined marginal rates on investment at the corporate and personal levels under the assumption of a constant real interest rate (fixed-r assumption) or constant real before-tax rate of return on investment (fixed-P assumption).

If we denote P and s as the real before-tax rate of return on investment net of economic depreciation rate (net capital cost) and the real after-tax rate of return on assets held by household, respectively, the total tax wedge can be defined as (P-s)/P. In this calculation assets are divided into machinery, buildings, and other, while investment is assumed to be financed by debt, retained earnings, and new share issues. Different discount rates on a firm's cash flow are attached to each financing method, due to the different tax treatment of debt, dividends, and capital gains and the arbitrage activity on the capital market at the personal level. The capital cost of a new share issue is the highest due to the heavier tax burden on dividend income, as compared with capital gain (=financing by retained earnings). Debt financing is the cheapest way to finance investment because of the deduction of interest payments from the tax base at the corporate level.

The personal sector is divided into individuals, tax-exempt institutions, and insurance companies, while industry is assumed to consist of manufacturing, commerce, and other. The 81 costs of capital are calculated and integrated into one marginal tax wedge as a weighted average. The cost of capital (P) net of economic depreciation rate is calculated, using the King-Fullerton (1984) formulation, as below:[1]

TABLE 1

Tax Parameters in the United States and Japan

	United States (1986)		Japan (1987)	
	Before Reform	After Reform	Before Reform	After Reform
Corporate Sector				
Effective corporate tax rate	0.495	0.383	0.568	0.528
Legal depreciation rate				
Machinery	0.3	0.4	0.241	0.241
Buildings	0.097	0.032	0.071	0.071
Investment grant rate				
Machinery	0.1	0	0.0088	0.0088
Buildings	0	0	0	0
Personal Sector				
Marginal tax rate				
Interest income	0.304	0.268	0.099	0.20
Dividends	0.406	0.350	0.285	0.285
Capital gain	0.052	0.134	0	0.20*

* The capital gains tax is the 20 percent withholding tax on putative 5 percent gain (similar to transaction tax). One can choose separate income tax of 20 percent plus 6 percent local tax.

$$(1-A) = \int_0^\infty (1-u)\,(P+\delta-t_p)e^{-(\rho+\delta-\pi)^t}dt$$

A:present value of tax saving

u:the effective corporate tax rate

t_p:the property tax rate

e:the required rate of return by investor

δ:the economic depreciation rate

π:the inflation rate of investment goods

Table 2 shows the calculated results of the total tax wedge by industry in the two countries, based on the fixed-P assumption; after the first reform the U.S. marginal tax rate of investment was significantly lower than that of Japan.[2] The second reform under the Reagan administration brought about the convergence of marginal tax rates in the two countries. Yet the Japanese marginal tax rate is still higher than the U.S. marginal rate, primarily reflecting its higher corporate tax rate. Several U.S. economists argue that lower capital costs due to the light tax burden on business investment reinforced the competitiveness of Japanese firms, but the calculated results do not confirm this hypothesis. Moreover, U.S.

TABLE 2

Total Tax Wedge under the Assumption of Constant Real Before-Tax Rate
of Return in the United States and Japan
[fixed-P(10%) case] (%)

	United States		Japan	
	Before Reform	After Reform	Before Reform	After Reform
Total tax wedge	26.1	31.8	42.8	46.9
Manufacturing	34.3	37.5	45.4	49.0
Others	13.7	18.9	40.9	45.6
Commerce	27.0	20.0	40.3	44.8

firms could have enjoyed an inflow of cheap capital from Japan in the presence
of international capital movements as discussed below. We should remember,
however, that mutual shareholding among related firms is abstracted in the
net-base calculation of capital cost; cross-shareholding tends to lower the cost
of a new share issue due to the low marginal tax on dividends received by firms
(often zero). Further, an equity price rise in the latter half of the 1980s significantly lowered the capital costs of equity financing by Japanese firms.

International Capital Movement
in the Absence of a Tax System

In the absence of a tax system and under the assumption of identical production functions, capital moves from a saving-abundant country to a saving-
shortage country. Hamada-Iwata (1989) made a simulation exercise under the
assumption of different saving ratios, labor growth rates, and technological
progress rates between the United States, Japan, and Germany. In a steady state
where population growth and technological progress rates are the same, the
different saving ratios determine the equilibrium distribution of debt and capital stock in the world economy.

If there were no international trade or factor movement, the equilibrium
real interest rates in the two countries would diverge, with the U.S. rate being
higher than the Japanese rate. If capital movement across the border is allowed,
capital moves from Japan to the United States; the size of the movement can
be measured by the distance AB in Figure 1A where investment demand and
saving in two countries are depicted as a function of the real rate of return on
capital. In the Hamada-Iwata simulation, Japan will provide 10–36 percent of
total U.S. capital stock by the year 2030 with the capital inflow amounting to

Case A: no tax system

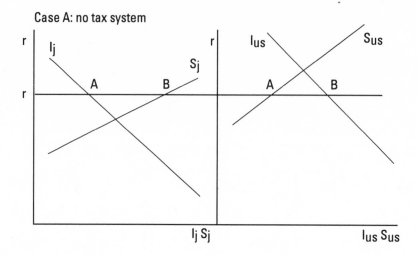

Case B: r*=r_us=r_j

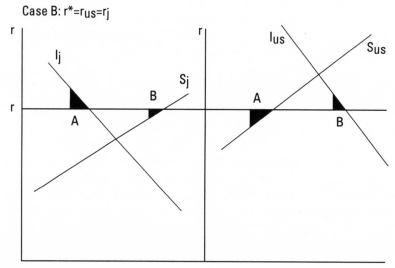

FIG. 1. Tax and international capital movements

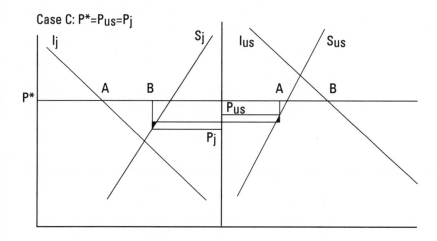

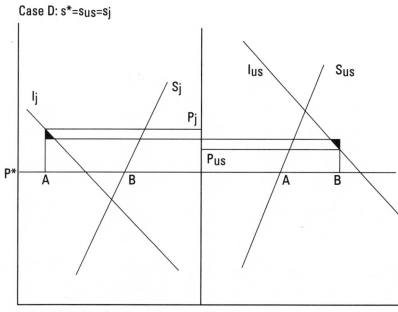

FIG. 1. (*continued*)

about 0.2–0.8 percent of U.S. capital stock annually; in terms of Japan's nominal GNP it is equivalent to a current account surplus of 0.7–3.0 percent. So it is not surprising, even if Japan registers a current account surplus amounting to two percent of nominal GNP vis-a-vis the United States, given the sizable difference in net national saving ratios.

Tax System on Capital Income and
International Capital Movement

In the presence of a tax system on capital income, we can distinguish three cases for assessing the effect of change in capital income tax on international capital movement. Thereby we assume that the tax on labor income does not affect investment and saving decisions.

In the first case, the real market interest rate (r) is assumed to be the same in the two countries. The development of offshore markets enables the economic agents in each country to borrow and lend at the same market interest rate. Under the condition that the exchange rate adjusts for differences in inflation rates, the residents of each country face the same real interest rate.

In the second case, the real before-tax rate of return (P) is assumed to be equalized in the two countries: it corresponds to the fixed-P assumption in the King-Fullerton framework on cost of capital, while the first is equivalent to the fixed-r assumption.[3]

In the third case, the real after-tax rate of return(s) is assumed to be equalized. This case can be named the fixed-s assumption, although it is rarely adopted in empirical studies on international comparison of capital costs.

Residence Principle and Fixed-P Assumption

What is more interesting is the fact that these three cases correspond to the different methods of avoiding international double taxation. The second case of fixed-P assumption can be justified if both countries adopt the residence principle of capital income at both the corporate and personal levels. The complete foreign tax credit system without deferral and excess credit can assure the residence principle strictly; it maintains production efficiency in the world economy because of the assurance of the same real before-tax rate of return (marginal productivity of investment) in allocating world investment. In this case the total tax wedge in each country determines the real after-tax rate of return which in turn affects the saving decision in each country differently.

Both the United States and Japan adopted the residence principle to avoid double taxation of foreign-source income. However, the residence principle is not perfectly maintained in reality because of several factors. First, portfolio investment dominates the international capital flow in gross terms, although it may be largely segmented into national markets on a net basis (Feldstein 1994). Domestic business investment can be financed by using funds of portfolio investment from abroad. In this case the corporate sector is subject to the domestic tax system, while asset holders (individuals or corporate firms) are under a personal or corporate tax system abroad.

Second, with foreign direct investment, the repatriation of the profits of multinational companies to their home countries is often delayed. In addition, excess credits could arise when the tax rate in the home country is lower than the foreign tax rate, although the firm is permitted to carry them over five years forward at zero interest in the United States and Japan, or two years backward in the United States against tax liability.

Hartman (1984) argued that investment financed by retained earnings by a mature foreign subsidiary is affected only by the host country's tax system, not by tax parameters of its home country.[4] Against the Hartman hypothesis, Jun (1989) showed that financial control by the home company and thus the home country's tax parameters influence the investment decision of the subsidiary. Yet under the assumption that the home company, instead of investors, engages in arbitrage activity between keeping and selling the subsidiary, only the host country's tax parameters matter in the case of investment financed by local borrowing by the subsidiary. Even in the case of equity transfer from the retained earnings of the parent company, only the host country's tax parameters affect the investment decision of the subsidiary, irrespective of whether it is a mature or immature subsidiary, if no deferral of repatriation takes place or the capital gains are taxed on an accrual basis. The cost of capital is similar to portfolio investment. While only the home country's corporate tax is imposed uniformly on all repatriated income from abroad, the corporate tax rate attached to the opportunity cost of keeping the subsidiary cancels out the tax parameter of the home country (see Appendix 1 for proof). In contrast, the residence principle is secured at the personal level, since individuals engage primarily in portfolio investment across the border and most tax treaties assure a lower withholding tax rate on dividend and interest income by the host country.

Third, tax sparing ("deemed foreign tax credit" which is equivalent to a tax exemption on foreign-source income) eliminates the home-country tax on foreign-source income. The United States disallows tax sparing, while Japan allows it with respect to foreign-source income generated in some developing countries. Tax sparing serves to make investment incentive measures in the host country effective, while it erodes the tax base of the home country.

Fourth, the difference in definitions of taxable income due to different methods of calculating depreciation allowances and investment-promoting measures between host and home country may lead to double taxation and violate the residence principle.

Fifth, the withholding tax on interest income and dividends also creates a deviation from the residence principle in the case of tax-exempt financial institutions.

The corporate tax on foreign subsidiaries may be regarded as a withholding tax by the host country. Frenkel, Razin, and Sadka (1992) argue convincingly that the optimal tax system in a small, open economy is a zero source-base tax rate on international movable factors. However, the non-zero corporate tax is required to secure the tax on capital gains because of the difficulty in tax collection at the individual level. It also serves to limit income-shifting between corporate income and labor income in the domestic economy or between the home company and foreign subsidiaries through transfer pricing.[5]

If the withholding tax rate on interest and dividend income is higher than the home country tax rate, the source principle becomes valid. Further, there is a well-known difficulty in tax collection regarding overseas financial investment because of bank secrecy and bearer security. This results in a withholding tax burden only as far as overseas financial investment is concerned.

Sixth, there is room for multinational companies to utilize a tax haven or low-tax country to save or defer tax imposed by the home country, even though the laws attempting to obtain tax revenues in tax havens have been strengthened in the two countries.

Multinational companies can exploit the excess credit on foreign-source income, thereby reducing their overall tax liability; if the after-tax tax haven income minus the foregone foreign tax credit carryforwards exceeds the foregone after-tax domestic income, they will choose to shift to a tax haven the subsidiary profits actually earned in a high-tax country. Further, they would never repatriate principal by investing on the world capital market, although the interest income earned in the tax haven (passive income subject to tax on tax-haven income) is repatriated to the home country.[6]

The use of a tax haven provides a channel to deviate from a tax system based on a strict residence principle. There is empirical evidence that U.S. multinational companies shift income out of high-tax countries into the United States, and from the United States to low-tax countries; multinational firms with subsidiaries in low-tax countries such as Ireland, the Asian NIEs, and tax havens tend to register relatively low U.S. tax liability per dollar of assets or sales (Harris, Morck, Slemrod, and Yeung 1991). A similar tendency can be observed among Japanese firms. The rate of return on foreign direct investment in the United States is relatively low (therefore the amount of repatriated profits from the United States to Japan is also limited), whereas the profit rate is high in the case of foreign direct investment by Japanese firms in Asian countries. The main channels of income-shifting may be transfer pricing, international factoring income, and intrafirm loans, which are discussed below.

The Source Principle and Fixed-s Assumption

The third case (constant-s assumption) is valid if both countries adopt the source principle vis-a-vis the foreign-source income. This ensures efficiency in allocating world saving, because the after-tax real rate of return is internationally equalized. In this case the total tax wedge in each country determines the real before-tax rate of return with different capital costs applying to the two countries. However, no major country has adopted the source principle on foreign-source income at the personal level.

Fixed-r Assumption

The first case of constant real market interest rate is in between the two cases; the residence principle applies only to foreign-source income at the personal level, while that of the corporate sector is subject to the source principle. As mentioned above, this is the case with respect to portfolio investment and foreign direct investment under certain conditions. In regard to foreign direct investment, France and Belgium adopted the source principle at the corporate level and Germany, the Netherlands (depending on tax treaties), and Canada have done so in part.

In these cases the total tax wedge can be decomposed into two parts, namely, the corporate and the personal tax wedges, defined as follows:

$$\text{corporate tax wedge (CW)} = \frac{(P-r)}{P}$$

$$\text{personal tax wedge (PW)} = \frac{(r-s)}{P}$$

It may be noted that the corporate tax could affect saving indirectly through its influence on private wealth and income and the distribution of income across generations.

These three cases are depicted in Figure 1B, 1C, and 1D. The II curve has a downward slope due to the diminishing return on capital investment, while the SS curve has an upward slope reflecting the positive (compensated) interest rate sensitivity of saving. The size of international capital movements is measured by the distance AB in each case. In the presence of a distortionary tax on capital income, the dead-weight loss arising from tax wedges between investment and saving cannot be avoided in all three cases.

However, it is well known that the residence principle on foreign income taxation secures capital export neutrality, because individuals face the same effective tax rate on domestic and foreign investment. Thus, capital export neutrality ensures the equalization of marginal productivity of investment, while it is accompanied by distortion on saving decisions due to different after-tax rates of return on saving in the two countries. On the other hand, the source principle achieves capital import neutrality which ensures equalization of after-tax rates of return on saving, yet impedes efficiency in allocating investment due to the difference in pretax rates of return on investment.

We can show easily how world welfare is lowered by distortion even under capital export and import neutrality. In the case of capital export neutrality, which implies a tax credit system with no deferral and no limit on foreign tax credit to avoid international double taxation, the distortion remains in allocating world saving. If the same after-tax rate of return on saving between the two countries is applied, world welfare can be improved by the reallocation of saving without changing world saving. In Figure 1C the shaded triangle areas indicate the potential welfare improvement arising from reallocation of saving by applying the same after-tax rate of return in the two countries.

In the case of capital import neutrality, world welfare can be improved through reallocation of investment without changing world investment, if the same pretax rate of return on capital investment is applied. Assuming the same pretax rate of return on investment, Japan's output increases by the area below the I_j, while U.S. output is reduced by the area above the I_{us} curve in Figure 1D. The difference in the areas below the I_j and above the I_{us} curves measures the potential welfare gain to the world economy that could be distributed through transfer among the two countries. Thus the potential welfare improvement can be measured by the two shaded triangle areas.

If the interest sensitivity of saving is small, the world welfare loss under capital export neutrality is minor, compared with the loss under capital import neutrality. Moreover, the Diamond-Mirrlees production efficiency theorem suggests that capital export neutrality (residence principle) in the absence of adjustment cost of investment is a necessary condition for optimal tax in a second-best world (Frenkel, Razin, and Sadka 1992).

Asymmetric Tax Burden between Corporate and Personal Sectors

In the following analysis on international capital movements, I take up the first case of fixed-r assumption. There are several reasons to focus on the case of the same real market interest rate.

Under the fixed-P assumption, the allocation of capital stock would not be affected by different tax systems on capital income, while the ownership pattern of capital stock could be affected as far as the compensated interest rate sensitivity is different from zero. The size of the total tax wedge (as presented in Table 2) simply determines the real after-tax rate of return, as is shown in Figure

1C. However, the actual scheme to avoid international double taxation is far from the residence principle as discussed above.

On the other hand, almost all advanced countries do not adopt the source principle in taxing foreign-source income at the household level. Thus, the real after-tax rate of return for the personal sector is not likely to be equalized internationally, implying that the fixed-s assumption is not realistic enough to carry out further analysis.

Under the conditions that the offshore market is well developed and the intermediation cost is disregarded, it seems reasonable to assume that each country can borrow and lend at the same real market interest rate. Alternatively, we can assume that tax-exempt institutions or investors located in tax havens engage in arbitrage activity and provide the same rate of return to lenders and borrowers adjusted for risk and exchange rate changes. In this case the direct economic effect of the two tax wedges can be separated neatly. The corporate tax wedge affects primarily the investment decision by firms, while the personal tax wedge mainly influences saving behavior.

Table 3 shows the total tax wedge, corporate tax wedge, and personal tax wedge in the United States and Japan, based on the fixed-r assumption. While there are some differences in the size of the tax wedges between Tables 2 and 3, the same tendency can be seen from the two tables. In particular, Table 3 demonstrates that a disproportionately large tax burden was imposed on the corporate sector in Japan before tax reform. A disproportionate tax burden at the corporate level may induce income-shifting from corporate income to labor income (by buying equity and enjoying capital gain, instead of receiving labor income). Yet income-shifting is limited because the top labor income tax rate (currently 65 percent) is much higher than the effective corporate tax rate in Japan.

In contrast, the tax burden was shared equally between the corporate and personal sector in the United States before the second tax reform; the tax burden had been somewhat smaller at the corporate level. After the second tax reform, the corporate tax wedge increased significantly and the difference in the corporate tax wedge between the two countries became smaller. As a result, the tax burden could be minimized, if the lower tax wedge for the personal sector in Japan were combined with the corporate tax wedge in the United States through international capital flow before the second reform (Table 4).

Effect of Tax Reform on International Capital Movement

Under the assumption that the capital income tax at the personal level is based on the residence principle with the source principle being applied to capital income at the corporate level, the change in international capital movement due to tax reform can be described by parameter changes embodied in

TABLE 3

Total Tax Wedge, Corporate and Personal Tax Wedge in the United States and Japan:
[fixed-r(5%) case] (%)

Year:Country	Total Tax Wedge	Corporate Tax Wedge	Personal Tax Wedge
1980:U.S.	39.1	20.1	19.0
1983:U.S.	32.6	15.0	17.6
1986:U.S.	44.4	30.6	13.8
1983:Japan	50.6	41.3	9.3
1988:Japan	53.4	38.7	14.7

NOTE: (1) The tax wedges are calculated by the author, except for the figures for the United States in 1980 which are derived from King-Fullerton (1984). (2) The personal sector includes the household, insurance companies, and tax-exempt institutions.

the corporate and personal tax wedge. Assuming that competitive firms in the two countries produce one good based on the Cobb-Douglas production function, the capital market equilibrium in terms of stock can be described as follows:

$$K_j^D(P_j) + K_{Dus}(P_{us}) = K_j^S[s_j] + K_{Sus}[s_{us}]$$

whereby

$$P_j = r[1+CW_j(r)]$$
$$P_{us} = r[1+CW_{us}(r)]$$
$$s_j = r(1-PW_j)$$
$$s_{us} = r(1-PW_{us}).$$

It may be noted that the world real interest rate changes are due to changes in tax parameters and that the corporate tax wedge (CW) is in turn affected by changes in the real market interest rate, due to its effect on tax saving relating to the present value of depreciation of capital stock. A higher real interest rate causes a lower present value of legal depreciation of capital stock. Thus, the capital market equilibrium can be calculated by iterative procedure.

The labor supply is assumed to be immobile across the border and constant (inelastic to changes in tax parameters) in the two countries. This assumption enables us to concentrate on the effects of tax parameter changes relating to capital income on international capital movement. Further, we assume that the utility function is also of Cobb-Douglass form. This implies that intertemporal substitution is unity, and that the saving ratio is insensitive to changes in the after-tax real interest rate.

TABLE 4

Tax Saving by Combining Two Tax Schemes to Attain Minimum Tax Burden:
[Fixed-r(5%) case] (%)

	U.S. Investment Financed by Japanese Saver	
	Before Tax Reform	After Tax Reform
Total tax wedge	21.92	43.19
Corporate tax wedge	12.62	28.47
Personal tax wedge	9.30	14.72

NOTE: The corporate tax wedges lower than those in Table 3 are due to the different weights in sources of financing. The personal tax wedge is the same since the residence principle in international taxation holds true.

Under these assumptions we can calculate the effect of change in the corporate tax wedge on international capital movement between the United States and Japan. The change in the corporate tax wedge is accompanied by change in capital costs which, in turn, affects domestic business investment. In calculating the effect of capital cost changes on business investment, I assumed that the inelasticity of investment to capital cost is 0.84. This estimate is derived from an empirical study on the investment function using cross-section data in Japan (Iwata, Suzuki, and Yoshida 1987).

The results are presented in Table 5. The first U.S. tax reform under the Reagan administration invited a significant capital inflow from abroad ($11.1 billion). Even more remarkable is that the second reform yielded a sizable reduction in investment demand in the United States ($33.5 billion). While the Japanese tax reform brought about a minor change in the corporate tax wedge, the increase in investment demand was significant ($8.8 billion). If we combine the effect of tax reform in the United States (1986) and Japan (1988), the reduction of capital outflow from Japan to the United States was substantial. Further, if the corporate tax wedge in Japan were lowered to the level of the United States in a future tax reform, the capital outflow from Japan to the United States would be reduced by $48.4 billion.

Certainly the results may exaggerate the effect of tax parameter changes on international capital flow, since we abstract from changes in the exchange rate and the existence of third countries as well as substitution among different goods.[7] Moreover, the interest sensitivity of the saving rate may be positive and counteract international capital movements induced by tax parameter changes. Despite these shortcomings we may say that tax reform in the late 1980s exerted a nonnegligible impact on international capital movements between the two countries.

If the actual taxation system on foreign-source capital income at the cor-

TABLE 5

Impact of Change Corporate Tax Wedge on International Capital Movement
between the United States and Japan ($billion)

	United States	Japan
1981 (Reagan I)	+11.1	−11.1
1986 (Reagan II)	−33.5	+33.5
1987 (Nakasone-Takeshita)	−8.8	+8.8
(The same corporate tax wedge)	−48.4	+48.4

NOTE: The sign (+) indicates capital inflow, while the sign (−) denotes capital outflow.

porate level is closer to the source principle, instead of the residence principle, there is an incentive for the host country to reduce the corporate tax wedge with the aim of inviting capital inflow. Multinational firms choose to register larger profits in a lower-tax country. This profit-shifting through intrafirm transactions is enabled by fiscal transfer pricing and debt financing concentrated in subsidiaries in high-tax countries. The tax system based on the source principle combined with private incentive to achieve minimum tax liabilities through income-shifting promotes the tendency to move the corporate tax rate to zero. Yet this is not desirable in view of the role of corporate tax as a withholding tax on capital gains and a backstop to labor income.

TAX FRICTION: TRANSFER PRICING AND THIN CAPITALIZATION

Strengthening the Transfer Price Tax in the United States

The calculation of the tax effect on international capital flows in the preceding section assumed implicitly that profit-shifting through fiscal transfer pricing to a low-tax third country does not take place. However, there is a tendency for multinational firms to register larger profits in a low-tax country.

The United States moved to strengthen its taxation system on foreign firms after the mid-1970s. The U.S. subsidiaries of Japanese automobile (Toyota and Nissan) and electric machinery (Matsushita and Fujitsu) firms were requested to pay taxes, based on the U.S. rules of transfer-pricing taxation. In the case of Nissan and Toyota, any doubt on the thin margin due to low sales prices was dispelled after the dumping petition against Japanese automobiles was rejected. Yet it raised another doubt on the possibility of tax evasion through transfer pricing to home companies.

After acrimonious debate between the U.S. and Japanese tax authorities, a substantial amount of tax revenue was transferred from Japan to the U.S. tax authority (for instance, ¥80 billion in 1987 and ¥15 billion in 1993) (Appendix

2). Recently, the Japanese tax authority, in turn, requested that Japan Coca Cola Company pay additional tax on the excessive royalty payment for a new product adapted to Japanese tastes.

After the mid-1970s transfer-pricing taxation became one of the most serious tax frictions between Japan and the United States. The competition to increase tax revenue from multinational companies by both countries and arbitrary rules in restricting transfer pricing may, however, lead to double taxation and discourage foreign direct investment.

New Rules on Transfer Pricing

The release of Section 482 in January 1992 formed a watershed in U.S. transfer pricing rules. Section 482 regulations were originally adopted in 1968 and amended by the Tax Reform Act of 1986. The newly introduced transfer pricing rules follow proposals made in a 1988 white paper (by the Treasury Department and the IRS). They included detailed rules for the treatment of interest, services, use of tangible property, use or transfer of intangible property, and sale of tangible property.

In 1968 the Internal Revenue Service (IRS) identified the following four methods based on the application of arm's-length standards:

(1) the comparable uncontrolled prices (CUP) method, which relies on matching or comparable transactions with unrelated parties;

(2) the resale price (RP) method, which defines the price as the price at which the good was sold to unrelated parties minus an appropriate margin for distribution services by foreign subsidiaries;

(3) cost plus (CP) method, which defines the price as the sum of manufacturing costs and an appropriate profit margin; and

(4) other reasonable methods.

The first three methods are based on transaction, while the fourth includes the profit split and the comparable profit method. The IRS preferred the first method and ranked the methods by priority. Yet the hierarchical approach was ultimately abandoned and was replaced by the best rule method.

The actual application of the first method was not dominant due to the difficulty in determining the comparable arm's-length price; it is often the case that a unique good is traded among related parties and the market structure deviates from perfect competition in the case of differentiated products. In addition, the trade or transfer of intangible property (royalties and license fees) became important in intracompany trade in the 1980s. Obviously it is almost impossible to provide comparable prices for services. Further, the substantial transfer of tangible property is included in the transfer of intangible property; for example, the sale of cans of tuna fish under a brand name falls under intangible rules.

In a white paper of 1988, the Treasury and the IRS introduced the "commensurate-with-income standards" with respect to payments of sales or license of intangible property ("super-royalty clause"). It states that the division of R&D expenses should reflect the income that each company expects to receive from its territorial application of newly developed technologies.[8] More concretely, in 1988 the IRS proposed four methods to determine correct transfer price for intangibles: (1) uncontrolled comparable price method, (2) inexact comparable price method, (3) an arm's-length return method, and (4) profit split method.

Following this white paper, the Treasury in 1992 proposed three methods for the transfer price of intangibles: (1) matching transaction method (uncontrolled price of transfer of the same intangibles); (2) comparable adjustable transaction method (uncontrolled price of the same or similar intangibles under substantially similar circumstances); and (3) comparable profit method (comparison of profit level with equivalent uncontrolled parties).

The last method (CPM) plays a central role in the 1992 Section 482 proposed regulations. The CPM presumes that even if the controlled parties adopt the first two transactional methods, operating income must fall within margins of profit set by the comparable profit method. The profit interval is calculated by using various profit indicators of equivalent U.S. firms. This profit interval test is also extended to the transfer of tangibles. The 1993 temporary and proposed Section 482 regulations weakened somewhat the application of the ex post "comparable profit interval" or "arm's-length range," but did not eliminate the use of the CPM.

Problems of the Comparable Profit Method

The comparable profit method can be employed only if the comparison is just, valid, and accords with business reality. Past experience has already demonstrated the difficulty in finding comparable arm's-length prices between independent firms. Yet it may be more difficult to find comparable profit. The comparison based on a functional analysis of the firm's activity, instead of transactional prices, can be arbitrary, because of the many differences in location of firms and managerial skills. Furthermore, it is difficult to collect financial data from a foreign entity because of differences in accounting standards and information disclosure obligations. Thus, the U.S. tax authority may tend to use similar U.S. firms as comparable firms. Comparison with U.S. firms, however, tends to exaggerate the actual profit of U.S. subsidiaries of Japanese firms.

For instance, the basic objectives of firms are different. Japanese firms are oriented toward market share rather than profit maximization. Table 6 shows the marked difference in profit rates between U.S. firms and foreign-controlled firms in the United States.[9] The profit rate of Japanese firms is the lowest among

TABLE 6
Net Income of Foreign-Controlled U.S. Firms (1987) (%)

Country	Net Income Before Deficit	Net Income Less Deficit
Canada	3.6	0.9
Japan	2.7	0.1
United Kingdom	2.3	3.3
Netherlands	3.0	0.6
Germany	2.4	0.2
France	2.7	2.7
Antilles	2.1	−1.4
Total	2.8	0.9
Other countries	3.1	0.4
U.S. firms	4.9	3.4

SOURCE: SOI Bulletin, Spring 1991

these seven countries. The low profit rate may partly reflect the tax saving by Japanese firms through engaging in takeovers and mergers and acquisitions or investing in energy, thus reducing the tax on repatriation (trapped equity effect); it is more advantageous to buy the equity of other U.S. firms and receive tax-free dividends than to repatriate profits to Japan and pay a higher corporate tax. This operation involves debt financing and thus reduces the profit rate. It may also reflect the poor performance of Japanese firms in the United States (for instance, securities companies and financial services). Further, a large number of subsidiaries were established after mid-1985 in the case of Japanese firms; the existence of a "maturation effect" arising from large depreciation costs and interest deductions tends to reduce the profit rate.

Solution of Tax Friction on Transfer Pricing

The OECD (1993) criticized the U.S. move on the risk of double taxation. It recommended limiting the use of the comparable profit method to abusive cases or as a last resort. In July 1994 it reiterated the limited use of the CPM only in the case where the transactional method is not available. In response to this criticism, the IRS admitted in the 1994 final regulations that the CPM is a last resort, though both the CPM and the profit split method constitute the other specified methods.

One way to avoid the excessive tax burden based on the comparable profit method is the use of an "advanced pricing agreement" (APA). This system was introduced in March 1991. General Motors had initiated advance pricing agreements with 16 European countries in the 1980s, and the company's success prompted the introduction of the APA into the U.S. tax system. It allows the IRS and a firm to formulate a method for calculating transfer pricing rules for a period of years. It predetermines the pricing zones under consultation with the IRS. This ensures that the company will avoid the risk of additional tax, if the transfer price is within the margin of pricing zones. Sumitomo Capital Markets, Matsushita, and other Japanese firms entered such agreements with the IRS.

However, the APA is also expensive and time consuming. It is hard to predetermine an adequate arm's-length price in industries where technological changes are rapid and economies of scale are significant. It is desirable to standardize the APA procedure to save costs.

Japan's Tax System on Transfer Pricing

Japan legislated transfer pricing taxation for the first time in 1986. The Japanese system was influenced by the U.S. and German taxation systems as well as the 1979 OECD report on "Transfer Pricing and Multinational Enterprises." Japan adopts the CUP, RP, and CP methods in measuring "arm's-length price" without priority (the "best rule method"), but does not acknowledge the application of the comparable profit method. It is noteworthy that Japan introduced a preconfirmation system similar to the APA when the transfer pricing tax system was established, preceding the APA in the United States. In this system firms can preconfirm the arm's-length price of intracompany transactions after consultation with tax offices on the method of calculating transfer prices. Although the use of the preconfirmation system is still limited (about 20 cases), the tax authority has moved to enhance the use of the preconfirmation system by amending rules to allow the application of the profit split method in assessing the value of intangible assets. It could serve to augment efficiency in narrowing the gap between firms and the tax authority on adequate transfer prices and determining the arm's-length prices of intangible assets.

Need for International Cooperation

It goes without saying that there is a need to strengthen the mutual consultation system between the U.S. and Japanese tax authorities and to establish an internationally consistent method of calculating transfer prices if the APA or preconfirmation system is utilized. Moreover, it is also important to establish an international arbitration procedure when disputes on different assessments of transfer prices arise among different tax authorities. Japan and the United States should establish an arbitration procedure in a tax treaty, following the suit of the U.S.-German tax treaty that admits a binding decision by the arbitration boards.

Although the transactional price approach to transfer pricing is more adequate than the CPM, it must be noted that the shadow price of internal transactions for multinationals aiming at global profit maximization diverges from arm's-length price in the presence of market imperfections and distortionary implicit taxes such as tariffs, trade-restricting measures, and capital control. Further, multinational firms can manipulate market prices to some extent. Certainly the shadow price in the absence of trade barriers and market imperfection may come closer to market price regardless of the different international taxation systems between home and host country when the tax rate on capital income at the corporate level is the same.

The difficulty in measuring the intrafirm transaction price correctly leads to the adoption of a unitary tax system among states in the United States. Yet, the apportionment approach and the transactional approach involve a similar difficulty due to the lack of a globally recognized accounting system and arbitrary weightings in turnovers, labor, and capital stock. What is more important is to diminish the tax incentive for manipulating transfer pricing. Again a strict residence principle on foreign-source income is needed, with no deferral and no excess credit or limitation in providing tax credit in order to achieve the goal.[10]

Thin Capitalization

In addition to stricter transfer price taxation, the Clinton administration has proposed to tax interest payments on all loans guaranteed by the parent company. This proposal aims at limiting the deduction of interest payments if the subsidiaries rely on excessive borrowing (earnings stripping); in the present law the tax is imposed on subsidiaries if their equity-asset ratio is lower than 40 percent and the interest payments exceed 50 percent of taxable income.

The "thin capitalization" by multinational enterprises erodes the tax base. Thus many countries, notably countries with higher corporate tax rates, impose a tax on thin capitalization. The U.S. Treasury published a draft of regulations on thin capitalization in 1981, based on section 395 of the Internal Revenue Code. Yet it was withdrawn in 1983. Since 1983 case-by-case judgments have been made broadly in line with the 1981 regulations. Foreign companies can escape taxation on thin capitalization if one of the following conditions is met: (1) the equity-debt ratio exceeds one-third and interest and principal are paid by the due date (safe-harbor rule); (2) external debt ratio is below one-tenth, and internal debt ratio is also below one-third; or (3) loan conditions are set based on transaction criteria with third parties.

In 1989 section 163 of the Internal Revenue Code was amended to limit the interest deduction of U.S. subsidiaries on loans from parent companies, if the foreign related companies enjoyed diminished tax burdens due to the tax treaty. In April 1992 a stricter limit on interest deductions was imposed on subsidiaries in the United States based on the calculated average debt and deemed debt of the U.S. subsidiary, instead of the book value of interest payments. Subsequently, in February 1993 the Treasury announced that the limit would be imposed on loans assured by parent companies and "back-to-back loans" in which borrowing by the U.S. subsidiary from a branch bank at whose parent bank in Japan the parent company has deposits. The U.S. subsidiaries of Japanese banks were the most seriously hit by the new tax rules on thin capitalization.

Japan's Rule on Thin Capitalization

Japan also moved to introduce a tax on thin capitalization in 1991. If a foreign subsidiary in Japan registers an amount of borrowing from foreign-related companies more than three times its own capital, then the interest deduction is not allowed. Japan also introduced a measure to prevent the deferral of the capital gains tax on land sales by foreign companies that avoid capital gains tax by utilizing the tax deferral in the form of capital subscription in kind (land) to establish the subsidiary.

Solution to Thin Capitalization

In the present income taxation system there is an inherent tax incentive to utilize debt financing, as far as the deduction of interest payments from the tax base is allowed. The most powerful measure for preventing thin capitalization would be to abolish the deduction of interest expense combined with a reduction in the corporate tax rate. This may lead to the adoption of a cash-flow corporate tax system that is neutral to financing methods. However, one of the difficulties with a cash-flow tax system is the taxation on financial institutions incurring large debt.

It must be remembered that the foreign tax credit system without excess credit (deferral does not occur in the case of interest payment) removes the incentive to shift profit by manipulating the interest rate on intrafirm loans, because the same tax treatment applies to all types of foreign-source income, when foreign-source income is repatriated. The existence of a tax-exemption country (more typically, a tax-haven country) provides the opportunity for multinational firms to save tax by thin capitalization, since there is room for multinationals to exploit the differential tax treatment of dividend and interest income in the host country. This gives rise to the establishment of conduits and investment companies as well as complicated financial intermediation. Yet it is also clear that income shifting through thin capitalization is not profitable if the withholding tax rate on interest income is set at the same level as the corporate tax rate in the host country: in this case the attempt to transform the dividend into interest income is unprofitable.

To conclude, it is desirable to harmonize tax rules on foreign-source income with other countries relying on the source principle, notably the European Union, if thin capitalization is to be avoided. However, if thin capitalization is the real problem between the United States and Japan, it implies that the actual taxation system on foreign-source income at the corporate level is closer to the source principle.

CONCLUSION

In the 1980s we saw a move in tax reform in many advanced countries aimed at simplified and more efficient taxation systems. At the same time we observed tax competition to strengthen international competitiveness by reducing the tax burden on domestic companies and to intensify efforts to collect tax from foreign companies. Although the attempt to establish a more efficient and neutral tax system, in contrast to supply-side-oriented tax reform, has not exerted a distortionary impact on international capital movement between the United States and Japan, tax collection efforts through imposition of strict tax rules on transfer pricing and thin capitalization gave rise to tax friction between the two countries.

In this paper I have argued that significant change took place in international capital movement due to tax reform in the United States and Japan. Under several assumptions the change in capital costs arising from changes in the corporate tax wedge induced a significant amount of international capital movement ranging from $9 billion to $34 billion. Yet the difference in the tax burden on the corporate sector is now somehow diminished, thus working to narrow the external imbalance between the United States and Japan. It seems desirable to further narrow the gap of the corporate tax wedge in future tax reform, in order to minimize the tax-distorted international capital movement.

With a view to establishing a more efficient international taxation system on foreign-source income, it is necessary to implement the residence principle more strictly; we should prohibit the deferral of the profit of a subsidiary to the home company. Excess credit under a foreign credit system should be eliminated by adopting a common corporate tax rate. The strict implementation of the residence principle not only assures production efficiency in the world economy, but also makes income-shifting through transfer pricing and thin capitalization unprofitable.

In reality the actual international taxation system is closer to the source principle at the corporate level; it provides the incentive to manipulate transfer price and financial transactions of multinationals aiming to minimize their global tax burdens. The residence principle is also undermined by the existence of other countries adopting the source principle. The European Union embarked on harmonizing the taxation systems of member countries, thereby relying on the source principle on foreign-source income at the corporate level. This adds to the difficulty in implementing the residence principle strictly.

At least it is desirable to adopt a common corporate tax rate among advanced countries. We need also to establish a common standard for calculating transfer pricing and common rules on thin capitalization. It also seems necessary to establish an international arbitration procedure with a view to solving tax friction in taxing multinational companies.

APPENDIX 1

The formulation of the capital cost of investment by a subsidiary under the control of a parent company is developed by Jun (1989) and Sinn (1990). In the following I derive the cost of capital of a subsidiary by extending Sinn's model to include local borrowing and intrafirm loans, in addition to equity transfers from the parent company.

(1) Let us consider the case where the subsidiary finances investment by equity transfer from the retained earnings of the parent company and local borrowing. The arbitrage activity by the parent company leads to the equilibrium that the after-tax return from equity transfer (dividends plus capital gains) is equal to the opportunity cost of keeping the subsidiary. Thus,

$$(1-m_p)D_t^* + (1-m_G)\left(\frac{dV_t^*}{dt-S_t^*}\right) = \rho V_t^* \tag{1}$$

whereby

D_t^*:repatriated profits from subsidiary to home company
V_t^*:market value of subsidiary firm
S_t^*:equity transfer from parent company to subsidiary
m_p:marginal tax rate on repatriated profits
m_G:marginal tax rate on capital gain on equity
ρ:required rate of return by home company.

Under the transversality condition

$$\lim_{t \to \infty} V_t^* e^{-\rho t/(1-m_G)} = 0 \tag{2}$$

the market value of the subsidiary can be expressed as:

$$MAX:V^* = \int_0^\infty [mD_t^* - S_t^*]e^{-\rho t/(1-m_G)} dt : m = \frac{1-m_p}{1-m_G} \qquad (3)$$

The subsidiary is assumed to maximize its market value, given the cash flow constraint. Thereby it is also assumed that the subsidiary has a target debt-finance ratio. The before-tax repatriation of profits can be written as follows:

$$D_t^* = (1-u^*)[p_t^* F^*(K_t^*, L_t^*) - W_t^* L_t^* - R_t^* - t_p^* q_t^* K_t^*$$

$$-q_t^* K_t^*(1-A^*)\beta^* i_t^*] + \beta^* q_t^*(1-A^*)(\pi_t^* + I_t^*) \qquad (4)$$

$$- (1-A^*)q_t^*(\delta^* K_t^* + I_t^*) + u^* D_t^* + S_t^*$$

whereby

q_t^*:price of investment goods

p_t^*:product price

K_t^*:capital stock

I_t^*:net investment

L_t^*:number of employed workers

W_t^*:wage rate

R_t^*:royalty payment to parent company

i_t^*:market interest rate in host country

π_t^*:inflation rate in host country

β^*:target debt ratio

t_p^*:property tax rate in host country

A^*:present value of tax-saving effect arising from legal depreciation
and investment tax credit in host country

u^*:effective corporate tax rate in host country.

The problem of optimization for the subsidiary is to maximize its market value (V^*) under the additional conditions as below:

$$\dot{K}_t^* = I_t^* \qquad (5)$$

$$D_t^* \geq 0 \qquad (6)$$

$$S_t^* \geq 0 \qquad (7)$$

Equation (7) implies that there is no tax-exempt repatriation of profits to the home company; in other words, capital redemption by the parent company through repurchase of the subsidiary's shares is regarded as repatriation of profits and thus is taxable.

The current value of Hamiltonian can be expressed as:

$$H = [mD_t^* - S_t^*] + \mu_t I_t^* + \eta_{1t}(1-u^*)D_t^* + \eta_{2t}S_t^* \qquad (8)$$

In addition to the multiplier with respect to the equation of motion of capital stock, two Kuhn-Tucker multipliers representing nonnegative conditions on the repatriation of profits and equity transfer appear in the Hamiltonian.

The first order condition for maximization can be written as follows:

$$\frac{\partial H}{\partial L_t} = P_t^* \frac{\partial F^*}{\partial L_t^*} - W_t^* = 0 \qquad (9)$$

$$\frac{\partial H}{\partial I_t^*} = -(1-\beta^*)(1-A^*)q_t^*\left(\frac{m}{1-u^*} + \eta_{1t}\right) + \mu_t = 0 \qquad (10)$$

$$\frac{\partial H}{\partial S_t^*} = \left[\frac{m}{1-u^*} - 1\right] + \eta_{1t} + \eta_{2t} = 0 \qquad (11)$$

$$\dot{\mu}_t - \frac{\rho}{1-m_G}\mu_t = -\frac{\partial H}{\partial K_t^*} = -[m+(1-u^*)\eta_{1t}]$$

$$\left[p_t^* \frac{\partial F^*}{\partial K_t^*} - t_p^* q_t^* - \frac{(1-A^*)q_t^*(\beta^*(i_t^*(1-u^*)-\pi_t^*)+\delta^*)}{1-u^*}\right] \qquad (12)$$

We assume that under the deferral-cum-tax-credit system the deferral is more advantageous than immediate repatriation of profits. The presence of the deferral implies that the marginal tax rate on repatriated profits is higher than the tax rate on profit retention. Thus:

$$m = \frac{(1-m_p)}{(1-m_G)} < (1-u^*) \qquad (13)$$

Under this condition, the applied tax rate on repatriated profits is the effective corporate tax rate in the home country ($m_p = u$).

The Kuhn-Tucker multipliers satisfy the complementary slackness conditions as follows:

$$\eta_{1t}D_t^* = 0, \ \eta_{1t} \geq 0, \ D_t^* \geq 0 \qquad (14)$$

$$\eta_{2t}S_t^* = 0, \ \eta_{2t} \geq 0, \ S_t^* \geq 0 \qquad (15)$$

The two complementary conditions combined with equations (11) and (13) imply that repatriation of profits and equity transfer do not take place simultaneously. It may be noted that for an immature subsidiary, equity transfer from the parent company is positive ($S^*>0$), while the repatriation of profits is zero ($D^*=0$). For a mature subsidiary the opposite holds true ($S^*=0, D^*>0$). In between both of them can be zero ($S^*=D^*=0$): the subsidiary finances investment by all the retained earnings.

The transversality condition can be written as:

$$\lim_{t \to \infty} \mu_t e^{-pt/(1-m_G)} K_t^* = 0 \qquad (16)$$

From equations (10) and (12) we can obtain the cost of capital including economic depreciation as:

$$p_t^* \frac{\partial F^*}{\partial K_t^*} = q_t^* \frac{1-A^*}{1-u^*} \left[(1-\beta^*) \left(\frac{\rho}{1-m_G} - \pi_t^* \right) \right.$$
$$\left. + \beta^*(i_t^*(1-u^*) - \pi_t^*) + \delta^* \right] + t_p^* q_t^* \qquad (17)$$

The cost of capital is represented as the weighted sum of equity financing and debt financing. The first term indicates the cost of capital financed by equity transfer from the parent company, while the second term represents the capital cost financed by local borrowing. It may be recalled that the required rate of return by the parent company is equal to

$$\rho = (1-u)i_t \qquad (18)$$

whereby i_t: market interest rate in home company.

If the capital market is integrated between the two countries in the absence of exchange rate changes, then $i_t=i_t^*$. It is easy to see that in the case of local financing, the home country's tax parameters do not affect the capital cost of investment by the subsidiary. Further, under the condition that the marginal tax rate on capital gains is equal to the effective corporate tax rate in the home country (capital gain tax on accrual base: $m_G=u$) or the deferral is absent (in equation (13) the equality holds true), the home country's tax parameters vanish even in the case of equity transfer financing, irrespective of a mature or immature subsidiary.

In the case of a tax-exempt system on foreign-source income (source principle), no tax is imposed on repatriated profits: $m_G=u=0$. Thus the cost of capital is identical to the case of a capital gains tax on an accrual base.

On the other hand, the Hartman hypothesis presumes that deferred tax in the home country is capitalized in the market value of the firm and thus the home country's tax parameters do not appear in the cost of investment capital financed by the retained earnings of the subsidiary.

Yet we must use caution with respect to the difference in tax bases. Some investment-promoting measures such as the accelerated depreciation scheme and investment tax credit in the host country are not acknowledged as deductible in the home country. This creates a difference in the definition of taxable income (A is not always equal to A*).

So far, we have assumed that the parent company engages in arbitrage activity. However, if we take the view that the parent company is simply a liaison for investors in the home country, the required rate of return for investors is equal to:

$$\rho = (1-m_I)i_t \qquad (19)$$

whereby

m_I:marginal tax rate of interest income at personal sector.

Then the tax parameters of both countries affect the capital cost in the case of equity transfer financing. The applied marginal tax rates on capital gains and dividends are those of the personal sector in the home country. The investor in the home country looks through the parent company as a financial intermediary and engages in arbitrage activity on the capital market. Thus, the home country's tax parameter affects the cost of investment capital by the subsidiary.

(2) In the case of borrowing from the parent company, there are two different treatments. First, the applied interest rate on intrafirm loans can diverge from the market interest rate. However, under the tax credit system, intrafirm profit-shifting using in-trafirm loans is washed out in the consolidated cash-flow constraint. In the case of intrafirm loans to a subsidiary from the retained earnings of the parent company, the cash flow constraint of the parent company is written as:

$$D_t + (1-A)q_t(\delta K_t + I_t) + S^*{}_t = (1-u)[P_t F(K_t, L_t) - W_t L_t$$
$$- \beta q_t K_t(1-A)i_t - t_p q_t K_t + R_t^* + D_t^* + \beta^* i_{It}(1-A^*)q_t^* K_t^*]$$
$$+ \beta q_t(1-A)(\pi_t + I_t) + S_t \qquad (20)$$

whereby

S_t:new share issues by home company.

Note that $D^*{}_t$ denotes the before-tax repatriation of profits. Thus it is not necessary to gross up $D^*{}_t$ before tax in the home country.

$$D_t + (1-A)q_t(\delta K_t + I_t) + \frac{1-u}{1-u^*}(1-A^*)q_t^*(\delta^* K_t^* + I_t^*)$$

$$-\frac{u-u^*}{1-u^*}S_t^* = (1-u)[P_t F(K_t, L_t) + P_t^* F^*(K_t^*, L_t^*) - W_t L_t$$

$$- W_t^* L_t^* - \beta q_t(1-A)K_t i_t - t_p q_t K_t - t_p^* q_t^* K_t^*]$$

$$+ \frac{1-u}{1-u^*}\beta^* q_t^*(1-A^*)(\pi_t^* + I_t^*) + \beta q_t(1-A)(\pi_t + I_t) + S_t \quad (21)$$

Using equation (4) both the interest payment on intrafirm loans and royalty payments disappear in the consolidated cash-flow constraint with a subsidiary (when $i_t^* = i_{lt}$).

The second difference from local borrowing lies in the fact that the cost of capital depends on the method of financing used by the parent company to facilitate the intrafirm loan. If the parent company borrows and lends to the subsidiary, the cost of capital is similar to local borrowing: the corporate tax rate attached to the market interest rate in the host country must be replaced by the home country's parameter. On the other hand, the cost of investment capital financed by intrafirm loans from the retained earnings of the home company is reduced to the case of equity transfer from retained earnings.

The consolidation of cash flow constraints implies that we deal with the case of branch companies. Yet in the case of subsidiaries, there can be deferrals on the royalty payments through underpricing ($R^{*\prime} < R^*$:transfer pricing): the tax burden is saved by $[(u-u^*)(R^*-R^{*\prime})]$. But in the case of intrafirm loans, the deferral is excluded by definition.

APPENDIX 2

1928	The U.S. Government legislated the transfer pricing taxation system.
1968	The U.S. Treasury published the Regulations concerning transfer pricing taxation.
1975	The IRS initiated investigation of the case of transfer pricing concerning the subsidiaries of Toyota and Nissan in the U.S. and requested them to pay tax amounting to Yen 250 billion.
1986	The Japanese Government legislated the transfer pricing taxation system.
1987: Autumn	The Japanese Government paid back tax revenue amounting to Yen 80 billion to Nissan and Toyota which in turn made tax payment to the IRS for the transferred income of the period from 1974 to 1984.
October	The Japanese Government introduced the Preconfirmation System.

1988: October	The U.S. Treasury and the IRS published "A Study of Intercompany Pricing: SEC 482 White Paper."
1989: November	The U.S. Congress passed the Bill to strengthen tax collection from foreign companies.
1990: June	The IRS requested the U.S. subsidiary of Matsushita to pay tax amounting to Yen 50 billion.
November	The IRS requested the U.S. subsidiary of Fujitsu to pay tax amounting to $614 million.
	The U.S. Congress passed the Bill to further strengthen the tax collection from foreign companies.
1991	The U.S. Government introduced the Advance Pricing System.
February	The Japanese Tax Agency requested the AIU Insurance Company in Japan to pay Yen 20 billion for transferred income to the U.S. parent company.
Spring	The U.S. Fujitsu invoked petition to the Appeals Office against the request of tax payment by the IRS.
Autumn	The agreement was reached between the U.S. and Japanese Government on tax payment concerning the U.S. Matsushita.
1992: January	The U.S. Treasury published the draft on the amendment of regulations on transfer pricing taxation including the adoption of Comparable Profit Method.
April	Mr. Hunter made statement on the tax revenue shortage in regard to foreign companies at the Revenue Committee. According to his estimate the shortage amounts to $30 billion since 1990.
Autumn	Matsushita agreed to adopt the Advanced Pricing Agreement with respect to transaction with its U.S. subsidiaries.
Autumn	President Clinton announced the measures to increase tax collection centering on transfer pricing taxation by $4–5 billion in forthcoming four years.
October	The U.S., Canada, Australia, and Japan agreed to cooperate in the joint-investigation concerning transfer pricing taxation at the Pacific Association of Tax Administration.
1993: January	The IRS published the amended SEC 482 of the U.S. IRC and the draft to change rules and regulations on transfer pricing taxation.
November	The Japanese Tax Agency paid back Yen 17 billion to Nissan for the tax payment amounting to Yen 15 billion to the IRS; the tax was imposed for the transferred income from the U.S. Nissan in California to home company for the period from 1985 to 1988.
1994: March	The Japanese Tax Agency requested the Japan Coca Cola Company to pay Yen 15 billion for transferred income to the U.S. parent company.

NOTES

1. The King-Fullerton framework can be regarded as a simplified version of Jorgenson-type formulation of capital cost; the latter approach is adopted in the Appendix, which derives the cost of capital of investment by a subsidiary under the control of a parent company. Only one minor difference between King-Fullerton (1984) and Jorgenson and Yun (1991) can be found in the case of capital financed by new share issue; in the latter, the inflation rate is multiplied by $(1-m_D)/(1-m_G)$.

2. The estimate by Shoven-Tachibanaki (1988) records the higher U.S. total tax wedge. A major difference can be traced in the assumption on different economic depreciation rates in Japan (see Iwata and Yoshida 1990).

3. Hamada and Iwata (1986) examined whether the before-tax rate of return on net corporate capital stock or the after-tax rate of return is equalized between the United States and Japan. Yet the data did not discriminate the difference.

4. The "new view" of corporate taxation provided a theoretical base for Hartman's hypothesis. See Hartman (1984) and Slemrod (1990) for empirical evidence.

5. Gordon and MacKie-Mason (1994) view the corporate tax as primarily a backstop to the personal tax on labor income, and formulate an optimal tax system in home and host countries in the presence of income shifting in the domestic economy and across the border.

6. Hines and Rice (1990) report that American companies register extraordinarily high profit rates in tax havens, although tax havens enhance tax collection by the U.S. government due to high after-tax returns and small foreign tax credit on income repatriated from tax havens.

7. A more comprehensive analysis including exchange rate changes and substitution between different goods and intertemporal substitution is carried out by Bovenberg (1989).

8. Hines (1990) recommends allocating total profits based on the share of expenditure for developing multiple intangibles.

9. Grubert, Goodspeed, and Swenson (1991) did empirical research on the difference in profit rates between U.S. firms and foreign firms in the United States and concluded that about half of the difference is due to the maturation effect, trapped equity effect, and the dollar depreciation after 1985, while the remaining difference is attributable to transfer pricing. They denied the importance of thin capitalization and capital cost differences in explaining the profit rate difference.

10. Alworth (1988) confirms that the tax credit system without deferral in the case of a debt financing and tax depreciation rate equal to the economic depreciation rate remains neutral with respect to transfer pricing, while the source-base taxation system (tax exemption system) provides an incentive to transfer profit out of the home country to a low-tax country.

REFERENCES

Alworth, Julien S. 1988. *The finance, investment, and taxation decisions of multinationals.* Oxford: Basil Blackwell.

Bovenberg, Lans. 1989. The effect of income taxation on international competitiveness and trade flows. *American economic review* 79(5):1045–64.

Feldstein, Martin. 1994. The effects of outbound foreign direct investment on the domestic capital stock. NBER working paper no. 4668.

Frankel, Jacob A.; Razin, Assaf; and Sadka, Efraim. 1992. *International taxation in an integrated world.* Cambridge, Mass.: MIT Press.

Gordon, Roger H. and MacKie-Mason, Jeffrey K. 1994. Why is there corporate taxation in a small open economy? The role of transfer pricing and income shifting. NBER working paper no. 4690.

Grubert, Harry; Goodspeed, Timothy; and Swenson, Debrah. 1991. Explaining the low taxable income of foreign-controlled companies in the United States. Paper presented at NBER conference.

Hamada Koichi and Iwata Kazumasa. 1986. The significance of different saving ratios for the current account: The U.S.-Japan case. NIRA output.

Hamada Koichi and Iwata Kazumasa. 1989. On the international capital ownership pattern at the turn of the twenty-first century. *European economic review* 33:1056–85.

Harris, David; Morck, Randall; Slemrod, Joel; and Yeung, Bernard. 1991. Income shifting in U.S. multinational corporations. NBER working paper no. 3924.

Hartman, David. 1984. Tax policy and foreign direct investment in the United States. *Tax journal* 37(4):475–87.

Hines, James R. 1990. The transfer pricing problem: where the profits are. NBER working paper no. 3538.

Hines, James R. and Rice, Eric M. 1990. Fiscal paradise: Foreign tax havens and American business. NBER working paper no. 3477.

Iwata Kazumasa and Yoshida Atsushi. 1990. Capital cost of business investment in Japan and the United States under tax reform. *Japan and the world economy* 2(1):23–45.

Iwata Kazumasa; Suzuki Ikuo; and Yoshida Atsushi. 1986. Zeisei to setsubi tōshi no shikon kosuto. *Keizai bunseki* 107 (Economic Research Institute, Economic Planning Agency, February).

Jorgenson, Dale W. and Yun, Kun-Young. 1991. *Tax reform and the cost of capital.* Oxford: Oxford University Press.

Jun, Joosung. 1989. Tax policy and international direct investment. NBER working paper no. 3048.

King, Marvyn A. and Fullerton, Don. 1984. *The taxation of income from capital: A comparative study of the United States, the United Kingdom, Sweden, and West Germany.* Chicago: University of Chicago Press.

Organization for Economic Cooperation and Development (OECD). 1979. *Transfer pricing and multinational enterprises.* Paris: OECD.

————. 1993. Tax aspects of transfer pricing within multinational enterprises: The United States proposed regulations. Tax documents. Paris: OECD.

Shoven, John B. and Tachibanaki Toshiaki. 1988. The taxation of income from capital in Japan. In *Government policy towards industry in the United States and Japan*, ed. John Shoven. Cambridge: Cambridge University Press.

Sinn, Hans-Werner. 1990. Taxation and the birth of foreign subsidiaries. NBER working paper no. 3519.

Slemrod, Joel. 1990. Tax effects on foreign direct investment in the United States: Evidence from a cross-country comparison. In *Taxation in the Global Economy*, ed. Assaf Razin and Joel Slemrod. Chicago: University of Chicago Press.

Treasury Department and Internal Revenue Service. 1988. A study of intercompany pricing. Discussion draft (October 18).

U.S. Taxation and International
Capital Flows Since 1980

JOEL SLEMROD

THE OBJECTIVE OF this paper is to examine what impact the changes in the U.S. federal tax system since 1980 have had on capital flows between the United States and foreign countries, with particular emphasis on the flows between the United States and Japan. It will investigate the flows of both portfolio investment and foreign direct investment.

The paper is organized as follows. Part I offers a chronological overview of the important U.S. tax changes since 1981. Part II provides additional detail on the changes that affected foreign direct investment flows, and Part III briefly summarizes the changes affecting portfolio investment. Part IV examines the relationships between taxation and inflation, and Part V reviews the issues involved in establishing a link between the tax changes and capital flows.

I. TAX CHANGES SINCE 1981

The Economic Recovery Tax Act of 1981 (ERTA)

Ronald Reagan had campaigned on a promise to reduce the size of government and the taxes it levies, and once in office his administration began to put together a package of individual tax rate reductions and investment incentives. There were two principal planks in his original proposal. The first would lower all individual tax rates by ten percent a year for three years. The second would shorten the depreciable lifetimes of capital assets, to ten years for all plant and buildings, and to either five or three years for machinery and equipment.

170

After some initial resistance from the opposition Democratic party, the political dynamic changed so that the Democrats and Republicans began to add more and more tax relief to the legislation. The final piece of legislation contained a slightly less drastic overall cut in individual rates (five percent in the first year followed by a further ten percent cut in each of the following two years), but provided an immediate drop in the highest rate from 70 percent to 50 percent. It also added a host of other revenue-reducing provisions. These included the introduction of tax-exempt savings certificates (called "All-Savers" Certificates); extending eligibility for Individual Retirement Accounts (under which up to $2,000 per earner can be designated to a special account, entitling the contributor to a tax deduction, with the proceeds taxable upon withdrawal); a limited deduction for the earnings of one spouse in a two-earner family; and a large increase in the tax-exempt amount for estate tax purposes.

The investment incentives were embodied in the new tax depreciation schedules, contained in the Accelerated Cost Recovery System. Under its provisions, most buildings and structures could be written off over a 15-year period, with a five-year period for most equipment. The act also provided that a further acceleration of depreciation schedules would begin in 1984. Furthermore, there was a significant liberalization of the conditions under which a company without current tax liability could benefit from the investment incentives, by allowing the users of capital assets to be treated for tax purposes as leasing the assets from another firm with tax liability ("safe harbor" leasing), with the tax benefits shared between the lessor and lessee.

One other aspect of ERTA has proven to have lasting importance. It called for indexing of tax brackets, personal exemptions, and the standard deduction, beginning after 1984. This change eliminated the automatic increase in real tax revenues due to inflation-driven "bracket creep."

The tax changes were just one part of the Reagan administration's strategy for the budget and national security. The other parts envisioned were substantial cuts in non-defense expenditures and substantial increases in defense expenditures. It soon became apparent, however, that large non-defense cuts were not likely to be enacted. This left the combination of tax reductions and expenditure increases, a scenario that was inconsistent with another campaign pledge of Ronald Reagan—to eliminate the budget deficits that had become standard federal fiscal practice in the late 1970s.

Ardent supply-siders maintained that the reduced tax rates would induce enough additional labor supply and other taxable-income generating activities that the predicted revenue loss would be substantially mitigated. Second, the macroeconomic projections on which the revenue forecasts were based were exceedingly optimistic; the set of economic assumptions has been known as the "Rosy Scenario."

Faith that either of these two factors would forestall large deficits was not, however, widespread. The ink on ERTA had hardly dried when many within the administration and Congress began to look for ways to increase tax revenues, though without rescinding the basic features of ERTA. This momentum led to revenue increases (not officially "tax increases") in the years after 1981. Because of the political untouchability of the individual income tax rate structure, the increases instead took the form of "base-broadeners," "loophole closures," or improved tax enforcement.

The Tax Equity and Fiscal Responsibility Act of 1982 (TEFRA)

TEFRA took back some of the investment incentives introduced by ERTA. First, the depreciable basis of a fixed asset was to be reduced by one-half of the applicable investment tax credit. Next, the second round of depreciation speedups, scheduled for 1985 and 1986, was abandoned. Third, "safe harbor" leasing was repealed. These provisions, plus a series of other miscellaneous base-broadeners, several of which served primarily to accelerate tax payments that would otherwise have been made later, were estimated to raise $20 billion per year.

The Social Security Amendments of 1983

Sparked by the prospect that the pay-as-you-go Social Security system would run out of funds in the near future, in 1981 the Reagan administration created a bipartisan task force, chaired by Alan Greenspan, to address the funding and benefits of the Social Security system. The proposals of the Greenspan commission were largely adopted as the Social Security Amendments. They addressed the short-term crisis by accelerating increases in payroll taxes planned for 1990 to 1984. In addition, new civilian employees of the federal government and non-profit organizations were brought into the Social Security system, providing short-term revenues in excess of benefits paid. The payroll tax on self-employed individuals was increased toward the sum of the employer and employee rate on employees. Finally, up to half of Social Security benefits was made subject to federal income tax, for high-income families only. Changes in Social Security benefit payments, other than a six-month delay in benefit increases, were entirely prospective—phasing in between the years 2000 and 2022 an increase in the retirement age for full benefits from 65 to 67.

The Deficit Reduction Act of 1984 (DEFRA)

The tax legislation passed in 1984 continued in the spirit of TEFRA by raising revenues without resorting to explicit increases in tax rates. It also continued to rescind some of the investment incentives offered in the 1981 legislation. In particular, it increased the depreciable life of buildings from 15 years to 18 years and put further restrictions on asset leasing. On the individual side, it increased the holding period required for preferential long-term capital gains treatment from six months to one year, and repealed (before its scheduled enactment date) an ERTA provision that would have exempted from taxation a limited amount of interest income.

The Tax Reform Act of 1986 (TRA)

The complex set of forces that produced TRA can be reduced to the uneasy coalition between "supply-side" Republicans, who favored lower marginal tax rates on individuals, and reform-oriented Democrats, who wanted to rid the tax system of horizontal inequities and tax "loopholes" that could be exploited by some to the detriment of others. Encouraging this coalition from the sidelines, and to an important extent within the government, were economists who favored a comprehensive income tax and restoring a "level playing field" for alternative investments and economic activities.

Proposals to move the income tax system in line with a broad-base, low-rate philosophy (the most prominent of which were the Bradley-Gephardt bill and Kemp-Kasten bills) had been seriously discussed since the early 1980s. Perhaps partially in anticipation of the Democratic presidential candidate promising tax reform, President Reagan called for a Treasury Department study of the tax system in his January 1984 State of the Union Address. Soon after the 1984 election, won resoundingly by Reagan, the Treasury delivered its report, entitled *Tax Reform for Fairness, Simplicity, and Economic Growth*. This plan proposed to compress the 14 (15, for single filers) brackets, with a top rate of 50 percent, into three brackets with rates of 15, 25, and 35 percent. Overall individual tax liability was to fall by eight percent, with the shortfall made up by corporation tax increases. Several base-broadeners were proposed for the individual income tax, including eliminating the deduction for state and local taxes and a floor for deductible charitable contributions. The standard corporation tax rate was to be reduced from 46 to 33 percent. At the same time, the Treasury proposed that the investment tax credit be repealed, and the accelerated cost recovery system be replaced by a system closer to economic depreciation.

There were two innovative aspects of the proposal with regard to capital income taxation. The first was a comprehensive scheme for indexing the measurement of capital income, including capital gains, interest income and deductions, inventory and depreciation allowances. The indexing was to work as follows. For property other than inventory assets and debt instruments, the taxpayer's original cost basis used to calculate taxable capital gains would be indexed for inflation during the period the property was held. The cost basis adjustment was to be based on inflation tables using the Consumer Price Index for Urban Households (CPI), which would specify inflation adjustment factors by calendar quarters that the asset was held.

For inventories, taxpayers would be permitted to use an indexed FIFO (first in, first out) method in addition to the standard LIFO (last in, first out) and FIFO methods. Under this proposed method, inventories would be indexed using inflation adjustment factors based on the Consumer Price Index by, for example, applying the percentage increase in the CPI to the FIFO cost of the number of units in beginning inventory which does not exceed the number of units in ending inventory.

The indexing proposal with respect to indebtedness applied to interest rather than principal. A fraction of interest receipts would be excluded from taxable income and a corresponding fraction of interest payments would not be deductible. The fraction was designed to proxy for the portion of the nominal interest rate due to expected inflation, and was to be modified annually to reflect changes in the rate of inflation. The fraction was calculated assuming a constant six percent real, before-tax, interest rate. For example, for an inflation rate of two percent, the fraction was 0.25; at a six percent inflation rate it was 0.50, etc. Notably mortgage interest was not subject to the proposed indexing, so that mortgage interest secured by the taxpayer's principal was to remain fully deductible. The proposal was to apply to corporations' interest income and expense.

The proposed new system of capital cost recovery, dubbed the Real Cost Recovery System (RCRS), would adjust depreciation allowances by means of a basis adjustment. Under RCRS, the remaining unrecovered basis of an asset would be increased each year by the inflation rate and the fixed depreciation rate applicable to the asset's class would be applied against the resulting adjusted basis.

The second particularly innovative proposal allowed corporations to deduct from taxable income 50 percent of dividends paid out of previously taxed earnings, a proposal designed to relieve the double taxation of dividends inherent in the classical system of taxing corporate income, which arguably distorts a variety of decisions concerning corporate financial policy.

This proposal, commonly known as Treasury I, was not embraced by President Reagan and, after gauging public reaction to the plan, a second plan, dubbed Treasury II, was presented in May 1985. This plan retained the basic Treasury I philosophy of broadening the base while lowering statutory rates, but altered several key details. The comprehensive indexing of capital income measurement was dropped, the 50 percent dividend-paid deduction was reduced to 10 percent, and a 50 percent exclusion for long-term capital gains was back.

Congress then began lengthy deliberations about the tax reform. Many observers and participants in the debate were critical of a process devoting so much time to debating a revenue-neutral change in the tax system, while the specter of large deficits loomed. After a long process featuring several periods when the process looked to be derailed, a tax reform bill was passed by both houses of Congress and signed into law by President Reagan on October 22, 1986—the Tax Reform Act of 1986 (TRA).

TRA compressed the multiple bracket rate structure into two brackets, taxed at 15 percent and 28 percent. The threshold for being subject to individual income tax was greatly enlarged by increasing the standard deduction (for joint filers from about $4,000 to $5,000) and increasing the personal exemption allowances from slightly over $1,000 to $2,000. It repealed several deviations from a comprehensive tax base, such as the two-earner deduction, the sales tax deduction (but not the deduction for state and local income or property taxes), and consumer interest deduction. It also eliminated the 60 percent exclusion of long-term capital gains, increasing the top rate on realized long-term capital gains from 20 to 28 percent.

On the corporate side, the standard rate was reduced from 46 to 34 percent, with the investment tax credit eliminated, depreciation schedules stretched out, and the alternative minimum tax tightened. Neither the indexing nor dividends-paid deduction of Treasury I were included in the bill.

The bill was designed to be approximately revenue neutral and distributionally neutral. Total individual income tax revenues were to fall by seven percent, with the revenue shortfall made up by higher corporate tax revenues. The total effective tax rate on new investment probably increased (by one estimate from 38 to 41 percent), because the lower corporate rate did not offset the loss of the investment tax credit and accelerated depreciation. The dispersion of effective tax rates by asset type and sector did decline significantly.

The Omnibus Budget Reconciliation Act of 1990

Soon after President Bush abandoned his "no new taxes" pledge in 1990, a budget package was passed in Congress that would reduce the deficit by $500 billion over a five-year period, of which slightly less than $200 billion was to come from tax increases. A new top individual tax rate of 31 percent was established, although the top rate on capital gains was kept at 28 percent. Phaseouts for the benefits of the personal exemptions and itemized deductions increased the implicit top marginal tax rate above 31 percent. The alternative minimum tax rate was raised to 24 percent from 21 percent. Federal excise taxes on gasoline, tobacco, and alcoholic beverages were increased, and a new luxury goods tax, 10 percent on the price above a specified amount for cars, boats, jewelry, furs, and planes, was adopted. The payroll tax for Medicare was extended, as was the earned income tax credit.

II. CHANGES IN THE TAXATION OF
FOREIGN DIRECT INVESTMENT[1]

Indirect Influences of ERTA and TRA on the
Attractiveness of Foreign Ownership of U.S.-Located Assets

The tax acts passed before 1986 did not contain any major changes in the provisions that directly affect the incentives for foreign direct investment (FDI). The acceleration of depreciation allowances in ERTA applied to all businesses operating in the United States, regardless of whether they are domestic or foreign owned. On the surface these changes made investment located in the United States more attractive relative to investment abroad, regardless of who owns the investment. That view has, though, been challenged by Scholes and Wolfson (1990), who argue that a decrease in taxes on U.S.-located investment such as in ERTA will be a deterrent to foreign ownership of this capital, and an increase in effective tax rates as in TRA will cause greater foreign ownership of U.S. local capital. To see their argument, consider a foreign firm resident in a country that taxes on the basis of worldwide income and offers a tax credit for income taxes paid to foreign governments. If the U.S. average tax rate is below the foreign statutory rate, and ignoring the benefits of deferral, the total effective tax rate on a U.S. investment will be unchanged by the increase in the U.S. effective tax rate. To put it another way, the increased U.S. taxation is offset by increased credits offered by the foreign government. If the total effective tax rate faced by foreigners stays unchanged, when the tax rate faced by U.S. investors increases, the relative tax rate of foreigners declines, causing a shift in ownership of U.S.-located assets to foreign corporations. Thus the counterintuitive prediction of this analysis is that increases in U.S. corporate taxation will increase foreign ownership of U.S.-located capital, and decreases in U.S. effective tax rates will decrease foreign ownership.

The analysis rests on two assumptions that are subject to some qualification. First, of the six principal countries exporting capital to the United States, only two (Japan and the United Kingdom) operate a worldwide system with foreign tax credit. France and the Netherlands operate a territorial system, so that foreign-source income of their resident multinationals is untaxed by the home country. Although Canada and Germany in theory have a worldwide system, by treaty with the United States repatriated dividends bear no further taxation. For multinationals in these latter four countries, the effective tax rate on FDI in the United States is no different than for U.S. companies, so that the analysis does not apply. Japan and the United Kingdom have, however, accounted for slightly than half of the six countries' FDI in the United States in the past several years. Nevertheless, the assumption that the investing country operates a worldwide system of taxation does not apply universally. Furthermore, even for Japan and the United Kingdom, the Scholes-Wolfson argument applies only to the extent the multinationals are in an excess limitation position and are repatriating income that is subject to additional taxation in the home country. If most income is retained by the U.S. subsidiaries, then the U.S. tax rate is the relevant one for all investors and an increase does not reduce the relative tax rate faced by Japanese or U.K. investors.

Second, the Scholes-Wolfson hypothesis says that an increase in U.S. corporate taxation reduces the relative tax burden on foreign-owned investment, but certainly does not imply a decline in the absolute level of taxation. Thus the hypothesis suggests a change in the ownership pattern of existing capital, but is consistent with a decline in the rate of increase of foreign-owned capital due to the heavier absolute tax burden imposed by TRA.

The Scholes-Wolfson model was certainly consistent with the sharp increase in inward FDI from Japan and the United Kingdom following TRA. FDI from these two countries accounted for about three-quarters of the 1985–88 increase in inward FDI to the United States and of outlays by foreigners for acquisition and establishment of U.S. business enterprises. To some extent, though, this large rate of increase simply reflected the worldwide increase in FDI from these two countries. For example, worldwide FDI from Japan (measured in dollars) doubled between 1986 and 1988, though the share going to the United States did increase over this period.

Swenson (1992) provided some corroborating evidence for this hypothesis, finding a positive association between a manufacturing sector's average effective tax rate and inward FDI, and a higher estimated coefficient on the tax rate for investment from countries with worldwide tax systems than for investment from countries with territorial tax systems. Somewhat troubling, though, she also found a negative relation between marginal effective tax rates and FDI.

More recent research has cast doubt on the empirical significance of this finding. Auerbach and Hassett (1993) point out that the Scholes-Wolfson argument applies to new asset purchases rather than to foreign acquisitions of existing assets, but the surge in Japanese and U.K. FDI was largely in acquisitions, and is thus not consistent with the model. They conclude that taxes do not explain recent FDI trends in the United States. Collins, Kemsley, and Shackelford (1993) cast doubt on the Scholes-Wolfson hypothesis in their examination of the U.S. tax returns of a sample of corporations that were acquired by U.K. and Japanese investors between 1987 and 1989. They conclude that, in general, the tax advantages of these acquisitions were very small relative to the size of the acquisitions, and that TRA "did not significantly enhance the competitive advantage of foreign firms in the U.S. acquisition market" (p. 23).

I conclude that the provisions of ERTA and TRA not directly applicable to FDI did not tilt the playing field for or against foreign ownership. However, the Tax Reform Act of 1986 did have major implications for the taxation of multinationals' income, and therefore for the incentives for foreign direct investment to and from the United States. These changes did not, though, occur because of any premeditated shift in views about the appropriate tax regime. On the contrary, most of the changes were the side effects of a domestically focused strategy of lowering corporate tax rates while broadening the tax base. A second element was that, in order to keep the reform package revenue-neutral in the face of drastically lowered tax rates, there was a need for provisions that either raised revenue or limited that revenue loss from other aspects of the tax reform package. Many of the international tax changes in TRA fall into the latter category, as will be discussed further below.

Before detailing the important tax changes in TRA, I next offer a brief overview of the rules that govern the taxation of multinationals.

An Overview of the Taxation of the Income from Foreign Direct Investment

Each country in the world asserts the right to tax the income that is generated within its borders, including the income earned by foreign multinational corporations. Countries do, however, differ widely in the tax rate they apply, the definition of the tax base, and in the special incentives they offer for investment. Nevertheless, the first and quantitatively most important tax burden on FDI comes from the government of the country where the investment is located (known as the "host" country).

Many countries, including the United States, Japan, and the United Kingdom also assert the right to tax the worldwide income of their residents, including resident corporations. As a rule, the income of foreign subsidiaries is recognized only upon repatriation of earnings through dividends, interest, or royalty payments. In order to avoid the potentially onerous burden of two layers of taxation, those countries that tax on a worldwide basis also offer a credit for income and withholding taxes paid to foreign governments. The total credit available in any given year is usually limited to the home country's tax liability on the foreign-source income, although credits earned in excess of the limitation may often be carried forward or backward to offset excess limitations for other years. Several other countries, including France and the Netherlands, operate a "territorial" system of taxing their resident corporations, under which foreign-source business income is completely exempt from home-country taxation.[2]

This would be the end of the story if the geographical location of income was not a matter of dispute. In fact, even if all the information necessary to ascertain the location of income was costlessly available, the conceptual basis for locating income is controversial (Ault and Bradford 1990). In reality corporations do not have the incentive to fully reveal all the information on which to base a determination of the geographical source of income. For any pattern of real investment decisions, a multinational has the incentive to shift the apparent source of income out of high-tax countries into low-tax countries. This can be accomplished through, for example, the pricing of intercompany transfers of goods and intangible assets, or doing borrowing through subsidiaries in high-tax countries. Note that this incentive applies regardless of whether the home country operates a territorial or worldwide system of taxation.

Much of the complexity of the taxation of foreign-source income arises from the attempt of countries to defend their revenue base against the fungibility of income tax bases. Complex rules cover standards for acceptable transfer pricing, allocation rules for interest expense and intangibles, and taxing on an accrual basis certain types of income. It is impossible to concisely summarize the variety of rules that countries employ to determine the location of income. In some countries the statutes are not as important as the outcomes of case-by-case negotiations between representatives of the multinationals and the countries involved. In other cases the source rules are governed by bilateral tax treaties. What is clear, however, is that the de facto rules that govern the sourcing of income are at least as important for understanding the effective taxation of foreign direct investment as the tax rates, depreciation rules, and tax credits.

The U.S. System of Taxing the Income from Foreign Direct Investment

The United States operates a worldwide system of taxation. Thus both domestic-source and foreign-source income of U.S. multinationals is subject to U.S. taxation. The income of foreign subsidiaries[3] is not, however, taxed as accrued but instead enters the tax base of the U.S. parent only upon repatriation of dividends, at which time it is "grossed up" by the average tax rate paid to foreign governments. The grossed-up dividend, minus certain expenses of the multinational allocated to foreign-source income, enter into the taxable income of the parent. Foreign-source income of the parent also includes interest and royalty payments from subsidiaries and certain types of "passive" income on an accrual basis, plus the foreign-source income of foreign branch operations.

In general, income taxes paid by foreign affiliates to foreign governments can be credited against U.S. tax liability. This credit is, however, limited to the U.S. tax liability on the foreign-source income, which is approximately equal to the U.S. statutory corporation tax rate multiplied by the net foreign-source income of the subsidiary. Multinationals whose potentially creditable foreign taxes exceed the limitation on credits are said to be in an excess credit position. These excess credits may be carried forward for five years (or backward for two years) without interest to be used if and when the parent's potentially creditable taxes fall short of the limitation. If the potentially creditable taxes are less than the limit on credits to be taken in a given year, the corporation is said to be in an *excess limitation* (or *deficit of credit*) position. Distinguishing the excess credit and excess limitation situation is critically important, because the tax-related incentives for real and financial behavior are often quite different for a corporation depending on which situation it is in.

The Tax Reform Act of 1986 and the Changed Incentives for Outward Foreign Direct Investment

The three most significant aspects of TRA for outward investment, in order of importance, were as follows:

1. the reduction in the statutory corporate rate from 46 percent to 34 percent, and the resulting increase in the number of firms in an excess credit situation;

2. the change in the rules governing the sourcing of income and the allocation of expenses (most significantly, interest) between domestic and foreign-source income; and

3. the tightening of the foreign tax credit limiting the averaging of different types of income.

The single most important aspect of TRA for outward FDI was the reduction in the statutory rate of corporation income tax from 46 percent to 34 percent. Many of the repercussions of the new law follow from this change.

To see this, a brief digression on the impact of TRA on domestic investment is required. It is well known that the net effect of the tax system on the incentive to invest depends not only on the statutory rate but also on, among other things, the schedule of depreciation allowances, the rate and scope of investment tax credits, the source of financing, and the rate of inflation. TRA eliminated the investment tax credits that previously applied to equipment and machinery, and provided generally less generous depreciation allowances, both of which tended to offset the tax rate reduction. Most analysts concluded that the net effect of these provisions was to slightly increase the effective corporate-level tax on new domestic investment, an important alternative to FDI.

An analysis of how these same changes affected the effective tax rate on FDI must proceed quite differently because, with certain exceptions, foreign-source income of foreign subsidiaries enters the parent's tax base only to the extent that dividends are repatriated. There is thus no calculation of foreign-source taxable income from which depreciation allowances are deducted and against which investment tax credits can be offset. The tax base is simply dividends received minus allocable deductions, grossed up by the average rate of foreign taxation (calculated using an earnings and profits measure of taxable income, which is not sensitive to legislated changes in the tax depreciation schedules used for domestically located assets,[4] investment credits, etc.). To that base is applied the corporate statutory tax rate.

Thus, ignoring the source-of-income rules discussed below, the corporate tax changes of TRA reduced the statutory rate from 46 percent to 34 percent but did not broaden the tax base, resulting in an unambiguous reduction in the tax rate on income from FDI. Assuming that the taxes imposed by the foreign governments remained unchanged,[5] it follows that the amount of additional taxation imposed by the United States upon repatriation either stayed the same or declined. It stayed at zero for multinationals whose average[6] tax rate paid to foreign governments exceeds 46 percent. Any multinational subject to an average tax rate by foreign governments between 34 percent and 46 percent had formerly been paying taxes upon repatriation, but under the new rate would no longer be liable for any additional taxes. For firms paying less than a 34 percent average tax rate to foreign governments, the tax due upon repatriation would fall substantially, although not to zero.[7]

The other important implication of the reduction of the U.S. statutory rate from 46 percent to 34 percent is that a much higher fraction of U.S. multinationals are likely to be in an excess credit situation, because the average tax paid to foreign governments exceeds 34 percent.[8] For a firm in excess credit status, every additional dollar paid in tax to a foreign government generates a foreign tax credit that cannot be used immediately, and has some value to the multinational only if the firm will be in an excess limitation position either in the next five years (the carryforward limit) or had been in an excess limitation position in the previous two years (the carryback limit). Thus a U.S. multinational in an excess credit position is likely to be much more sensitive to difference in foreign effective tax rates than a firm in an excess limitation situation.[9] This increases the relative attractiveness of investment in a low-tax foreign country such as Ireland compared to a high-tax country such as Germany.

A firm in excess credit status can reduce the present value of its tax burden to the extent it can increase the limit on foreign tax credits. This increases the importance of the rules determining the source, for U.S. tax purposes, of worldwide income. Holding worldwide income constant, if a dollar of income is shifted from domestic source to foreign source, it increases the foreign tax credit limitation by one dollar and allows 34 cents more of foreign taxes to be credited immediately against U.S. tax liability. Only to the extent that foreign governments enforce the same source rules will there be an offsetting increase in foreign tax liability.

One existing source rule that becomes more important applies to production for export. According to current regulations, between 40 and 50 percent of the income from domestic U.S. production of export goods can effectively be allocated to foreign-source income. For a multinational in an excess credit position, this has the effect of reducing the effective tax rate on domestic investment for export by as much as a half. Thus, if a contemplated FDI is to produce goods for sales outside the United States, the alternative of domestic

U.S. production has become relatively tax favored for those firms that have shifted into excess credit status, in spite of the base-broadening aspect of TRA. This reasoning would not, though, apply to FDI designed to reexport to the United States, because the alternative of domestic production for internal consumption does not benefit from the export source rule.

Interest expenses of the U.S. parent corporation must be allocated to either U.S. or foreign-source income. The general rule is to allocate on the basis of the book value of assets, so that interest expenses deductible from foreign-source income are equal to total interest payments multiplied by the fraction of worldwide assets represented by assets expected to generate foreign-source income. Although TRA did not significantly alter this allocation formula, it did add a "one-taxpayer" rule, under which corporations that are members of an affiliated group are consolidated for the purpose of allocating interest expenses between U.S. and foreign sources.[10] In the absence of this rule a multinational could load its debt into a U.S. subsidiary with no foreign-source income and have the interest expense be allocated entirely to U.S.-source income, thus maximizing foreign-source income and the limitation on foreign tax credits. With the one-taxpayer rule, a fraction of these interest payments has to be allocated to foreign-source income regardless of the legal structure of the multinational.

For multinationals in excess credit position that are forced to reallocate interest payments, this provision increases the average cost of capital of domestic or foreign investment to the extent debt finance is used. It also increases the marginal cost of foreign investment, because foreign investment increases the amount of interest payments that must be allocated abroad, which decreases foreign-source income and therefore the amount of foreign taxes that are immediately creditable.[11] This provision is obviously most important for multinationals with a high debt-to-capital ratio.

TRA also changed the operation of the foreign tax credit by creating separate ("basket") limitations for certain categories of income. Foreign taxes imposed on taxable income in a particular basket can only offset U.S. taxes due on that category of income. There are eight separate baskets, including passive income, high withholding tax interest, and financial services income. In some cases (e.g., passive income), the objective was to prevent fungible income from being earned in low-tax rate foreign jurisdictions and thus increasing the amount of available foreign tax credits that could offset taxes paid on other income to foreign governments. In other cases (e.g., high withholding tax interest), the objective was to prevent multinationals (often banks) in an excess limit position from paying effectively high withholding taxes (which, due to the excess limit, could be immediately credited against U.S. tax liability) in return for favorable pretax terms of exchange (i.e., higher than otherwise pretax interest rates on loans). These objectives share the common thread of limiting the revenue loss to the United States that can arise from manipulation of the foreign tax credit mechanism.

In general, the creation of separate foreign tax credit baskets increases the effective taxation of foreign-source income, because it makes it more difficult in certain cases to credit foreign income taxes against U.S. tax liability. In addition, the baskets can add significant complexity to the typical multinational's compliance procedure, and to this extent the provisions add a hidden tax burden to multinational operation.

The Tax Reform Act of 1986 and the Changed Incentives for Inward Foreign Direct Investment

Foreign corporations, and U.S. corporations controlled by a foreign corporation, that are engaged in a trade or business in the United States are subject to taxation according to rules that are roughly comparable to those that apply to U.S. corporations. Thus, the reduction of the statutory rate, elimination of the investment tax credit, and changes in depreciation schedules in TRA apply directly to foreign subsidiaries. Whether changes made inward FDI more attractive was discussed above. The United States also imposes a "withholding" tax of 30 percent, modified by treaty to a much lower figure for many countries, on payments from corporations within the United States to foreign corporations. These withholding tax rates were not affected by TRA.

TRA did introduce a new branch profits tax, which imposes a 30 percent tax (often reduced by treaty) on the repatriated profits and certain interest payments of a U.S. branch of a foreign corporation. This tax, which affects primarily financial institutions, was designed to equalize the tax treatment of foreign corporations operating through a U.S. branch and those operating through a wholly owned domestic subsidiary.

III. CHANGES IN THE TAXATION OF FOREIGN PORTFOLIO INCOME

Foreign investment can also occur through the purchase of debt and equity securities by individuals. In this case the corporate tax system of the individual's resident country is not relevant. Relevant are the corporate and withholding tax systems of the host country, and the personal tax system of the home country of the investor, including whether foreign withholding taxes are creditable against domestic tax liability, and the relative taxation of income from interest, dividends, capital gains, and foreign exchange.

Bovenberg, Andersson, Aramaki, and Chand (1990) have done a careful study of the evolution of taxation on portfolio flows between the United States and Japan in the 1980s. Their results are summarized in Table 1. From the point

TABLE 1

Tax Wedges on Foreign Portfolio Flows between the U.S. and Japan:
1980, 1984, and 1987

	U.S. Saver Investing in Japan			U.S. Saver Investing in the U.S.			Japanese Saver Investing in the U.S.		
	1980	1984	1987	1980	1984	1987	1980	1984	1987
Debt Instrument									
Host country	−1.20	−0.47	−0.22	−5.57	−6.55	−2.49	−4.43	−6.55	−2.49
Residence country	1.95	1.35	1.00	3.27	3.23	1.88	0.13	1.26	0.82
Total	0.75	0.88	0.78	−2.30	−3.32	−0.61	−4.30	−5.29	−1.67
Equity Instrument									
Host country	6.64	7.71	6.50	1.76	0.66	1.81	1.78	0.72	1.87
Residence country	1.00	0.85	1.28	0.82	0.80	1.19	0.05	0.12	0.12
Total	7.64	8.57	7.78	2.58	1.46	3.00	1.83	0.84	1.99

SOURCE: Bovenberg, Andersson, Aramaki, and Chand (1990).

of view of a U.S. saver, the total tax rate on a U.S. investment fell between 1980 and 1984, but then rose above 1980 levels in 1987; this was primarily due to the investment incentives in the 1981 tax act, repealed by 1986. These tax changes are, of course, irrelevant for a U.S. investor contemplating investing in Japanese assets; the time pattern was opposite for this case, with the 1984 tax wedge being the highest, but 1987 ending up approximately at its 1980 level.

From the point of view of investment in the United States, the tax wedge fell between 1980 and 1984, and rose by 1987 to a higher level than in 1980, for both Japanese and U.S. savers.

IV. TAXATION AND INFLATION

One potentially important factor in the 1980s is the link between inflation and taxation. Because the U.S. tax system (as well as the Japanese and all other countries') mismeasures real taxable income in the presence of inflation, basing tax liability on nominal rather than real capital income, exogenous changes in inflation can have important effects on the effective rate of tax on the returns to saving and investment. For example, because depreciation allowances are based on historic rather than replacement cost, increased inflation reduces the real value of these allowances and increases the effective rate of tax on investment. Similarly, the effective tax rate on inventories increases as inflation increases, in the absence of some form of inflation adjustment to the value of inventories. At the same time, nominal rather than real interest payments are allowed as deductions to leveraged investors, and are taxed fully as income to savers. Nominal, rather than real, capital gains are subject to tax.

The inventory, capital allowance, and capital gains effects raise the effective tax rate, but nominal interest deductibility lowers it. The net effect depends on the details of the tax system. A careful study by the OECD (1991) concluded that in the United States (and Japan) increased inflation would increase the effective combined corporate and personal tax rate for retained earnings and new equity-financed investment, but reduce it for debt-financed investment, so as to leave the overall average tax rate unchanged.

In an international context, there is another interaction between taxes and inflation that must be considered. In principle, the United States levies personal tax on a residence basis, meaning that the effective personal tax rate does not depend on the country where the capital income originates. One reason this fails in practice is that, even though the United States applies the residence principle to nominal returns, real returns are taxed differently to the extent that inflation rates diverge across countries. In particular, portfolio investments denominated in the currency of low-inflation countries benefit from the preferential tax treatment of capital gains, because these securities earn a large part of their returns in the form of an exchange rate appreciation, which until 1986 were taxed at the preferential capital gains tax rate in the United States.

As Bovenberg *et al.* point out, this is important because during the 1980s Japan had a lower expected inflation rate than the United States. Assuming that this was reflected in exchange rates, this implies that the yen was expected to appreciate relative to the dollar throughout this period. This in turn means that Japanese assets were expected to yield a larger part of their return to U.S. investors in the form of preferentially taxed capital gains. Thus the personal tax system favored Japanese debt instruments over U.S. debt instruments, although according to Bovenberg *et al.* this was more than offset by favorable U.S. tax treatment at the corporate level.[12]

V. U.S. TAX POLICY AND NET CAPITAL FLOWS

The organizing framework for this section is that total net capital flows from the United States are equal to the difference between national saving and national investment, and therefore the effect of taxation on capital flows depends on how it affects saving and investment. For this reason in what follows I will investigate each of these two components separately. Of course, the two may be interrelated to the extent that tax-induced changes in one may, through their effect on real interest rates and exchange rates, affect the other.

According to this framework the flows of direct foreign investment to and from the United States are presumed to be determined by separate, primarily

industrial organization, forces. In a subsection below, I discuss a recent chal-
lenge to this view.

U.S. National Saving

There are two issues here. The first is how changes in tax policy that affect
the government deficit affect national saving. The second is how changes in tax
policy that affect the after-tax rate of return influence the rate of private saving.

Whether these changes in government saving will have a dollar-for-dollar
impact on national saving depends on how much weight one gives to the notion
of "Ricardian equivalence," i.e., the idea that taxpayers realize that current
government deficits must be offset by future net tax increases, and so increase
their private saving to offset this future liability. To the extent that this occurs,
deficits will be accompanied by little if any change in national saving, as private
saving increases offset the declines in government saving.

The empirical relevance of the Ricardian equivalence proposition is, of
course, highly controversial, and cannot be resolved here. The general consensus is that it does not hold in its purest form, so that changes in the time pattern
of government tax collections will not be exactly offset by private saving.

Once the Ricardian equivalence framework is abandoned, the deficit is not
a sufficient statistic to understanding the impact of government fiscal policy on
private saving—one needs to know more details about the intergenerational
transfers engendered by the fiscal policy. For example, a tax cut for elderly
taxpayers will be less likely to be offset by an increase in private saving than a
tax cut that applies primarily to taxpayers at the beginning of their working
lives.

The other potential avenue of tax policy's impact on national saving is
through its effect on the after-tax rate of return received by private savers. The
average personal tax rate on capital income has fallen consistently since 1980,
with discrete drops in 1981 and 1987. Special incentives to save, in particular
the IRA programs, were also introduced in 1981, although largely withdrawn
in the 1986 Act.

In gauging the effect of these changes on private saving, one other change
since 1980 needs to be considered—the change in the economics profession's
views about the interest elasticity of saving. In 1980 many prominent economists argued that this elasticity was high, often citing the 0.4 estimated elasticity
from Michael Boskin's influential 1978 empirical study of saving. However, the
experience of the 1980s, with its widely fluctuating after-tax real rates of interest,
accompanied by steadily declining rates of saving, has tempered this view
somewhat. In a review of the evidence of the 1980s, Skinner and Feenberg
(1990) recently concluded that there was little convincing evidence that private
saving reacts in a significant way to tax changes affecting the rate of return to

saving, and that "positive interest elasticity estimates. . . are fragile and fleeting" (p. 63).

Investment

There is wide agreement that ERTA lowered the cost of capital for investment in the United States, and that DEFRA and TEFRA took back some, but not all, of this reduction. There is less agreement about the impact of TRA on the cost of capital, due to the offsetting effects of the corporate tax rate cut and the elimination of both the investment tax credit and accelerated depreciation; most analysts have concluded that it slightly raised the cost of capital.

How responsive investment is to changes in the cost of capital is a more controversial question. Auerbach and Hassett (1990) concluded, based on an econometric investigation of U.S. investment behavior since 1957, that tax policy may have been given too much prominence in earlier discussions of investment behavior, and that the Tax Reform Act of 1986 played a relatively unimportant role in explaining the level and pattern of investment in equipment and structures after 1986.

Views on U.S. Tax Policy and Capital Flows

Sinn (1988) argued forcefully that the 1981 and 1986 tax reforms "reinforced, if not caused" (p. 327) the major international economic fluctuations of the 1980s, including the wide swings in the dollar exchange rate, massive U.S. capital inflows, and the worldwide recession of the early 1980s. He stresses the importance of ACRS, the accelerated depreciation reform in the 1981 Act, in explaining the capital outflows of the early 1980s. In support of this notion he refers to the fact that U.S. investment "not only failed to shrink in the years following the 1981 reform, it even rose and stayed high despite an excessively high level of U.S. interest rates" (p.328).

With regard to the 1986 tax reform, Sinn concludes that the effective tax on domestic U.S. investment slightly increased, and the tax rate on U.S. savers decreased. To the extent that investment and saving are interest-elastic, these two aspects of the tax reform were self-reinforcing with regard to their effect on capital flows—both would increase net capital outflows from the U.S.

Sinn goes on to argue that the theory that international economic movements were largely driven by U.S. tax policy is fully compatible with movements in exchange rates. The rise of the dollar began in 1981, at the time the investment-oriented tax reform was being designed. Sinn associates the dollar peak in February 1985 with the publication, in November 1984, of the Treasury I tax reform proposal that removed the investment incentives introduced in 1981. This, he argues, is a more plausible trigger for the dollar decline than the Plaza

Accord of 1985, since that came seven months after the dollar's peak and did not produce significant changes in the time path of the exchange rate. Rather, he argues, Treasury I was the important event, because it signaled to far-sighted investors to expect lower interest rates in the United States and a lower value of the dollar in the long run.

Feldstein (1992) has also argued that there was a clear causal link between the increased budget deficit of the early 1980s on the one hand and the higher dollar and enlarged trade deficit—and capital inflows—on the other hand. It was no coincidence, he claims, that both the budget deficit and the trade deficit increased by about three percent of GNP between the beginning and the middle of the 1980s.

Feldstein, though, goes on to caution that these parallel movements should be thought of as a special case rather than as a general phenomenon. More generally, any decrease in national savings will be offset by some combination of decreased national investment and net exports (capital inflows). In the absence of the business investment incentives in ERTA, there might have been less investment and a smaller increase in capital inflows and the trade deficit. He argues that, in the long run, changes in domestic saving are balanced by parallel changes in domestic investment; his own empirical research suggests that each incremental dollar of domestic saving is associated with about 70 cents of increased domestic investment. His conclusion is that, in the long run, sustained increases in budget deficits crowd out domestic investment and are not financed by capital inflows from abroad. This pattern was not observed in the early 1980s because of the extraordinary domestic investment incentives and the incomplete adjustment to the long-run equilibrium.

Frankel (1989) rejects the argument that the investment incentives in ERTA were an important factor in the capital inflow of the early 1980s, and the high real interest rates that accompanied it. This argument is flawed, he argues, because the investment rate always rises in expansions, and the investment increase in the 1983–84 recovery was no greater than its decline in the 1981–82 recession; by 1985 the investment rate was not significantly different from its average level during the 1970s. Furthermore, Frankel claims that the net benefit of the ERTA tax incentives was less than the increase in real interest rates, so that the after-tax real cost of capital to firms was not reduced, and the investment boom was concentrated in sectors such as office computers, suggesting a technological, and non-tax-related, explanation.

The controversy boils down to the relative importance to assign to the relative price effects of the 1981 and 1986 changes and to the deficit-increasing effects of ERTA. How one evaluates this relative importance depends in turn on one's views on the price elasticities of saving and investment and on the degree of Ricardian farsightedness that consumers are endowed with. My own views are that (at least the short-term) elasticities are fairly low, and that consumers are largely not Ricardian. These views imply that the most important aspect of the tax changes of the 1980s for capital flows was the tax cut in 1981 that amounted to three percent of GDP. Thus I favor the Feldstein-Frankel view over that expressed by Sinn.

Does Foreign Direct Investment Matter for Net Capital Flows?

The foregoing discussion leaves untied one loose end concerning the effect of U.S. taxation on net capital inflows: the role of foreign direct investment. Section II of this paper documented the many changes in the taxation of FDI to and from the United States in the 1980s, but in Section V I have adopted a conceptual framework in which the taxation of FDI plays no critical role in aggregate net capital flows; the framework implies that any flow of FDI is offset by a flow of portfolio capital, so that the net capital inflow position is unaffected by the incentives (tax or otherwise) to FDI.

This view has recently been challenged by Feldstein (1994). This paper builds on an earlier work in Feldstein and Horioka (1980), which documents the fact that, across countries, there is a high correlation between domestic saving and domestic investment; they estimate that, for OECD countries, between 70 and 90 percent of a marginal dollar of domestic saving is invested domestically. This is the empirical basis for Feldstein's view, discussed in Section V, that sustained increases in budget deficits eventually crowd out domestic investment.

Feldstein (1994) presents evidence that an extra dollar of national saving remains in domestic portfolio assets *unless* it is used by a multinational corporation to finance a cross-border investment. Thus, such an outbound FDI would reduce the funds available for domestic investment by an equal amount, an effect not offset by any international flow of capital. The cross-country evidence Feldstein examines suggests that each dollar of outbound FDI reduces domestic investment by approximately one dollar, holding national saving constant.

Feldstein's hypothesis has not yet been tested on U.S. time series data, so that it is not known to what extent it can explain the capital flows of the 1980s. Dooley (1990) has argued that in the 1970s and 1980s U.S. net direct investment flows were dominated by net inflows through other financial markets, but he does not directly address Feldstein's (1994) hypothesis. One need not accept the extreme version of the hypothesis to see that it implies that, in order to understand the effect of taxation on net capital flows, one has to consider separately its influence on direct foreign investment flows and on aggregate domestic saving and investment.

VI. CONCLUSIONS

Because the 1980s was a decade marked by both extraordinary capital outflows from the United States to Japan as well as major tax changes in the United
States, it is natural to contemplate the causal relationship, if any, between these
two phenomena. Based on this review of the theory and evidence regarding the
U.S. tax changes and capital flows, I tentatively conclude that the 1981 tax act
was an important cause of the capital flows, mostly because of the large increase
in the federal budget deficit associated with it, and only secondarily because of
its induced increase in domestic investment.

The tax act of 1986 contained some important changes in the taxation of
foreign direct investment of U.S. multinationals. Although a simple analysis
suggests that the net incentives to FDI increased, because there were also
technical changes that made outward FDI less attractive it is difficult to establish
how the net tax incentive changed. Although the standard theory suggests that
any changed incentive to FDI should have little effect on capital flows, recent
empirical evidence has challenged that view.

The prospect of lower U.S. deficits in the 1990s by itself suggests that capital
outflows from the United States to Japan will be lower than in the 1980s. The
conspicuous absence of any prospect for further fundamental U.S. tax reform
in the 1990s implies that it is the path of deficits that will be the principal fiscal
influence on capital outflows in the near future.

NOTES

1. The material in this section is adapted from Slemrod (1990a).

2. By statute, Canada and Germany have worldwide systems of taxation. However,
their tax treaties with the United States provide that repatriated dividends are generally
subject to no further tax liability.

3. The income of foreign branches of U.S. corporations is taxed as accrued. Partly
for tax reasons, most foreign activity of U.S. corporations is carried out by subsidiaries
rather than branches.

4. The depreciation rules used in the calculation of earnings and profits do, however,
change. For example, since 1980 the depreciation rules that apply to property used
overseas have been made less generous. These schedules have tax implications because
they affect the calculation of tax deemed paid by subsidiaries to foreign governments
and the amount of foreign tax credit available, for any given amount of dividends
remitted.

5. Since the passage of TRA, many other countries have enacted tax reforms that
share some of the corporate-rate-reducing, base-broadening aspects of TRA. To the
extent that TRA caused these reforms (or increased their likelihood), the host country

effective tax rate was influenced by the U.S. tax reform. The analysis that follows holds constant the foreign tax system.

6. The average tax rate paid to foreign governments is subject to a degree of control by the multinational via its repatriation policy. By repatriating income primarily from high-tax countries, the average tax rate on its foreign-source income is high and less likely to attract additional U.S. tax liability.

7. Hartman (1985) has argued that, regardless of the excess credit status of the U.S. parent, the level of repatriation tax is irrelevant for the incentive to undertake FDI financed by earnings of the foreign subsidiary. This is because the repatriation tax reduces equally both the return to investment and the opportunity cost of investment (reduced dividends). This argument would not apply to the infusion of new equity capital from the parent. See Jun (1989) for a critique of this view.

8. Grubert and Mutti (1987) quote U.S. Treasury estimates that the fraction of manufacturing multinationals (weighted by worldwide income) in excess credit would increase from 20 percent to 69 percent. Goodspeed and Frisch (1989), using updated corporate tax return information, estimate that the fraction of foreign-source income subject to excess credits would rise from 50 to 78 percent, and from 32 to 82 percent in manufacturing. These calculations, however, consider only the change in statutory rate and do not consider changes in the allocation rules or the separate baskets, discussed below. In addition, neither analysis considers changes, perhaps induced by the U.S. reform, in other countries' tax rates. Perhaps most importantly, the analyses do not take into account any behavioral response of the multinationals.

9. Of course, Hartman's argument implies that, for investment financed by retained earnings, only the host country's tax rate matters even for firms in an excess limitation position, so that no post-TRA increased sensitivity to host country tax rates should be observed.

10. The one-taxpayer rule already effectively applied to the allocation of expenses on research and development.

11. This analysis presumes that the interest allocation rules of foreign governments have not changed.

12. Note that Japanese savers could not deduct the expected capital losses on U.S. assets from their personal taxable income, although they were fully taxed on the higher nominal returns on these assets.

REFERENCES

Auerbach, Alan and Hassett, Kevin. 1990. Investment, tax policy, and the Tax Reform Act of 1986. In *Do taxes matter?: The impact of the Tax Reform Act of 1986,* ed. Joel Slemrod. Cambridge, MA: The MIT Press.

———. 1993. Taxation and foreign direct investment in the United States: A consideration of the evidence. In *Studies in international taxation,* ed. Alberto Giovannini, R. Glenn Hubbard, and Joel Slemrod. Chicago: University of Chicago Press.

Ault, Hugh J. and Bradford, David. 1990. Taxing international income: An analysis of the U.S. system and its economic premises. In *Taxation in the global economy,* ed. Assaf Razin and Joel Slemrod. Chicago: University of Chicago Press and NBER.

Boskin, Michael. 1978. Taxation, saving, and the rate of interest. *Journal of political economy* 86: S3–S27.

Bosworth, Barry P. 1993. *Saving and investment in a global economy.* Washington: The Brookings Institution.

Bovenberg, A. Lans; Andersson, Krister; Aramaki Kenji; and Chand, Sheetal K. 1990. Tax incentives and international capital flows: The case of the United States and Japan. In *Taxation in the global economy,* ed. Assaf Razin and Joel Slemrod. Chicago: University of Chicago Press and NBER.

Collins, Julie; Kemsley, Dean; and Shackelford, Douglas. 1995. Tax reform and foreign acquisitions: a micro analysis. *National tax journal.*

Crooks, Ed; Devereux, Michael; Pearson, Mark; and Wooley, Charles. 1989. Transnational tax rates and incentives to invest. Manuscript. Institute for Fiscal Studies, London. March.

Dooley, Michael P. 1990. Comment on "U.S. tax policy and direct investment abroad," by Joosung Jun. In *Taxation in the global economy,* ed. Assaf Razin and Joel Slemrod. Chicago: University of Chicago Press.

Feldstein, Martin. 1992. The budget and trade deficits aren't really twins. National Bureau of Economic Research Working Paper No. 3966, January.

———. 1994. The effects of outbound foreign direct investment on the domestic capital stock. National Bureau of Economic Research Working Paper No. 4668, March.

Feldstein, Martin and Horioka, Charlie. 1980. Domestic savings and international capital flows. *Economic journal* 90:314–29.

Frankel, Jeffrey. 1989. International capital flows and domestic economic policies. In *The changing role of the United States in the world economy,* ed. Martin Feldstein. Chicago: University of Chicago Press.

Goodspeed, Timothy J. and Frisch, Daniel J. 1989. U.S. tax policy and the overseas activities of U.S. multinational corporations: A quantitative assessment. Manuscript. July.

Graham, Edward M. and Krugman, Paul R. 1989. *Foreign direct investment in the United States.* Washington: Institute for International Economics, April.

Grubert, Harry and Mutti, John. 1987. The impact of the Tax Reform Act of 1986 on trade and capital flows. In *Compendium of tax research 1987.* Washington: Office of Tax Analysis, Department of the Treasury.

———. 1989. Taxes, tariffs and transfer pricing in multinational corporation decision making. Manuscript. March.

Hartman, David E. 1985. Tax policy and foreign direct investment. In *Journal of public economics* 26: 107–21.

Hines, James R., Jr. and Hubbard, R. Glenn. 1990. Coming home to America: Dividend repatriations by U.S. multinationals. In *Taxation in the global economy*, ed. Assaf Razin and Joel Slemrod. Chicago: University of Chicago Press and NBER.

Jun, Joosung. 1989. What is the marginal source of funds for foreign investment? National Bureau of Economic Research Working Paper No. 3064, August.

Mutti, John and Grubert, Harry. 1988. U.S. taxes and trade performance. *National tax journal* 41: 317–25.

Organization for Economic Co-operation and Development. 1991. *Taxing profits in a global economy: Domestic and international issues.* Paris: OECD.

Scholes, Myron, and Wolfson, Mark A. 1990. The effect of changes in tax laws on corporate reorganization activity. *Journal of business* 63: 5141–64.

Sinn, Hans-Werner. 1988. U.S. tax reform 1981 and 1986: Impact on international capital markets and capital flows. *National tax journal* 41: 327–40.

Skinner, Jonathan and Feenberg, Daniel. 1990. The impact of the 1986 tax reform on personal saving. In *Do taxes matter?: The impact of the Tax Reform Act of 1986*, ed. Joel Slemrod. Cambridge, MA: The MIT Press.

Slemrod, Joel. 1990a. The impact of the Tax Reform Act of 1986 on foreign direct investment to and from the United States. In *Do taxes matter?: The impact of the Tax Reform Act of 1986*, ed. Joel Slemrod. Cambridge, MA: The MIT Press.

Slemrod, Joel. 1990b. Tax effects on foreign direct investment in the United States: Evidence from a cross-country comparison. In *Taxation in the global economy*, ed. Assaf Razin and Joel Slemrod. Chicago: University of Chicago Press and NBER.

Steuerle, Eugene. 1991. *The tax decade*. Washington: The Urban Institute Press.

Swenson, Deborah L. 1992. The impact of U.S. tax reform on foreign direct investment in the U.S. Fuqua School of Business, Working Paper.

Effects of Financial Liberalization on Banks, Corporations, and Monetary Policy

Asset Price Inflation and Money Flow from Japan

NAOYUKI YOSHINO

THIS PAPER ANALYZES the impact of banking and corporate behavior with special emphasis on the so-called asset price inflation period of 1987–90, when banks extended huge speculative loans to real estate and non-bank financial institutions, subsequently resulting in default losses. Monetary policy in the late 1980s focused more on exchange rates than money supply because prices were stable due to the appreciation of the yen. The Plaza Accord in September 1985 pushed Japan to lower interest rates in order to stimulate the domestic economy and also to expand the fiscal stimulus in order to lower the balance of payment surplus.

The first section briefly reviews the progress of financial liberalization of Japan.

The second section surveys the principal reasons for the international money flow from Japan. City banks, long-term credit banks, and trust banks in Japan supplied their funds to the Euro-dollar market in the 1980s. Foreign securities investment by Japanese financial institutions increased when government capital controls were eased due to the appreciation of the yen in 1971–72, 1977–78, 1980, and 1985–87. However, the outflow of foreign capital slowed after the implementation of the Bank for International Settlements (BIS) capital requirement rule in 1989.

The third section examines changes in the conduct of monetary policy using quarterly data with special focus on those variables that are carefully watched

194

by the central bank of Japan. The examination reveals that structural change in monetary policy occurred between 1979 and 1980. However, when monthly data are analyzed, structural change is seen between September 1985 and October 1985, following the Plaza Accord. The exchange rate became important as a monetary target variable after October 1985. In order to avoid too rapid an appreciation of the yen, the central bank of Japan lowered its interest rate, thus encouraging domestic investment and accelerating capital outflow from Japan. This in turn led to more imports and depreciation of the yen.

The fourth section analyzes the behavior of private banks and businesses utilizing various data. Loans made to real estate-related concerns, non-bank financial institutions, and construction firms were substantial during the "bubble" period because demand in these sectors was steady. The gap between lending and deposit rates narrowed at city and long-term credit banks. In order to keep their profits, these institutions competed with higher volumes of loans. Deregulation of deposits was gradually implemented starting in 1979 with large-denomination deposits and CDs, then extended to smaller-denomination deposits. Private banks could set higher interest rates in deregulated, large-denomination deposits in order to collect more deposits from customers, while regulated, small-denomination deposits were kept at low interest rates. Because of the share competition among private banks, a higher interest rate for larger deposits allowed commercial banks to absorb a large inflow of deposits. Therefore, city banks and long-term credit banks expanded their overseas operations by supplying enormous funds to the Euro-market, together with the credit expansion to real estate, construction companies, and non-bank financial institutions due to lack of loan demand by large corporations.

While large corporations started to rely more on stocks and bonds for financing, small businesses continued to rely heavily on bank loans. Because stock prices rose until November 1989, and people were expecting high capital gains due to future stock price hikes, it was easy for large corporations to issue stocks (or convertible bonds) in order to finance their investments. Therefore, large corporations reduced their bank borrowing, while banks kept on absorbing deposits to maximize their market shares.

The fifth section examines household asset portfolio behavior. Bank deposits are still the main financial instrument, but their share is declining while the shares of insurance and postal savings are increasing. Because of the high stock prices in the late 1980s, the stocks and investment trusts held by households increased greatly in 1989. However, their share had started to shrink after 1989 due to the collapse of stock prices. The share of postal savings increased until 1994. Big shifts in postal savings were observed in 1980 and 1991 when market interest rates were falling. Private banks reduced their interest rates on deposits quickly; interest rate changes on postal savings, however, were delayed. Therefore, sudden shifts occurred from other financial assets to postal savings.

The last section deals empirically with the impact of monetary policy and exchange rates on asset prices and other macroeconomic variables. A VAR estimation of the causal relationship is conducted. The impulse response function shows that land prices were affected by changes in the money supply more strongly after 1980 than in the 1970–79 period.

PROGRESS OF FINANCIAL LIBERALIZATION

Postwar financial flow in Japan was mainly through private financial institutions, especially private banks. Approximately 60 percent of total funds flow went through private banks. Prime Minister Tanaka initiated a nationwide land development plan in 1972 to expand economic activities not only in large cities but also in rural regions. Easy monetary policies and expansionary fiscal policies were adopted by the authorities to pursue large-scale public investments all over Japan, which raised land prices by 25.1 percent in 1973.

In 1973 OPEC countries raised crude oil prices, and the first oil crisis hit the Japanese economy severely: 99.7 percent of Japan's oil at that time was imported from abroad. The high oil price raised wholesale prices and then the consumer price index (CPI). The rate of inflation rose to 31.6 percent in 1974 and the real growth rate in GNP was negative (-0.4 percent) for the first time since World War II. The Japanese economy was thus stricken with a high rate of inflation and high land prices. Private investment fell to about 15 percent of nominal GNP in 1974, compared to the period 1960–70 when the ratio was 16–21 percent.

In order to offset sluggish private investment, the government was forced by falling tax revenues to increase its expenditures through the general account by issuing deficit bonds in 1975 for the first time since World War II. The government increased its loans through the Fiscal Investment and Loan Program at the same time in order to stimulate the sluggish economy.

The ratio of new bond issues to total government revenue climbed to 24.6 percent in 1975, 32.2 percent in 1980, and 22.8 percent in 1985. A large portion of government bonds were held by private and government financial institutions: in March 1980, 41.3 percent were held by private financial institutions, and in March 1975 39.4 percent were held by government financial institutions (i.e., the Trust Fund Bureau of the Ministry of Finance).

The high share of holdings of government bonds by private banks forced the government to allow the liquidation of government bonds into the financial market. In 1977 the government allowed private banks to resell government bonds, and in 1978 medium-term government bonds were issued by setting their price based on market demand. Also in 1978 private banks were allowed to sell the new government bonds over the counter. In 1979 private banks were allowed to deal in existing government bonds. By 1980 investment banks (security companies) were allowed to sell the pooled funds of medium-term government bonds. This deregulation of the government bond market shifted the financial flow from banks and insurance companies to the securities market.

The financial flow into private banks dropped to 48.0 percent in 1979 and then to 41.5 percent in 1980. In order to compete with securities, private banks issued certificates of deposit (CDs) in 1979, and mutual money-market funds (MMCs) and deregulated, large-denomination time deposits in 1985. Small-denomination MMCs were issued by private banks in 1989. Time deposits were completely deregulated by June 1993 and all demand deposits were deregulated in October 1994. The progress of the deregulation of interest rates was thus gradual; it took 15 years to complete all the deregulations.

FINANCIAL OUTFLOW FROM JAPAN

Until the mid-1970s, only city banks and long-term credit banks invested in overseas securities markets. Sudden increases in overseas securities investments can be seen in 1971–72, 1977–78, and 1985–87 when the Japanese yen appreciated. These sudden increases in foreign securities investment are related to the relaxation of government capital controls.

In June 1971 and September 1977, the relaxation of the control of foreign capital investment made city banks and long-term credit banks increase their overseas securities investment in FY 1972 and 1978. In December 1979, the capital control law was revised substantially so that inflow and outflow of capital from Japan, in principle, could be free. City banks, long-term credit banks, and trust banks increased their Euro-yen deposits from 1980. The share of their Euro-yen operations became more than 15 percent of all assets between 1983 and 1990 because large private banks in Japan were seeking to expand their market share during the 1980s. However, the implementation of the BIS capital rule led these banks to stop expanding their market share in the Euro market, which made these shares fall to the 10 percent level in 1993.

In March 1986, life and non-life insurance companies were allowed to increase their holdings of foreign securities from 10 to 25 percent of their total assets. In FY 1986, life insurance companies increased their foreign securities investment to 61.2 percent compared to the previous year, and non-life insurance companies increased it to 45 percent. Insurance companies were seeking so-called income gains rather than capital gains to pay higher returns to customers. Therefore, they invested in foreign securities, the yields on which were higher than yields on securities in Japan at that time, despite their future expected capital losses due to the high appreciation of yen.

Between 1984 and 1988, more than 40 percent of total overseas securities investment went into the United States, and the total net outflow trend was upward from 1984 to 1989. However, it dropped from $113.67 billion in 1989 to $39.46 billion in 1990 due to the tightening of monetary policy by raising interbank money market rates in late 1989. Overseas real estate investment rose in FY 1989 from ¥860 billion (1986–88 average) to ¥1,201 billion; 47.2 percent of overseas real estate investment went to the United States and 30.9 percent went to Europe. However, this figure dropped to ¥194 billion in 1992 and ¥115 billion in 1993 because of the recession in Japan.

CHANGES IN MONETARY POLICY

The purpose of this section is to examine how Japan's monetary policy changed between 1965 and 1991 by estimating the monetary policy reaction function by use of the call lending rate. Japanese monetary policy can be briefly summarized as follows (Suzuki 1993). The monetary policy of the Bank of Japan during the 1960s was aimed at tightening the money market when the balance of payments went into deficit. It was eased when the balance of payments came back to a normal level. However, the balance of payments went into surplus after 1968 and the wholesale price index (WPI) started to rise after 1968. Monetary policy during the 1960s was tightened because of a high inflation rate even when the balance of payments was in surplus.

The Japanese yen appreciated from 360 to 308 to the dollar in December 1971 for the first time since the end of the Second World War. The Bank of Japan was expecting appreciation of the yen to discourage export-oriented Japanese industries. Therefore, the central bank started to loosen monetary policy during 1972 and 1973 in coordination with the expansion of fiscal policy.

When OPEC raised the price of oil in 1973, the import price of oil in Japan increased 77.4 percent over the previous year. High oil prices raised the WPI by 37.2 percent and the CPI also increased 24.9 percent in 1974. Japan also experienced a huge trade deficit during this period. The government started to rely on government bonds in order to stimulate the economy after the first oil crisis due to lack of private investment. More than 30 percent of all government spending was financed by issuing government bonds. This huge amount of government bonds forced the deposits market to be deregulated; otherwise, the financial disintermediation would have developed much further.

Interest rates on CDs were deregulated in 1979, and the foreign exchange control law was abolished in 1980. Both these events resulted in changes in monetary policy to pay attention to the exchange rate and other factors and the behavior of the private banking sector became more competitive in the search for larger market shares.

Japanese monetary policy was changed after the Plaza Accord (September 1985) partly because of foreign pressures to encourage domestic investment judging from the structural change test applied to the monthly monetary policy reaction function (see Yoshino and Yoshimura 1995). The Japanese economy experienced high prices for stocks and bonds from 1986 until 1990.

A summary of the estimated results of the monetary policy reaction using quarterly data is shown in Table 1. The dependent variable in the table is the inverse of the call lending rate, which became better specified to estimate the monetary policy reaction function. The left side of Table 1 presents empirical results between the second quarter of 1968 and the fourth quarter of 1979, and the right side shows the results for the period between Q2 1980 and Q4 1991 from the use of quarterly data. Structural changes in the monetary policy reaction function are observed between 1979 and 1980 from the estimates of the quarterly data (see Table 1).

The growth rate of the money supply (M2+CD) and the rate of inflation (WPI inflation rate) were the two important target variables of the central bank for the entire period between 1968 and 1991. The policy weight of the rate of inflation (WPI) as a monetary policy target variable became stronger between Q1 1974 and 1979 due to the high rate of inflation, since the coefficient of WPI changed from -1.0685 to -0.0878 ($=-1.0685+0.9807$).

Conversely, the policy weight of the rate of inflation became smaller after Q4 1985 due to the very low inflation rate partly caused by the fall of import prices. It can be seen in the changes of the coefficient of GWPI from -0.2202 to -0.974 ($-0.2202-0.7538$) between Q4 1985 and Q4 1991.

The exchange rate became an important monetary target variable after 1980 judging from the t-value (t=-1.835) of the LREX variable (exchange rate). Furthermore, it became more important from Q4 1985, judging from estimates from monthly data (see Yoshino and Yoshimura 1995). Land prices were not a significant monetary policy target between Q4 1985 and Q4 1991 since the t-value (t=-0.8508) of the growth rate of land prices was not statistically significant.

The lagged value of the dependent variable, i.e., the inverse of the call rate denoted as 1/Call rate ($1/r(t-1)$) in Table 1, shows statistical significance, because the central bank of Japan tried to avoid too much fluctuation in the call rate. A similar smoothing of the call lending rate has been observed elsewhere from monthly and daily data (Yoshino and Yoshimura 1995).

CHANGES IN PRIVATE BANKING BEHAVIOR IN JAPAN

Assets and Liabilities of All Banks in Japan

This section observes the behavior of banks in Japan from balance sheet data. A breakdown of the assets of all banks (city banks, long-term credit banks, trust banks, and regional banks) in Japan from March 1954 to December 1992 reveals that the share of long-term government bonds to total assets of all banks

TABLE 1

Definition of Financial Institutions in Japan (March 1994)

	Number of Banks	Loan Share (%)	Number of Branches
City banks	11	25.5	3,568 (97%)
Regional banks	64	14.8	7,861 (76%)
Regional banks II	65	5.9	4,843 (85%)
Foreign banks in Japan	88	0.9	
Long-term credit banks	3	5.5	77 (100%)
Trust banks (domestic+foreign)	7+9	6.7	400 (100%)
Financial institutions for small business			
Shinkin banks	429	8.1	11,383 (79%)
Credit cooperatives	383	2.3	
Labor credit associations	47	0.6	660 (90%)
Shōkō chūkin bank	1	1.4	
Financial institutions for agriculture, forestry, and fishery			
Agricultural cooperatives	2,688	5.0	18,045 (49%)
Fishery cooperatives	1,556	0.2	
Mutual insurance federations of agricultural cooperatives	47	1.0	
Insurance companies			
Life insurance companies	27	7.4	
Nonlife insurance companies	25	0.8	
Securities finance companies	213	0.1	
Government financial institutions	11	13.9	24,293* (62%)

* Post offices.

increased approximately 2 percent every year from March 1975 (1.53 percent) to March 1979 (9.96 percent) due to the high level of issues. After the first oil crisis, the central government was able to increase expenditures by increasing bond issues to compensate for sluggish economic growth. Private banks purchased a substantial portion of government bonds in the late 1970s.

The share of corporate bonds and stocks of all assets held by all banks increased during 1988–89 (1.2 percent) and 1988–92 (5.2–6.3 percent), respectively, reflecting the heavy reliance on stocks and bonds for financing by large corporations. Stocks held by financial institutions (asset side) are evaluated by the book value.

The share of all bank loans to total assets declined from 1954 (86.7 percent) until 1990 (74.4 percent) due to the development of various financial instruments. However, the loan shares of all banks increased again from 1991 (76.1 percent), since the sudden drop in stock prices in 1989 made it difficult for large corporations to issue stocks on the financial market.

As for the liabilities of all banks, the share of demand deposits declined from 35.2 percent in March 1954 to 14.9 in March 1992, since corporate sectors were minimizing their demand deposit balance by investing in higher-yield financial instruments. The share of time deposits increased from 1954 (38.0 percent) until March 1981 (49.5 percent). However, it declined from 1981 until 1987 (43.5 percent) because of the shift from regulated time deposits to unregulated deposits such as CDs. It increased again in the 1990s (50.5 percent in 1991) when small-denomination time deposits were deregulated. The ratio of regulated deposits with city banks to all time deposits has declined since 1987, while that of deregulated deposits, such as large-denomination time deposits and CDs, increased from 4.3 percent in 1985 to 78.9 percent in June 1993. Deregulation of time deposits was completed on June 16, 1993, and the deregulation of demand deposits was completed in November 1994.

The issuance of stocks by city banks, long-term credit banks, and trust banks increased from 1988 (2.18 percent of city banks' total liabilities) until 1993 (3.44 percent) so that banks were able to attain the BIS capital adequacy ratio. The share of Bank of Japan loans to total liabilities declined from 1954 (15.3 percent) until 1985 (0.498 percent), though it increased during the asset "bubble" period of 1987–89 (1.2 percent), reflecting lower call rates and other interest rates. (See Yoshino 1995.)

Changes in the Balance Sheets of City, Regional, Long-term Credit, and Trust Banks in Japan

The assets and liabilities of various kinds of banks are characterized as follows. The growth rate of reserves for possible loan losses, other reserves, and reserves under special laws has been very high since the collapse of the asset price bubble in 1991 (6.67 percent in 1991, 20.5 percent in 1992, and 35.9 percent in 1993). Amortization of default loans grew large compared to net operating profits in 1993 and in 1994 due to bad loans extended to non-bank financial institutions, real estate developers, etc. as shown in Table 2. This may be seen from intensified competition among banks due to the loosening of the regulatory environment (such as deregulation of deposit rates and lending "window guidance"[1]) encouraging expansionary behavior in lending by simply relying on the collateral value of land.

The share of CDs to total liabilities of long-term credit banks (LTCB) and trust banks was high during 1988–89 (5.65 percent for LTCB) and 1989–90 (3.96 percent for trust banks) compared to the mid-1980s (2–3 percent for

LTCB and 3–4 percent for trust banks) and declined after 1991. The figure has fallen to 1.77 for LTCB and 1.63 percent for trust banks because of the sluggish economy. The share of bank debentures issued by long-term credit banks was around 65 percent of total liabilities in the 1975–79 period. However, it was low during 1987–90 (45.2 percent in March 1990) because their source of funding shifted from bank debentures to deposits (especially CDs).

On the asset side of the balance sheets of various banks, it is apparent that the share of deposits with other banks in the assets of city and long-term credit banks increased to around 20 percent during 1986–89 from around 10 percent in 1979. This was because city banks and long-term credit banks extended funds supply into the Euro-market after the change in the foreign exchange control law in 1979.[2] The expansion of the supply of funds into the Euro-market continued until 1989 (20.6 percent), when the BIS capital requirement rule was implemented. The BIS rule has substantially changed the nature of Japanese banks' market-share expansion into more profit-conscious behavior. Since operations in the Euro-market turned out not to be so profitable, banks decreased their Euro-market operations judging from the share of cash and deposits with others of city banks (12.8 percent in 1993), long-term credit banks (9.5 percent in 1993), and trust banks (15.0 percent in 1993).

On the other hand, regional banks have not shown such an increase in the share of cash and deposits since they mainly operate in the domestic market; that share was around 6 to 7 percent from 1974 to 1993. The share of loans in assets fell between 1974 and 1989–90 at city, regional, and long-term credit banks: 57.4 to 49.6 percent, 68.4 to 59.9 percent, and 49.3 to 38.9 percent, respectively. This was due to less reliance on bank borrowing by large firms, reflecting the fact that they were beginning to rely on the capital market by issuing stocks and bonds. However, the share of loans extended by trust banks to non-bank financial institutions, real-estate-related firms, etc. increased somewhat during 1987–88 compared with 1981–86 (Table 3), while their share of securities' holdings and call loans declined.

Interest Rate Gaps and the Personnel Costs of Various Banks

The interest-rate gap between the lending and funding of city banks fell from 3.66 percent (January 1970–September 1985 average) to 1.56 (October 1985–March 1991 average). The interest rate for loans is computed from the average yield on loans, securities, and call loans. The funding cost of interest consists of deposit rates and call money.

The continued narrowing of the gap can be explained as the behavior of banks as market-share maximizers, despite their low margins. However, the gap widened again after 1990 because the introduction of the BIS capital requirement rule made Japanese banks more conscious about asset quality and

TABLE 2

Bank Reserves for Loan Losses and Default Claims

	City Banks, March 1993				City Banks, March 1994			
	Deferred Claims & Deferred Payments Claims (A)*	Net Operating Income (B)*	A/B	Capital Ratio	Default Claims & Deferred Payments Claims (A)*	Net Operating Income (B)*	A/B	Capital Ratio
Sakura	1,356,549	341,557	3.97	8.96	1,458,839	207,483	7.03	9.50
Sumitomo	1,043,027	341,557	3.05	9.37	1,112,730	302,271	3.68	9.89
Ichikan	1,305,731	237,384	5.50	9.36	1,327,242	235,595	5.63	9.40
Fuji	1,141,172	313,442	3.64	9.26	1,188,194	362,194	3.28	9.66
Sanwa	784,257	370,226	2.12	9.43	909,802	358,008	2.54	9.94
Mitsubishi	502,495	336,452	1.49	9.12	572,789	283,541	2.02	9.65
Tokai	828,852	186,525	4.44	8.97	768,185	180,259	4.26	9.49
Asahi	481,318	146,361	3.29	9.22	499,126	165,462	3.02	9.60
Tokyo	351,717	202,605	1.74	9.66	266,651	185,109	1.44	10.37
Daiwa	281,409	71,897	3.91	9.37	336,538	70,275	4.79	9.40
Hokkaido Takushoku	358,695	38,871	9.23	8.97	508,093	32,008	15.87	9.20

* Figures in ¥1 million.

TABLE 2
(continued)

	Reserves for Possible Loan Losses (A)†	Reserves for Retirement Allowance (B)†	Reserves under Special Law (C)†	Reserves Total A+B+C +Others (D)†	Default Claims (E)†	Deferred Payments Claims (F)†	Operating Income (G)†	D/G	(D+E+F)/G
City banks									
1990‡	18,864	4,174	912	23,972			311,493	7.70	
1991	19,931	4,029	991	24,351			358,088	6.80	
1992	22,686	3,886	967	27,539			327,761	8.40	
1993	28,287	3,731	1,221	33,240	13,820	70,532	246,260	13.50	47.75
1994	32,351	3,646	1,343	37,341	16,520	72,959	222,382	16.79	57.03
1995	38,486	3,578	1,418	43,491	17,689	63,427	221,289		
Regional banks									
1990	5,885	3,552	951	10,388			95,496	10.88	
1991	6,077	3,572	981	10,632			125,625	8.46	
1992	6,727	3,640	891	11,258			127,884	8.80	
1993	7,969	3,740	923	12,634	5,692		104,283	12.12	
1994	9,380	3,813	962	14,156	6,745		90,491	15.64	
1995	11,392	3,908	942	16,242	7,524		83,730		

Regional banks II									
1990	3,385	1,285	298	4,970			36,575	13.59	
1991	3,060	1,309	306	4,675			47,063	9.93	
1992	3,122	1,441	283	4,847			49,017	9.89	
1993	3,805	1,456	280	5,542	3,863		40,615	13.65	
1994	4,818	1,481	309	6,608	5,119		35,091	18.83	
1995	6,293	1,500	290	8,082	5,721		32,183		
Trust banks									
1990	2,790	798	501	4,095			66,103	6.19	
1991	2,802	818	373	3,993			73,931	5.40	
1992	3,072	834	345	4,252			64,872	6.55	
1993	3,984	830	377	5,192	1,753		53,080	9.78	
1994	6,017	828	476	7,322	2,201	14,159	49,483	14.80	
1995	7,818	824	479	9,123	2,969	13,123	48,892		
Long-term credit banks									
1990	4,064	630	479	5,174			59,887	8.64	
1991	3,862	648	453	4,963			65,940	7.53	
1992	3,885	673	214	4,773			65,673	7.27	
1993	4,711	697	237	5,646	2,831	15,673	61,058	9.25	
1994	7,098	723	248	8,071	2,805	16,074	63,453	12.72	39.55
1995	9,059	747	281	10,089	4,116	15,042	65,617		42.47

† Figures in ¥100 million.
‡ Figures for each year as of March.

probably because of the accumulation of default loan losses. Furthermore, the introduction of the new short-term prime rate in 1990 induced banks to make their lending rates much more flexible.

The ratio of personnel costs to total expenses of city banks fell from 16.3 percent in 1978 to 4.1 percent in 1990 in city banks. Equipment costs also dropped from 9.2 percent in 1978 to 4.0 percent in 1990. However, the pace of reduction in personnel costs has been slower at regional banks compared with city banks: the share of personnel costs to total expenses of regional banks declined from 25.4 percent in 1978 to 10.4 percent in 1990. Regional banks are still paying more in the form of personnel costs compared to large city banks. (See Yoshino 1995.)

Changes in the Lending Pattern of Banks during the Bubble Period

Long-term loans as a proportion of total loans increased in city banks and regional banks. The maturity of loans extended by city and regional banks has expanded since 1987. The share of long-term loans to total loans by city banks rose from 34.7 percent (1981) to 56.4 percent (1991) and those of regional banks rose from 36.6 percent (1981) to 50.2 percent (1991).

Bank loans to small businesses and individuals increased during 1985–90. The ratio of small-business loans to total loans of all banks rose 43.6 percent in March 1985 to 54.4 percent in March 1990, while the ratio of individual loans rose from 9.3 percent to 15.3 percent. Banks focused long-term loans on real-estate-related firms and building contractors.

Table 3 shows the share of loans to real estate-related firms, non-bank financial institutions, and building contractors. The share allocated to real-estate-related businesses increased from 1986 and is still high even after the collapse of the bubble economy. However, the share of lending to non-bank financial institutions, which rose to 16.7 percent in 1990, declined to 14.5 percent in 1992.

Banks have extended these loans mainly using the value of land as collateral when land prices were rising; however, falling land prices since 1992 (Table 2) have made banks face default loan losses because of the decline in the collateral value of land.

Behavior of the Corporate Sector

Assets and Liabilities of the Corporate Sector. The shares of various assets of the corporate sector are summarized in Table 4. The share of investment trusts held by corporations jumped from 0.14 percent in March 1986 to 0.83 percent in March 1987 and it has remained at the 0.6 to 0.8 percent level, since rising stock prices raised the yields on investment trusts.

TABLE 3

Share of Loans to Real Estate, Nonbank Financial Institutions,
and Construction Companies by All Bank (%; in December of each year)

	1981	1982	1983	1984	1985	1986	1987	1988	1989	1990	1991	1992	1993
1. Real estate	6.54	6.76	7.13	7.52	8.39	10.39	11.13	11.69	12.19	11.86	12.02	12.42	12.44
2. Nonbank	5.08	6.48	8.18	9.86	11.14	12.79	14.42	15.38	15.17	15.21	14.54	14.17	14.13
3. Construction	5.12	5.08	5.24	5.35	5.43	5.30	5.04	4.96	5.21	5.10	5.34	5.57	5.95
Total for 3 sectors	16.74	18.32	20.55	22.73	24.96	28.48	30.59	32.03	32.57	32.17	31.90	32.16	32.52
Total outstanding bank loans													
(trillion yen)*	167.0	183.5	201.2	223.0	245.5	268.0	293.5	314.3	384.6	408.8	421.1	421.6	425.4

* Banking accounts plus trust accounts.

TABLE 4

Assets' Share of the Corporate Sector (%)

Year Ending March	Currency	Demand Deposits	Time Deposits	Certificates of Deposit	Foreign Deposits	Trusts	Securities	Bonds	Stocks	Investment Trusts	Comm. Paper	Trade Credits	Other	Total
1955	1.39	14.79	16.96	0.0	0.0	1.13	6.17	0.85	5.16	0.16	0.0	57.22	2.34	100
1960	0.90	11.70	17.29	0.0	0.0	1.93	6.26	1.19	4.94	0.13	0.0	59.16	2.77	100
1965	0.63	11.85	17.66	0.0	0.0	1.86	6.88	1.62	5.10	0.15	0.0	61.11	0.0	100
1970	0.52	10.93	16.81	0.0	0.0	1.45	4.56	1.38	3.16	0.02	0.0	64.56	1.17	100
1975	0.60	13.36	17.04	0.0	0.0	1.76	4.38	1.24	3.13	0.02	0.0	60.48	2.37	100
1980	0.59	12.30	16.49	0.46	0.0	1.95	4.95	2.29	2.62	0.04	0.0	61.21	2.07	100
1985	0.53	10.97	17.16	1.90	0.0	2.26	5.92	3.50	2.30	0.12	0.0	55.30	5.96	100
1986	0.54	10.79	19.07	1.97	0.0	2.82	6.36	3.91	2.31	0.14	0.0	52.18	6.27	100
1987	0.55	10.31	20.09	2.21	0.0	4.77	6.36	3.34	2.19	0.83	0.0	48.63	7.08	100
1988	0.43	7.25	16.96	1.59	0.70	4.96	25.41	1.71	23.11	0.59	0.03	38.26	4.41	100
1989	0.45	7.17	18.57	1.61	1.04	4.98	27.21	1.39	24.91	0.91	0.40	35.05	3.54	100
1990	0.47	6.17	18.90	1.65	1.41	5.66	24.99	1.48	22.69	0.81	0.54	35.21	5.01	100
1991	0.47	6.63	18.56	1.49	1.82	5.79	23.45	1.85	20.87	0.73	0.56	38.12	3.11	100
1992	0.50	7.65	18.52	1.24	1.93	6.54	18.66	2.02	15.88	0.76	0.67	41.00	3.30	100
1993	0.50	7.96	17.43	1.39	1.52	6.91	17.81	1.89	15.15	0.77	0.40	37.10	NA	100

The share of stocks increased during 1988–89 (25.41 percent), though it declined after reaching a peak in March 1989 (27.21 percent) because of the fall in stock prices in 1988. The share dropped to 17.8 percent in March 1993. The share of trusts increased from March 1987 (4.77 percent) until March 1993 (6.91 percent) because the amount of loan trusts increased.

The share of demand deposits shown in Table 6 continues to fall because the interest rate on demand deposits was regulated until November 1994; therefore, corporations are minimizing their holdings of demand deposits by shifting from demand deposits to other financial instruments. However, the share of unregulated CDs started to rise in 1984 (1.54 percent) and reached a peak in March 1987 (2.21 percent). Thus, the asset side of the corporate sector recorded a shift from ordinary deposits to stock-related financial products and deregulated financial instruments during the 1987–90 period.

The liability side of the corporate sector is summarized in Table 5. Borrowing from private financial institutions dropped from 72.77 percent in March 1987 to 55.58 percent in March 1988. The corporate sector continued to reduce its reliance on private bank loans until March 1990 (68.9 percent) and thereafter increased private bank loans to 71.7 percent by March 1993.

The issuance of corporate bonds started to increase in March 1986 (4.93 percent) and continued to increase until March 1993 (7.55 percent). The share of foreign bonds also started to rise in March 1986 (2.02 percent) and continued to do so until March 1992 (5.77 percent). Partly because domestic corporate bond issuance was restricted by various regulations, corporations issued bonds abroad. The share of stocks issued by the corporate sector rose continuously from March 1986 (6.37 percent) to March 1992 (10.58 percent).

In summary, the corporate sector started to rely less on bank borrowing and increased its issuance of stocks and bonds around 1987 as shown in Table 5.

Asset Components of the Manufacturing and Non-manufacturing Sectors. Asset and liability components are somewhat different depending on the manufacturing and non-manufacturing sectors and the capital size of the corporations. The share of stocks held by very large firms (capitalized above ¥1 billion) has risen steadily since 1985 in both the manufacturing and non-manufacturing sectors.

However, small and medium-sized non-manufacturing firms show much more volatility in stock holding compared with their counterparts in the manufacturing sector. The share of land is relatively small for large firms capitalized above ¥1 billion. Nevertheless, firms of all sizes have tended to increase their land holdings since 1985. The share of short-term borrowing peaked during 1985–86 and started to fall, except at small firms (¥5–10 million) in the manufacturing sector. The non-manufacturing sector shows a similar pattern. Reliance on corporate bonds by large manufacturing firms (over ¥1 billion) has

TABLE 5

Liabilities' Share of the Corporate Sector (%)

Year Ending March	Securities	Corporate Bonds	Stocks	Foreign Bonds	Comm. Papers	Loans (A+B)	Financial Inst. (A)	Govt. Bank (B)	Trade Credits	Others	Financial Deficit	Total
1955	25.81	4.94	20.87	0.0	0.0	94.65	83.63	11.02	43.23	0.0	−63.69	100
1960	25.92	5.10	20.82	0.0	0.0	84.08	75.34	8.74	46.27	0.0	−56.27	100
1965	22.84	4.70	18.14	0.0	0.0	73.75	66.86	6.89	46.96	0.85	−44.40	100
1970	15.68	3.80	11.65	0.23	0.0	70.61	63.80	6.81	49.94	0.0	−36.23	100
1975	12.01	3.66	8.25	0.11	0.0	78.36	71.29	7.06	50.67	0.0	−41.04	100
1980	11.43	3.90	6.74	0.79	0.0	71.48	63.89	7.59	49.96	0.0	−32.87	100
1985	11.13	3.68	6.00	1.46	0.0	76.42	68.40	8.02	43.49	0.0	−31.05	100
1986	13.32	4.93	6.37	2.02	0.0	80.25	72.19	8.05	39.63	0.0	−33.19	100
1987	13.54	5.07	6.21	2.26	0.0	80.29	72.77	7.52	37.15	0.0	−30.98	100
1988	15.60	5.66	7.84	2.10	0.45	63.60	55.58	8.01	30.10	0.0	−9.74	100
1989	16.70	5.58	8.47	2.65	1.46	65.65	57.43	8.22	27.17	0.0	−10.97	100
1990	19.02	5.65	9.41	3.96	1.99	68.88	60.28	8.59	27.16	0.0	−17.06	100
1991	20.51	5.94	9.71	4.86	1.68	74.62	65.09	9.53	29.40	0.0	−26.20	100
1992	23.38	7.02	10.58	5.77	1.56	83.81	72.26	11.55	30.79	0.0	−39.53	100
1993	23.01	7.55	10.26	5.20	1.51	84.29	71.71	12.58	27.91	NA	−41.32	100

increased since 1982. However, small and medium-sized firms cannot rely on corporate bonds since only large firms satisfy issuing requirements.

The dependence on corporate bonds by large non-manufacturers peaked in 1988 but is still at a high level relative to the early 1980s. Large manufacturers (over ¥1 billion) reduced their reliance on long-term borrowing from financial institutions during 1975–89, but gradually began to increase it from 1990. In contrast, non-manufacturers of all sizes tend to rely increasingly on long-term borrowing. The share of stocks among assets has been increasing since 1975 in very large firms in the manufacturing sector. Large non-manufacturers have increased their stock issuance since 1985. The capital to asset ratios of small and medium-sized firms have not changed to any considerable degree. (See Yoshino 1995.)

CHANGES IN HOUSEHOLD BEHAVIOR

Table 6 summarizes the elasticity of demand for each financial asset by computing the growth rate of each asset divided by the growth rate of total household assets. When the value of each asset is greater than one, the growth rate of that asset is larger than the growth rate of total household assets. Notice that the growth rate is computed by using the real term.

The elasticity of bank deposits relative to total personal assets was less than one between 1966 and 1988 except for 1972. This suggests that the growth rate of bank deposits was less than the growth rate of total personal savings. However, the growth rate of bank deposits became larger than one in 1989 and 1990 when the deregulation of small-denomination deposits attracted customers. In 1991 the high interest rate on postal savings caused a shift from private bank deposits to postal savings. The elasticity of postal savings became 4.41 in 1991 when the ten-year maturity "teigaku" deposits of postal savings offered better rates of interest than private bank deposits. A similar shift from private bank deposits to postal savings was observed in 1980–81, when the discount rate was also lowered. Private banks lower their rates of interest quickly following monetary policy, but changes in the interest rates on postal savings are delayed, which made interest rates on postal savings higher than private bank deposits.

Of household financial assets, private bank deposits still hold the highest share (24.35 percent in September 1994), even though their share has fallen since 1975 (when the share was 31.10 percent). Second highest among household financial assets is insurance, including life and non-life insurance. Some of the pension funds dealt with by insurance companies are also included here. The share of insurance among household financial assets was 23.42 percent in September 1994 and it has increased since 1974 when its share was 14.96 percent. The third highest share is for postal savings whose share increased from 14.21 percent in 1974 to 20.97 percent in September 1994.

TABLE 6

Percent Share and Elasticity of Personal Savings

									Total			
					Percent Share of Financial Assets in Total Personal Savings							
	Total Deposits B+C+D+E	All Banks	Shinkin & Credit Coop.†	Agricult. Coop. & Credit Assoc.	Postal Savings	Trusts	Insurance	Bonds & Mutual Funds	Personal Savings (B thru H)	Equity	Personal Savings	Personal Savings/
Year*	(A)	(B)	(C)	(D)	(E)	(F)	(G)	(H)	(I)	(J)	(¥100 million)	GDP
1975–79	68.64	29.67	11.30	10.80	16.88	5.81	14.71	10.84	100	NA	1,832,636	0.81
1980–84	66.72	26.72	10.20	9.73	20.07	5.53	16.48	11.26	100	NA	3,453,712	1.24
1985	67.27	26.25	10.02	9.50	21.50	5.74	14.39	12.60	100	9.62	4,374,060	1.42
1986	66.37	25.81	9.78	9.29	21.50	5.52	15.26	12.85	100	10.97	4,791,112	1.48
1987	64.50	25.23	9.46	8.89	20.93	5.19	16.53	13.78	100	13.51	5,274,124	1.59
1988	62.87	24.95	9.21	8.53	20.17	4.82	17.86	14.44	100	15.14	5,820,051	1.67
1989	61.38	24.37	9.08	8.30	19.62	4.92	19.36	14.34	100	16.02	6,415,743	1.74
1990	61.38	25.05	9.17	8.22	18.94	5.00	20.11	13.52	100	14.33	7,105,065	1.85
1991	61.75	26.02	9.40	8.38	17.95	5.33	20.70	12.21	100	12.05	7,592,035	1.88
1992	62.32	25.45	9.19	8.48	19.19	5.51	21.27	10.90	100	8.21	8,079,234	1.93
1993	62.70	24.74	9.31	8.45	20.20	5.71	22.36	9.23	100	8.07	8,421,977	2.00
1994	62.74	24.41	9.22	8.37	20.75	5.62	23.31	8.33	100	8.31	8,845,121	2.11
1995	63.29	24.48	9.27	8.25	21.30	5.34	23.89	7.48	100	6.68	9,278,317	2.20

Elasticity of Assets‡

Year	Total Deposits B+C+D+E (A)	All Banks (B)	Shinkin & Credit Coop. (C)	Agricult. Coop. & Credit Assoc. (D)	Postal Savings (E)	Trusts (F)	Insurance (G)	Bonds & Mutual Funds (H)	Total Personal Savings (B thru H) (I)	Equity (J)
1975–79	0.97	0.86	0.80	0.85	1.37	1.05	0.98	1.22	1.00	NA
1980–84	0.90	0.78	0.80	0.78	1.19	0.94	1.35	1.13	1.00	NA
1985	1.98	1.89	1.90	1.79	2.19	1.79	−3.67	2.23	1.00	NA
1986	0.85	0.80	0.72	0.76	1.00	0.56	1.70	1.22	1.00	2.61
1987	0.69	0.76	0.64	0.52	0.71	0.35	1.91	1.79	1.00	3.54
1988	0.73	0.88	0.73	0.58	0.61	0.24	1.86	1.52	1.00	2.28
1989	0.74	0.75	0.85	0.72	0.71	1.23	1.90	0.92	1.00	1.62
1990	1.00	1.29	1.10	0.89	0.64	1.16	1.40	0.41	1.00	−0.09
1991	1.10	1.61	1.39	1.31	0.19	2.04	1.46	−0.51	1.00	−1.48
1992	1.15	0.63	0.63	1.21	2.15	1.54	1.46	−0.78	1.00	−4.28
1993	1.15	0.32	1.31	0.90	2.29	1.91	2.25	−2.77	1.00	0.57
1994	1.01	0.72	0.81	0.77	1.57	0.66	1.89	−1.04	1.00	1.61
1995	1.19	1.06	1.10	0.71	1.56	−0.07	1.53	−1.18	1.00	−3.21

* For fiscal years (ending March 31); first two periods represent five-year averages.
† Credit institutions for small businesses.
‡ Growth rate for each asset ÷ growth rate of total personal savings.

Deposits at financial institutions for small business and agriculture and fisheries have fallen since 1974. Shares for *shinkin* banks, credit cooperatives, and agricultural and fishing cooperatives fell from 9.22, 3.31, and 10.83 percent to 7.26. 1.94, and 7.35 percent, respectively, in September 1994. The share of public and corporate bonds also declined from 9.64 percent (March 1978) to 4.55 percent (September 1994).

Due to high stock prices in the late 1980s, the share of stocks rose to 16.02 percent in March 1989 but fell to 8.3 percent by September 1994. Similar fluctuation can be seen in investment trusts because rising stock prices raised the yields on investment trusts. Their share peaked in March 1989 and declined to 3.65 percent in September 1994 due to the fall in stock prices. Households are thus seen to have increased stock holdings and investment trusts relative to other financial assets in the late 1980s. However, their shares went down along with the fall of the stock prices. On the other hand, insurance and postal savings absorbed those funds in early the 1990s.

VAR ESTIMATIONS

Impact of Macroeconomic Variables on Land Prices

This section presents estimated results of VAR estimation of macroeconomic variables in Japan. As seen in Table 7, very high land and stock prices were experienced in the late 1980s. Therefore, the effects of macro variables on land prices are shown by using the impulse response function.

The set of variables used in the estimation is: (i) the call lending rate (percent level=Rcall), (ii) real output (the first difference of log of real GNP=ΔGNP), (iii) money supply (the first difference of log of M2+CD=ΔM2), (iv) price level (the first difference of log of WPI=ΔWPI), (v) exchange rate (the first difference of log of yen/dollar exchange rate=Δe), (vi) share price (the first difference of log of TOPIX=ΔPstock), and (vii) land price (the first difference of log of land price=ΔPLand).

The augmented Dickey-Fuller test was applied to each variable by using quarterly data from Q1 1971 to Q1 1992 (Dickey and Fuller 1979). The results show all of the variables do not show unit root at the significance level of 10 percent:

Rcall	ΔGNP	ΔM2	ΔWPI	Δe	ΔPstock	ΔPLand
$-4.28(^{**})$	$-4.44(^{**})$	$-3.35(^{*})$	$-4.29(^{**})$	$-4.24(^{**})$	$-3.15(+)$	$-3.40(+)$

where $(^{**})$, $(^{*})$, and $(+)$ denote significance levels of 1 percent, 5 percent, and 10 percent respectively. In each case, the four lags, constant, and time trend terms are used in the augmented Dickey-Fuller test.

TABLE 7
Land Price and Share Price

Year	Topic Price Index (yen)	Nikkei Stock Average (yen)	Growth Rate of Tokyo Housing Land Price (%)	Growth Rate of Tokyo Commercial Property Price (%)
1971	199.45	2,713.74	19.9	8.0
1972	401.70	5,207.94	15.1	7.4
1973	306.44	4,306.80	35.9	28.0
1974	278.34	3,817.22	35.4	23.7
1975	323.43	4,358.60	−11.5	−10.0
1976	383.88	4,990.85	0.6	0.1
1977	364.08	4,665.60	1.7	0.5
1978	449.55	6,001.85	3.5	1.1
1979	459.61	6,569.47	8.8	4.3
1980	494.10	7,116.38	18.3	10.8
1981	570.31	7,681.84	14.1	8.3
1982	593.72	8,016.67	7.4	5.7
1983	731.82	9,893.82	4.1	4.2
1984	913.37	11,542.60	2.2	5.5
1985	1,049.40	13,113.32	1.7	7.2
1986	1,556.37	18,701.30	3.0	12.5
1987	1,725.83	21,564.00	21.5	48.2
1988	2,357.03	30,159.00	68.6	61.1
1989	2,881.37	38,915.87	0.4	3.0
1990	1,733.83	23,848.71	6.6	4.8
1991	1,714.68	22,983.77	6.6	4.1
1992	1,307.66	16,924.95	−9.1	−6.9
1993	1,439.31	17,417.24	−14.6	−19.0
1994*	1,584.66	19,989.60	−7.8	−18.3

* Through October.

The VAR estimations using quarterly data are summarized in Figure 1 (Q1 1971–Q4 1979) and Figure 2 (Q1 1980–Q1 1992).

(1) The call lending rate depends on lagged changes in the price, money supply, and land price during the Q1 1971–Q4 1979 period. On the other hand, it depends on the lagged exchange rate and price after 1980. The results are somewhat similar and were obtained from the monetary policy reaction function (see Table 2).

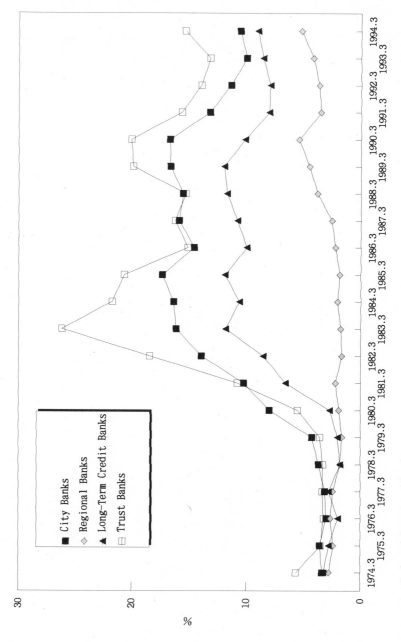

FIG. 1. Cash and deposits with others

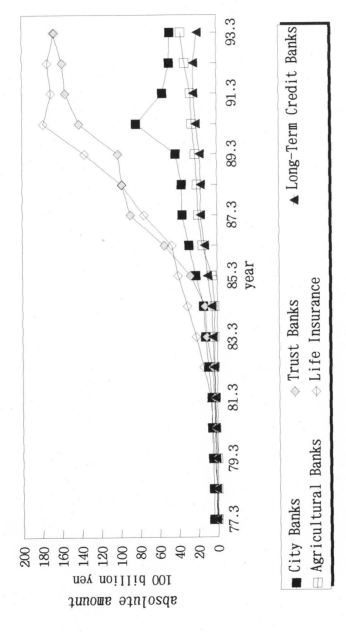

FIG. 2.   Foreign securities holdings by Japanese financial institutions

(2) Change in the real output depends on the call rate and money supply during Q1 1971–Q4 1979 period; however, it is affected more by the call rate and price after 1980. Causal relations of other variables are summarized in Figure 1 (Q1 1971–Q4 1979) and Figure 2 (Q1 1980–Q1 1992), respectively.

Impulse Responses of Land Prices to Macroeconomic Variables

A result of the VAR is presented in Figure 3 (Q2 1971–Q4 1979) and Figure 1 (Q1 1980–Q1 1992). The impulse responses of land prices by other macroeconomic variables are explained in this section, since much of the interest lies in the response of asset prices to other macroeconomic variables.

Figure 3 shows that land prices were influenced by the call rate, money supply, and the share price between Q2 1971 and Q4 1979. The call rate curve affects land prices negatively, showing a peak after six quarters in Figure 3. This says that when the call rate is lowered, land prices go up, taking six quarters to reach their peak. The money supply curve is shown as a positive hump denoting that the higher money supply raises land prices. There was a lag of about six months before the money supply brought land price hikes.

Figure 1 shows the impact of various macroeconomic variables on land prices for the period from Q1 1980 to Q1 1992. Land prices were much more influenced by the money supply and less affected by the call lending rate, exchange rate, etc. during this period than in the earlier period shown in Figure 3. The growth of the money supply is shown as a positive hump, just as in Figure 3, suggesting that the high growth of the money supply affected high land prices. Furthermore, the impulse of money supply is much larger in the later period compared to the earlier period. The time lag before the money supply affected land prices peaked after three quarters, shorter than the previous period's six quarters.

Commercial banks were competing with the volumes of deposits and loans even facing the deregulation of financial markets and financial instruments, just like the periods in a regulated environment. Since the deregulation of deposits started with large denominations, market-share competition forced commercial banks to expand their loans in both the domestic and overseas markets by setting the rate of interest on large-denomination deposits relatively high. Large corporations started to issue commercial papers at relatively lower rates to absorb funds in order to deposit in the commercial banks to get interest rate margins. Commercial banks had to find places to use their absorbed deposits in seeking higher rates of return such as stocks and real estate, etc. These activities raised the money supply which affected land prices in Japan.

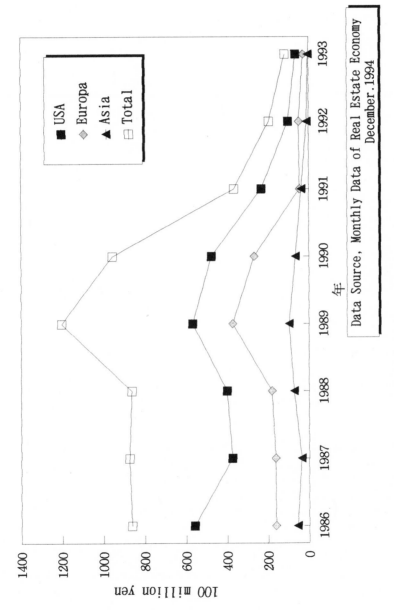

FIG. 3. Overseas real estate investment (*The Land Institute of Japan, Dec. 1994*)

CONCLUDING REMARKS

This paper examined the changing behavior of private banks, corporations, households, and the monetary policy with special focus on the 1980s and 1990s. The following is a brief summary of key findings.

(1) Increases in the overseas securities' investment can be seen in 1971–72, 1977–78, and 1985–87 in which the capital control by the government is relaxed due to appreciation of Japanese yen. City banks, long-term credit banks, and trust banks have increased their Euro-market operation since 1980 when the capital control law was revised substantially. However, the implementation of the BIS capital requirement rule led these banks to stop expanding in the Euro market. Overseas real estate investment rose in 1989. Forty-seven percent of overseas real estate investment went into the United States and 31 percent went into Europe. However, this figure dropped sharply in 1992 and 1993 due to recession in Japan.

(2) Structural changes in the monetary policy are observed in 1979 and 1985. The policy weight of the rate of inflation became smaller after 1985/4 due to a very low inflation rate. The exchange rate became an important monetary policy target after 1980/1 from the quarterly data and especially after 1985 from the monthly data. The bank of Japan relaxed monetary policy in order to cope with the high appreciation of yen.

(3) The share of stocks held by households went up from 9.6 percent (1985/3) to 16.02 percent (1989/3) due to high stock prices in late 1980s. Similarly the share of investment trusts went up to 6.51 percent in 1989/3. However, both shares fell to 8.3 percent and 3.65 percent respectively in 1994/9 after the corruption of stock prices.

(4) The growth rate of possible loan losses has been very high since the collapse of the asset price bubble in 1991 due to bad loans extended to non-bank financial institutions, real estate developers, etc. Private banks took an expansionary behavior of loans simply relying on the collateral value of land during the late 1980s.

(5) As for the behavior of the corporate sector, the share of stocks held by large firms has risen steadily since 1985 in both the manufacturing and non-manufacturing sectors. However, small and medium-sized firms show more volatility in stock holdings compared with their counterparts in the manufacturing sector. Large manufacturers reduced their reliance on long-term borrowing from financial institutions during 1975–89 issuing more stocks and bonds. However, small and medium-sized firms increased their long-term bank borrowing during the asset bubble period.

(6) The monetary policy focused more on the stability of inflation and money supply from 1965 to 1979. However, the exchange rate and the price levels were focuses after 1980.

(7) Impulse responses of land price show that the call rate and money supply had affected the fluctuations of land price between 1972 and 1979. However, the effect of money supply on land prices became bigger after 1980 due to the high volume of loans extended by the private banks.

NOTES

1. On window guidance, see Cargill and Royama (1988), pp. 79–80.

2. In the Euro-market, financial intermediaries set up offshore markets for assets denominated in U.S. dollars outside the United States because central banks in the 1950s and 1960s placed strict controls on financial markets. London has emerged as the premier Euro-market and all sorts of assets can be traded there. Tax evasion also motivates the existence of such markets in places such as Luxembourg, the Bahamas, and Singapore which offer lenient treatment on capital income. A particular feature of offshore markets is that the same assets, in the same currency, can be traded in both domestic and offshore markets.

REFERENCES

Cargill, Thomas F. and Royama Shoichi. 1988. *The transition of finance in Japan and the United States.* Stanford: Hoover Institution Press.

Dickey, D. A. and Fuller, W. A. 1979. Distribution of estimators for autoregressive time series with unit root. *Journal of the American statistical association* 74:427–32.

Suzuki Yoshio. 1993. *Nihon no kinyō seisaku.* Tokyo: Iwanami Shuppan.

Yoshino Naoyuki. 1995. *Changing behavior of private banks and corporations and monetary policy in Japan.* London: Macmillan.

Yoshino Naoyuki and Yoshimura Masaharu. 1995. Kinyō seisaku no hannō kansō to money supply. *Kinyō kenkyō* (Bank of Japan).

U.S. Government Expenditure Policy

in the 1980s

Internal and External Repercussions

STEPHEN J. TURNOVSKY AND MARCELO BIANCONI

IT IS GENERALLY agreed that the decade of the 1980s witnessed significant changes in the U.S. economy. This transformation occurred both within the domestic economy as well as in its international transactions, and most economists would agree that its relationship with Japan was an integral part of this process.

In the United States various domestic factors contributed to this development: several tax reforms with strong incentive effects; a period of volatile nominal interest rates mainly in the early part of the decade; and the economy experienced a period of expansion with a substantial increase in private net worth. More importantly, on the fiscal side, even though the growth of national income generated increased tax revenues, an ambitious program of government expenditure, associated largely with the build up of the defense industry, generated large budget deficits. For the first time, the U.S. became an international debtor nation and exchange rates followed a volatile pattern in the decade.

In summary, some of the facts that broadly characterize the behavior of the U.S. variables over the decade of the 1980s and its relations with Japan include:

(1) Real government spending in the United States grew faster than tax revenues, leading to large and growing budget deficits and an increased accumulated government debt. Most of the growth in expenditure occurred in defense, with a slower growth in social services and infrastructure.

(2) The overall growth of real capital in the United States grew modestly,

mainly in the form of equipment, with the growth of structures remaining relatively stable.

(3) The U.S. current account deteriorated dramatically mainly with Japan, and the United States is currently the largest debtor nation.

(4) After an appreciation during the first part of the decade, the U.S. dollar started a steady depreciation against the yen, from around ¥250 per U.S. dollar at its height to around ¥125 per U.S. dollar by the end of the decade.

The objective of this paper is to determine the extent to which the interrelationships among these and other key dynamic variables, which occurred in the U.S. economy throughout the 1980s, can be explained using a rigorous benchmark macroeconomic framework. The model we shall employ is that of the intertemporal optimizing representative agent, which has become increasingly adopted in contemporary macroeconomics. This framework includes the following key features:

(1) All consumption, saving, and labor supply decisions are carried out so as to maximize the intertemporal utility (welfare) of the agents in the domestic economy (United States) subject to an intertemporal budget constraint, which incorporates the accumulation of physical capital, and financial capital under perfect capital markets.

(2) A representative firm in the domestic country engages in production decisions in order to maximize the discounted present value of profits. These decisions involve determining a demand for labor (employment), the allocation of existing capital, and the rate of investment.

(3) The third agent is the government, which finances its expenditure by raising taxes and by possibly issuing debt.

The outcome of all these interrelated decisions is a benchmark dynamic macroeconomic equilibrium. This may be employed to analyze the macrodynamic adjustment of the economy as it responds to the various shocks impinging on it. These shocks may be of domestic origin, such as domestic expenditure shocks and domestic productivity shocks, or they may originate from abroad, as in the case of terms of trade shocks and the oil shocks of the 1970s. In addition, the shocks may be real, or they may reflect nominal rigidities. In principle, the dynamic adjustment in response to any specific shock can be analyzed using this framework.

The shock we choose to focus on in this paper takes the form of an increase in government spending which originates in the domestic (U.S.) economy. The reason for studying this particular disturbance is because the growth in government expenditure is one of the principal characteristics of the U.S. economy during the 1980s, and is generally viewed as a potential source of imbalance with the rest of the world in general, and with Japan in particular.

We should emphasize that the equilibrium we derive is only a benchmark. As such, it is important to note that it is consistent with several benchmark properties found in the literature. First, since the only form of taxation to be considered is of the lump-sum form, Ricardian Equivalence properties hold. Thus the analysis does not address issues relating to the effects of different forms of distortionary taxation. Second, the transversality condition guarantees that the long-run equilibrium is one in which the domestic economy achieves a zero current account balance with the rest of the world. However, this property does not mean that the domestic economy cannot maintain an indefinite current account deficit with a specific country. On the contrary, it is perfectly consistent with the United States running a long-run current account deficit with Japan, which is balanced by a corresponding surplus with Europe, say. Third, the model abstracts from monetary aspects, thereby ignoring any discrepancies between nominal and real quantities. By focusing on the latter, it abstracts from all monetary rigidities, which of course are an important real world phenomenon.

There are several advantages to adopting this kind of framework. First, it provides a rigorous analytical approach to addressing the dynamic aspects in the aggregate economy relating to both the domestic and foreign sectors. Since the accumulation of capital and debt are intrinsically dynamic processes, it is important that they be analyzed within such a framework, such as provided by the present approach. Second, central to this approach is the welfare of the representative agent. This is important if we want to address normative aspects pertaining to what are appropriate policies.

Within this framework, the case of fiscal shocks taking the form of government consumption expenditures induces certain patterns in the key endogenous variables that are surprisingly consistent with some of the characteristics of the U.S. economy during the 1980s, especially with respect to its interactions with Japan. In particular, the analysis shows that under the specific assumptions of the model, a domestic fiscal expansion will lead to an initial appreciation of the exchange rate, followed by a gradual depreciation. The capital stock accumulates gradually, while the stock of foreign assets declines over time. Thus the framework would seem to provide a promising starting point of departure.

At the same time, one needs to keep the limitations of this type of analysis in perspective. What will be analyzed is the result of just a single shock, albeit an important one. Yet in reality, the economy is continuously being subjected to a potentially infinite set of shocks of both domestic and foreign origin, occurring virtually continuously. It is clearly unrealistic to expect the type of analysis we shall undertake to replicate a complicated world with any degree of precision. Rather, the main merit of this approach is to aid in our understanding of the dynamics and to provide a framework within which the empirical patterns of behavior may be interpreted.

The remainder of the paper consists of five main parts. Section I examines some of the empirical regularities between the U.S. and Japan which existed in the 1970s and 1980s. We shall focus on key real variables, such as the rate of growth, the real current account, real exchange rate, and so on. Section II outlines the main features of the intertemporal model we shall use and some of its theoretical implications with respect to the variables we wish to study. The description of the model and its analysis will be at an intuitive level, with the formal details being available elsewhere. Section III summarizes some of the main implications of the theoretical model while Section IV parameterizes the model using data that might be representative of a stylized economy and the types of fiscal shocks that occurred during the period. Using these numerical values, the model is simulated and compared to the actual experience. Again, for reasons we have already noted, we should emphasize that our concern here is mainly with a qualitative comparison, rather than with attempting to replicate actual real world numerical magnitudes.

Section V uses the model, and other related models, as the basis for some empirical analysis. This part of the work has two aspects. First, we carry out some regressions directed at testing some of the implications of the model, particularly pertaining to the determination of the real exchange rate, the current account, and the growth rate of income and its response to fiscal shocks. The second part of our empirical work is devoted to estimating vector auto-regressive (VAR) systems consisting of the key variables in the theoretical model. We find this approach to be attractive in that it enables one to investigate the dynamic patterns in the data and to see the extent to which they match up with the theoretical responses discussed earlier.

One of the key disaggregations we consider in the empirical analysis is the distinction between military and nonmilitary fiscal expenditures in the United States. As indicated, these behaved differently over the period of the 1980s and one would expect them to impact on the economy in very different ways. Indeed, we show that government expenditure of the military type has a more pronounced short-run effect, while expenditures of the nonmilitary type tend to have longer-run effects.

I. SOME EMPIRICAL FACTS

We start by examining some empirical regularities in the data pertaining to the United States and Japan. We shall concentrate mostly on real variables and the reader is referred to Ito (1992) or the paper by Koichi Hamada in this volume for a more comprehensive survey. Our data are primarily from the International Financial Statistics (IFS) from the International Monetary Fund (IMF). We have quarterly observations mostly from 1975:2 to 1989:1, thus covering most of the decade of the 1980s. The following characteristics may be noted.

The quarterly growth of GNP for Japan is consistently higher than that of the United States until mid-1981, after which the two economies grow at comparable rates. Private consumption as a share of GNP is consistently higher in the United States than in Japan, and the gap widens after 1983. The data on gross investment as a share of GNP clearly indicate that investment in the United States is much more volatile than in Japan. In terms of total government expenditure as a share of GNP, the United States has about twice the size of government relative to Japan. While this characteristic is not surprising, given the differential military expenditures in the two countries, it has implications for the lack of impact of Japan's fiscal policy on the U.S. economy, as will be shown in Section IV below.

Turning to relationships with the rest of the world, measures of competitiveness of the two countries, and some additional series of interest, the following comments can be made. First, there has been an impressive widening of the U.S. current account deficit combined with a Japanese current account surplus. This began to occur at the beginning of the 1980s and reached a peak around 1987. The nominal exchange rate between the two countries indicates a sharp nominal depreciation of the U.S. dollar during the latter part of the 1970s, followed by a steady appreciation during the first half of the 1980s, again followed by a sharp decline to around ¥125 per U.S. dollar by the end of the decade, almost a 100 percent appreciation of the yen in nominal terms. This pattern is reflected by the behavior of the U.S./Japan real exchange rate, measured by the relative real price.

With respect to competitiveness, the real effective exchange rate and unit labor costs show that the United States holds an advantage over Japan in the sense that its currency is undervalued relative to Japan and its unit labor costs are lower relative to Japan. However, this U.S. advantage does not translate into a trade surplus in favor of the United States, see e.g. Backus (1993). Merchandise exports and imports show that the United States has a strikingly flat profile over the period. Japan consistently exports more as a share of its GNP relative to the same measure in the United States. The picture for imports shows that Japanese imports are much more volatile relative to U.S. imports both measured as a share of their respective GNP.

Long-term government bond yields show a consistently higher nominal interest rate in the United States relative to Japan in the 1980s. Given that the inflation rates in both countries were low and stable, this differential may well reflect differences in real rates of return across the two countries.

The trade imbalance of the United States in the 1980s certainly mirrors its poor performance along the fiscal dimension. Striking increases in both the U.S. domestic stock of government debt and the budget deficit occurred during the 1980s. In addition, the profiles of the military and nonmilitary expenditures in the United States demonstrate a hump-shaped build up of the former during the decade.

Finally, in terms of foreign direct investment, the data indicate that the large increase in interest rates in the United States in late 1979, coupled with other factors such as the tax reform of 1981, sparked large inflows of foreign capital from abroad, while the contrary is observed in Japan.

II. A STYLIZED EQUILIBRIUM MODEL

Our objective is to try to interpret and understand these empirical patterns in terms of a tightly specified macroeconomic model. For this purpose we shall use the representative agent framework, which has become a standard approach in the macroeconomic analysis recently. In this section we shall simply sketch the approach, and its implications, omitting all formal details. In doing so, we shall focus on a single economy.[1]

Macroeconomic Framework

The economy consists of a household and production sector, which for present purposes may be consolidated. The representative agent accumulates capital (k) for rental at its competitively determined rental rate and supplies labor (l) at its competitive wage. The agent is specialized in the production of a single commodity, using the stock of capital and labor, by means of a neo-classical production function $F(k,l)$. Expenditure on any given increase in the capital stock is an increasing function of the rate of capital accumulation. That is, there are increasing costs of investment associated with investment (I), which for simplicity we represent by the convex function $C(I)$; $C'(I)>0$; $C''(I)>0$. By choice of units, we assume

$$C(0) = 0; \quad C'(0) = 1$$

so that the total cost of zero investment is zero and the marginal cost of the initial installation is unity.

Domestic output is used in part for investment, in part as a domestic private consumption good (x), in part as a domestic government good (g_x), with the rest being exported. Thus domestic investment is a tradable good. In addition to consuming part of the domestically produced output, the private agent also consumes another good (y), which is imported from abroad. The domestic government similarly imports the quantity (g_y) of this latter good. While the price of the import good is taken as given, the economy is large enough in the production of the domestic good to affect its relative price and therefore the nation's terms of trade.

The agent can also accumulate net foreign bonds (b) that pay an exogenously given world interest rate (i^*). Equation (1a) describes the agent's instantaneous budget constraint, expressed in terms of units of foreign output:

$$\dot{b} = \frac{1}{\sigma}[F(k,l) - C(I) - x - \sigma y + \sigma i^* b - T] \tag{1a}$$

where σ = relative price of the foreign good in terms of the domestic good (the real exchange rate) and T = lump sum taxes. In addition, the rate of capital accumulation and investment are related by the constraint:

$$\dot{k} = I \tag{1b}$$

where for simplicity we continue to abstract from the depreciation of capital.

The agent's decisions are to choose his consumption levels, x, y, labor supply l, the rate of investment I, and the rates of asset accumulation $\dot{k}, \dot{b}$ to maximize:

$$\int_0^\infty [U(x,y) + V(l) + W(g_x, g_y)] e^{-\beta t} dt$$

$$U_x > 0, \quad U_y > 0 \quad V' < 0, \quad W_{g_x} > 0, \quad W_{g_y} > 0 \tag{1c}$$

The optimization is subject to the constraints (1a), (1b) and the given initial stocks $k(o) = k_o$, $b(o) = b_o$. For simplicity, the instantaneous utility function is assumed to be additively separable in the private consumption goods, x and y, labor l, and the public expenditures g_x and g_y. We also assume that the utility function is concave and that the two private goods are Edgeworth complementary, meaning that $U_{xy} > 0$.

The discounted Lagrangean for this optimization is expressed by

$$H \equiv e^{-\beta t}[U(x,y) + V(l) + W(g_x, g_y)]$$

$$+ \frac{\lambda}{\sigma} e^{-\beta t}[F(k,l) - C(I) - x - \sigma y + \sigma i^* b - T - \dot{b}] + q^* e^{-\beta t}[I - \dot{k}] \tag{2}$$

where λ is the shadow value of wealth in the form of internationally traded bonds and q^* is the shadow value of the agent's capital stock. Exposition of the model is simplified by using the shadow value of wealth as numeraire. Consequently, $q \equiv \sigma q^*/\lambda$ is defined to be the market price of capital in terms of the (unitary) price of foreign bonds.

The optimality conditions to this problem with respect to x, y, l, and I are respectively:

$$U_x(x, y) = \frac{\lambda}{\sigma} \qquad (3a)$$

$$U_y(x, y) = \lambda \qquad (3b)$$

$$V'(l) = -\frac{\lambda}{\sigma} F_l(k, l) \qquad (3c)$$

$$C'(I) = q \qquad (3d)$$

The first two equations equate the marginal utilities of the two consumption goods to the marginal utility of accumulating wealth, while the third equates the marginal utility of leisure to the opportunity cost of leisure, the real wage. Equation (4d) equates the marginal cost of investment to the market price of capital thereby determining the level of investment.

In addition, the shadow value of wealth and the market value of capital evolve in accordance with the conditions

$$\beta - \frac{\dot\lambda}{\lambda} = i^* \qquad (3e)$$

$$\frac{F_k(k, l)}{q} + \frac{\dot q}{q} = i = \left(i^* + \frac{\dot\sigma}{\sigma}\right) \qquad (3f)$$

These two equations represent efficiency conditions in world financial markets, which is a restrictive but important assumption underlying this approach. Equation (3e) asserts that in equilibrium, the rate of return on allocating a unit of output to consumption is equal to the rate of return on savings. The last equation describes the equality between the rate of return on investing in a unit of domestic capital, given by the left-hand side of this equation and the rate of return on investing in a domestic bond, which in turn is equal to the rate of return on investing in a foreign bond, the latter being equal to the foreign interest rate, plus the real rate of depreciation of the domestic currency.

A critical assumption we shall make is that both β and i^* are fixed. A consequence of this is that the ultimate attainment of a steady state is possible if and only if $\beta = i^*$. This implies that the marginal utility remains constant at its steady-state value $\bar\lambda$ to be determined below. In making these intertemporal allocation decisions, it is important to ensure that the private agent satisfies his intertemporal budget constraint, that is, the present value of expenditures cannot exceed the present value of resources. These conditions are described formally by

$$\lim_{t \to \infty} \lambda b e^{-i^* t} = \lim_{t \to \infty} q k e^{-i^* t} = 0 \qquad (3g)$$

The other agent in the economy is the government. Like the private sector, it is constrained in its actions by a budget constraint described by the equation

$$\dot{a} = \frac{1}{\sigma}[g_x + \sigma g_y + \sigma i^* a - T] \tag{4}$$

where a denotes the stock of (traded) bonds issued by the domestic government. This equation asserts that the domestic government deficit, which consists of the sum of its expenditures on the domestic good (g_x), on the imported good (g_y), the interest owing on its outstanding debt, less tax receipts, is financed by issuing additional debt.

Subtracting (4) from (3a) yields the national budget constraint:

$$\dot{n} = \frac{1}{\sigma}[F(k,l) - (x + g_x) - \sigma(y + g_y) - C(I) + \sigma i^* n] \tag{5}$$

where $n \equiv b - a =$ stock of net credit of the domestic economy. That is, the rate of accumulation of traded bonds by the domestic economy equals the balance of payments on current account, which in turn equals the balance of trade plus the net interest earned on the traded bonds. To rule out the possibility that the country can run up infinite debt or credit with the rest of the world, we impose the intertemporal budget constraint implied by the transversality condition

$$\lim_{t \to \infty} ne^{-i^*t} = 0 \tag{6a}$$

This relationship, together with the transversality condition (3g), imposes a corresponding intertemporal budget constraint on the domestic government, namely

$$\lim_{t \to \infty} ae^{-i^*t} = 0 \tag{6b}$$

The complete macroeconomic equilibrium can now be described as follows. First, there are the static optimality conditions (3a)–(3d), with $\lambda = \bar{\lambda}$, together with the domestic output market clearing condition

$$F(k,l) = x + Z(\sigma) + C(I) + g_x \tag{7}$$

where $Z(\sigma)$ is the amount of the domestic good exported, with $Z'(\sigma) > 0$; i.e., the quantity of exports increases as the domestic exchange rate depreciates (i.e.

as σ increases). Second, there are the dynamic equations (3b), (3f), (4), (5), together with the transversality conditions (3g), (6a), (6b).

The five static equations may be solved for x, y, l, I, and σ in terms of $\bar{\lambda}, k, q$, and g_x as follows:

$$x = x(\bar{\lambda}, k, q, g_x) \qquad x_{\bar{\lambda}} < 0, \quad x_k > 0, \quad x_q < 0, \quad x_{g_x} < 0 \qquad (8a)$$

$$y = y(\bar{\lambda}, k, q, g_x) \qquad y_{\bar{\lambda}} < 0, \quad y_k > 0, \quad y_q < 0, \quad y_{g_x} < 0 \qquad (8b)$$

$$l = l(\bar{\lambda}, k, q, g_x) \qquad l_{\bar{\lambda}} \gtrless 0, \quad l_k \gtrless 0, \quad l_q > 0, \quad l_{g_x} > 0 \qquad (8c)$$

$$\sigma = \sigma(\bar{\lambda}, k, q, g_x) \qquad \sigma_{\bar{\lambda}} > 0, \quad \sigma_k > 0, \quad \sigma_q < 0, \quad \sigma_{g_x} < 0 \qquad (8d)$$

$$I = I(q) \qquad I' > 0 \qquad (8e)$$

The explicit expressions for the partial derivatives can be obtained by the usual methods and the following intuitive explanation can be given.

(1) An increase in the marginal utility of wealth induces domestic consumers to reduce consumption of both goods and to increase their savings and labor supply. Being large in the market for the domestic good, this reduction in the demand for that good causes its relative price to fall, i.e., σ rises, thereby stimulating exports. The overall effect on the demand for domestic output depends upon whether this exceeds the reduction in x. If it does, then domestic output and employment and (given k) employment both rise; if not, both fall.

(2) An increase in the stock of capital raises output and the real wage. The higher domestic output stimulates the consumption of x, though by a lesser amount, and the relative price σ rises. With the two private goods being Edgeworth complementary ($U_{xy} > 0$), the increase in the consumption of the domestic good increases the demand for the imported good as well. While the rise in the real wage rate tends to decrease V', thereby stimulating employment, the rise in σ has the opposite effect and the net effect on employment depends upon which influence dominates.

(3) An increase in q stimulates investment. This increases the demand for the domestic good and its relative price rises; i.e., σ falls. This in turn raises the marginal utility of the domestic good, implying that the consumption of x must fall, and with $U_{xy} > 0$, y falls as well. On balance, the increase in investment exceeds the fall in demand stemming from the reduction in x and lower exports, so that domestic output and employment rise.

(4) An increase in government expenditure on domestic output raises the demand for that good, thereby raising its relative price (lowering σ). Employment and domestic output are therefore stimulated. However, the increased output, together with the reduced exports stemming from the fall in σ, is smaller than the increase in demand generated by the additional government expen-

diture, so that x must fall in order for domestic goods market equilibrium to prevail. With $U_{xy}>0$, the reduced demand for the domestic good spills over to the import good.

All this describes only the partial effects of a short-run change in government expenditure g_x. In addition, such an expenditure generates jumps in the marginal utility of wealth and the shadow value of capital, thereby inducing further responses. The complete short-run responses consist of a combination of these effects and will be discussed below. Finally, we may note that given the additive separability of the utility function in private and public goods, the short-run equilibrium does not depend directly upon g_y. However, as we will see presently, government expenditure on the imported good has an indirect effect through its impact on $\bar{\lambda}$ and q.

The evolution of the system is determined by substituting the short-run equilibrium into the dynamic equations and ensuring that the transversality conditions are met. In fact the dynamics can be determined sequentially. First, equations (1b) and (3f) can be reduced to a pair of autonomous differential equations in the capital stock k and its shadow value q and these constitute the core of the dynamics.

Next, (5) equates the accumulation of foreign assets by the economy to its current account surplus. Using the domestic goods market clearing condition (7), this may be expressed equivalently in terms of exports minus imports plus the interest service account

$$\dot{n} = \frac{1}{\sigma} [Z(\sigma) - \sigma(y+g_y) + \sigma i^* n] \qquad (7')$$

This equation may in turn be reduced to an autonomous differential equation in n, after substituting the solutions for q and k. The same applies to the government budget constraint (4).

Equilibrium Dynamics

Carrying out the procedure outlined above, along a stable adjustment path, the dynamics of the capital stock and its shadow value may be represented by:

$$k = \tilde{k} + (k_o - \tilde{k})e^{\mu_1 t} \qquad (9a)$$

$$q = \tilde{q} + \mu_1 C''(k - \tilde{k}) \qquad (9b)$$

where $\mu_1 < 0$. These two equations form the basis for determining the adjustment within the economy to any shocks. From these equations, together with the short-run solutions given in (8), the behavior of consumption, employment, the real exchange rate, and investment can be derived.

The behavior of the external economy is obtained by considering (7′) in the form

$$\dot{n} = \frac{Z\left[\sigma(\bar{\lambda}, k, q, g_x)\right]}{\sigma(\bar{\lambda}, k, q, g_x)} - [y(\bar{\lambda}, k, q, g_x) + g_y] + i^* n \qquad (7'')$$

Substituting (9a), (9b) into this equation, and solving, while imposing the intertemporal national budget constraint (6a), leads to the following relationship describing the rate of accumulation of foreign bonds by the economy, i.e., its current account:

$$n(t) = \tilde{n} + \frac{\Omega}{\mu_1 - i^*}(k_o - \tilde{k})e^{\mu_1 t} \qquad (10)$$

where

$$\Omega \equiv \frac{1}{\tilde{\sigma}}[\delta(\sigma_k + \sigma_q \mu_1 C'') - \sigma(y_k + y_q \mu_1 C'')] \quad \text{and} \quad \delta \equiv Z' - Z/\sigma.$$

Setting $t=0$ in equation (10) yields a linear approximation to the national intertemporal budget constraint and (10) itself describes the relationship between the accumulation of capital and the accumulation of traded bonds during the transition, if this condition is to be met. Of particular significance is the sign of this relationship. The definition of Ω emphasizes that capital exercises two channels of influence on the current account. First, an increase in k raises the relative price σ, both directly, but also through the accompanying fall in q, as seen in (9b). What this does to the trade balance depends upon δ. From the above definition of δ, $\delta > 0$ if and only if the relative price elasticity of the foreign demand for exports exceeds unity. Whether this is so, is an empirical matter. At the same time, the increase in k increases imports both directly and again through the fall in q, and this reduces the trade balance. While either case is possible, we shall assume in discussing the theoretical framework that the relative price effect dominates, so that $\Omega > 0$. However, we shall undertake some empirical analysis of this relationship.

Steady State

The steady state of the economy is obtained when $\dot{k} = \dot{q} = \dot{n} = 0$ and is given by the following set of relationships:

$$U_x(\tilde{x},\tilde{y}) = \frac{\overline{\lambda}}{\tilde{\sigma}} \tag{11a}$$

$$U_y(\tilde{x},\tilde{y}) = \overline{\lambda} \tag{11b}$$

$$V'(\tilde{l}) = -F_l(\tilde{k},\tilde{l})\frac{\overline{\lambda}}{\tilde{\sigma}} \tag{11c}$$

$$\tilde{q} = 1 \tag{11d}$$

$$F_k(\tilde{k},\tilde{l}) = i^* \tag{11e}$$

$$F(\tilde{k},\tilde{l}) = \tilde{x} + Z(\tilde{\sigma}) + g_x \tag{11f}$$

$$Z(\tilde{\sigma}) + \tilde{\sigma}i^*\tilde{n} = \tilde{y} + g_y \tag{11g}$$

$$n_o = \tilde{n} + \frac{\Omega}{\mu_1 - i^*}(k_o - \tilde{k}) \tag{11h}$$

These equations jointly determine the steady-state equilibrium solutions for $\tilde{x}$, $\tilde{y}$, $\tilde{k}$, $\tilde{l}$, $\tilde{q}$, $\tilde{\sigma}$, $\tilde{n}$, and $\overline{\lambda}$.

Several aspects of this steady state merit comment. First, the steady-state value of q is unity, consistent with the Tobin q theory of investment. Second, the steady-state marginal physical product of capital is equated to the exogenously given foreign interest rate, thereby determining the domestic capital-labor ratio. Third, (11g) implies that in steady-state equilibrium, the current account balance must be zero. Export earnings plus net interest earnings on traded bonds must just finance net imports. Equation (11h) describes the equilibrium relationship between the accumulation of capital over time and the accumulation of traded bonds, consistent with the nation's intertemporal budget constraint. Finally, we should recall that this steady state is sustainable only as long as the government maintains a feasible debt and taxing policy consistent with its intertemporal budget constraint.

Long-Run Effects of Fiscal Expansion

This model can be used to study the dynamic responses to all kinds of disturbances impacting on the economy and which may be either of domestic or foreign origin. Our emphasis is on fiscal policy and in particular on domestic government expenditure. This economy we have been describing has the characteristic of being forward-looking, so that to an important degree the short-run adjustments are driven by the expected long-run responses. It is therefore convenient to begin by focusing on the latter. In describing the behavior of the economy, at least as predicted by the model, our description shall be largely intuitive.

A convenient starting point is the observation that since the world interest rate i^* remains fixed, the marginal physical product condition (11e) implies that the long-run capital-labor ratio is constant, independent of either g_x or g_y. Capital, labor, and therefore domestic output all change in the same proportions (whether positively or negatively), so that the marginal physical product of labor and hence the real wage rate also remain constant. Whether the impact of the fiscal expansion on the domestic economy is expansionary or contractionary depends critically upon the elasticity of the foreign demand for domestic exports.

If this is large (say greater than unity), then the response of the relative price σ to an increase in g_x is relatively small in magnitude. Accordingly, the increase in taxes necessary to finance an increase in g_x raises the long-run marginal utility of wealth (measured in terms of domestic goods and $=\overline{\lambda}/\sigma$), inducing more labor supply, raising the productivity of capital, inducing an expansion in capital, and output, much as it does in an economy closed to international trade. However, in contrast to the closed economy, the stimulus to demand through government expenditure may, or may not, exceed the addition to output and the relative price σ of the import good may either rise or fall. At the same time, the increase in the steady-state stock of capital is likely to lead to a decline in the steady-state stock of traded bonds held by the domestic economy. The higher taxes, coupled with the reduction in net interest earnings by the economy, mean a reduction in real disposable income, a consequence of which is that the private consumptions of the two goods, $\tilde{x}$ and $\tilde{y}$, both decline. The fact that the marginal utility measured in terms of domestic goods rises, while the relative price σ may either rise or fall, means that the response of the marginal utility as measured in terms of the foreign good $\overline{\lambda}$ can also respond in either way, though it too will certainly be increased if the utility function is additively separable in the two goods.

Looking at (11g), we see that a fiscal expansion on the domestic good raises the equilibrium trade balance when measured in terms of the foreign good $(=-i^*\tilde{n})$. It will do the same even more strongly, in terms of the domestic good, as long as the domestic economy is a net creditor nation $(\tilde{n}>0)$. However, for a debtor country, the trade balance in terms of the domestic good may fall if the relative price effect is sufficiently strong.

However, these responses tend to be reversed if the foreign import demand elasticity is low. In this case, there is likely to be a larger response in the relative price, reducing the marginal utility $\overline{\lambda}/\sigma$. This leads to a reduction in labor supply, a decline in the long-run productivity of capital, inducing a contraction in domestic capital and in domestic output. In this case the parameter Ω which describes the comovement of the current account and capital, is negative, so that the decline in domestic capital is accompanied by a decline in net foreign assets. Furthermore, the decline in the marginal utility of wealth $\bar{\lambda}/\sigma$ will induce domestic residents to save less and consume more and the consumption of both the domestic and the import good will rise. The long-run trade balance will tend to decline.

Transitional Effects of Fiscal Expansion

Combining the solutions for k and q given in (9a) and (9b) leads to the negatively sloped relationship

$$q = 1 + \mu_1 C''(k - \tilde{k}) \tag{12}$$

As long as no future shock is expected, the economy must follow this locus, if long-run convergence is to prevail. This equation implies that an unanticipated permanent increase in g_x leads to an initial discrete change in the shadow value of capital $q(o)$, namely:

$$\frac{dq(o)}{dg_x} = -\mu_1 C'' \frac{d\tilde{k}}{dg_x} \tag{13}$$

The short-run response depends upon the long-run adjustment in the capital stock. If this is expansionary, then the shadow price of capital $q(o)$ will immediately rise. Since agents know that the fiscal stimulus is going to eventually raise the capital stock in the economy, the short-run marginal value of investing is increased.

The dynamics following an unanticipated permanent increase in g_x are illustrated in Fig. 1A and Fig. 1B. Part A describes the adjustment in q and k, while Part B describes the evolution of the stock of traded bonds. This is done in the case where the fiscal shock is expansionary. Suppose that the economy starts in steady-state equilibrium at the point P on the stable arm XX and that there is a permanent increase in g_x. The new steady state is at the point Q, with a higher equilibrium stock of capital $\tilde{k}$, and an unchanged shadow value of capital $\bar{q} = 1$. In the short run, q jumps from P to A on the new stable locus $X'X'$. From (13), it is seen that the increase in q has an immediate expansionary effect on investment and capital begins to accumulate.

The initial responses of other key variables include

$$\frac{dl(o)}{dg_x} = \frac{\partial l}{\partial g_x} + \frac{\partial l}{\partial \bar{\lambda}} \frac{\partial \bar{\lambda}}{\partial g_x} + \frac{\partial l}{\partial q} \frac{\partial q(o)}{\partial g_x} > 0 \qquad (14a)$$

$$\frac{d\sigma(o)}{dg_x} = \frac{\partial \sigma}{\partial g_x} + \frac{\partial \sigma}{\partial \bar{\lambda}} \frac{\partial \bar{\lambda}}{\partial g_x} + \frac{\partial \sigma}{\partial q} \frac{\partial q(o)}{\partial g_x} < 0 \qquad (14b)$$

$$\frac{dx(o)}{dg_x} = \frac{\partial x}{\partial g_x} + \frac{\partial x}{\partial \bar{\lambda}} \frac{\partial \bar{\lambda}}{\partial g_x} + \frac{\partial x}{\partial q} \frac{\partial q(o)}{\partial g_x} < 0 \qquad (14c)$$

$$\frac{dy(o)}{dg_x} = \frac{\partial y}{\partial g_x} + \frac{\partial y}{\partial \bar{\lambda}} \frac{\partial \bar{\lambda}}{\partial g_x} + \frac{\partial y}{\partial q} \frac{\partial q(o)}{\partial g_x} < 0 \qquad (14d)$$

which consist of two channels of influence. First, there are the direct effects, consisting of the partial derivatives such as $\partial l/\partial g_x$ and discussed previously. Second, there are the indirect effects, which operate through induced jumps in $\bar{\lambda}$ and q.

Despite the fact that the various effects may, or may not, work in the same direction (and in fact the effects through $\bar{\lambda}$ are ambiguous), we are able to establish that overall a permanent increase in g_x will have the same qualitative effect on employment and consumption in the short run, as it will have in the steady state. Namely, it will raise employment, while reducing the consumptions of the two goods. In addition, it will lower the relative price σ. How the magnitudes of these short-run responses compare with the long-run adjustments depends upon whether the short-run effects resulting from the rise in the shadow price of investment $q(o)$ dominate the long-run effects stemming from the eventual increase in the capital stock.

From (8d) and the fact that upon reaching the point A in Fig. 1A on the new stable locus $\dot{q}<0$, $\dot{k}>0$, we can infer that in the short run and during the subsequent transition $\dot{\sigma}>0$, i.e. the relative price of the import good must be increasing. This means that the short-run fall in the relative price overshoots its long-run response. At the same time, the fact that $\dot{\sigma}>0$ means that the fiscal expansion raises the domestic interest rate above the fixed real world rate, during the transition.

Differentiating (14a), (14b) analogously with respect to t, one can show using a similar argument that during the transition $\dot{x}>0$, $\dot{y}>0$, so that these consumptions also overreact in the short run. In both cases, the shadow price of investment effect dominates. In the case of employment, however, we are unable to determine the relative sizes of the short-run and long-run adjustments.

Part B of Fig.1 illustrates the relationship between n and k, which combining (9a) and (10) is

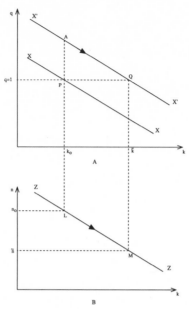

FIG. 1. Permanent fiscal expansion

$$n(t) - \tilde{n} = \frac{\Omega}{\mu_1 - i^*}(k(t) - \tilde{k})$$

This is a negatively sloped line, denoted by ZZ. Since $d\tilde{n}/dg_x = (\Omega/(\mu_1 - i^*))(d\tilde{k}/dg_x)$, this line remains fixed. The movement along A to Q in Fig. 1A corresponds to a movement along LM in Fig. 1B. From this figure, we see that an increase in government expenditure on the domestic good leads to an immediate decumulation of foreign bonds. This is brought about by the fact that the increase in g_x leads to an immediate reduction in the relative price σ, which with $\Omega > 0$ creates an immediate current account deficit. With the stock of traded bonds being predetermined, the trade balance, measured in terms of the foreign good, also falls, and with the fall in σ, the trade balance in terms of the domestic good falls even more. Over time, the rate of decline of the stock of foreign bonds is reduced. This occurs through the rising relative price σ, which causes the trade deficit to decline over time.

III. SOME EMPIRICAL IMPLICATIONS

We have presented a stylized macroeconomic model of an economy and used it to describe the likely theoretical response to a very precise policy disturbance, namely a once and for all permanent increase in government expenditure on a domestically produced good. Before trying to match up the implications with the data, it is convenient to summarize the main theoretical propositions suggested by the model. These include the following:

(1) If the foreign elasticity of demand for the domestic good is reasonably large, then an increase in government expenditure will be generally expansionary in the domestic economy. Over time capital will accumulate, while employment and output will also increase. If the foreign demand is relatively inelastic, then the capital stock, employment, and output should all contract over time in the domestic economy.

(2) If the foreign elasticity of demand for domestic output is large, then the accumulating capital stock may be accompanied by a decumulation of foreign assets. If the elasticity is small, then the decumulating capital stock will be accompanied by a decumulating stock of foreign assets. In either case, a fiscal expansion is accompanied by a current account deficit.

(3) A fiscal expansion will tend to crowd out the consumption of both the domestic good and the imported good, in both the short run and in the long run, leading to an unambiguous reduction in domestic consumption. However, the crowding out is more severe in the short run, and consumption increases over time, though it fails to reach its previous level.

(4) The fiscal expansion is likely to lead to an initial appreciation of the domestic real exchange rate, as the domestic government increases aggregate demand, followed by a subsequent depreciation.

(5) If the increase in government expenditure is expansionary, then during the transition $\dot{\sigma} > 0$ and the domestic interest rate will be above the foreign interest rate. If it is contractionary, then it will be below the world rate.

We need to emphasize that these propositions pertain to a one-time change only. Over the period of the 1980s (as well as other periods) policy is continually changing. We need to extrapolate from these theoretical propositions to observations about the data.

IV. NUMERICAL IMPLEMENTATION

To get some idea of how the formal analysis relates to the data, the model needs to be parameterized. That is, specific functional forms for the utility function, production function, etc. need to be chosen.

We shall assume that the utility of the representative household is of the form

$$Z = [\theta \ln(x) + (1-\theta)\ln(y)] + \left\{ \phi_1 \frac{(1-l)^{1-\phi_2}}{1-\phi_2} \right\} + W(g_x, g_y) \quad (15)$$

This instantaneous function consists of three subfunctions reflecting the separability of the utility function explicit in equation (1c). The utility attached to consumption is represented by the logarithmic subfunction, $U(x,y) = \theta\ln(x) + (1-\theta)\ln(y)$, where the parameter θ represents the share of expenditure devoted to the good. We choose $\theta = 0.5$, a value that is fairly standard in simulation exercises of this kind (see e.g. Stockman and Tesar [1990]) and serves as a reasonable benchmark.[2]

The second subfunction is associated with the labor-leisure choice, where we assume that $V(l)$ is of the CES type. The parameter $\phi_1 > 0$ represents the weight devoted to leisure relative to consumption and government expenditure in the instantaneous utility function. In our base data set we assume $\phi_1 = 1$.[3] The parameter $\phi_2 \geq 1$ is associated with the elasticity of labor supply of the representative household. In particular, the elasticity of demand for leisure is $-1/\phi_2$ and because the time endowment is given, the elasticity of labor supply is $1/\phi_2$. In our base set, we choose $\phi_2 = 1$, which yields the logarithmic function for leisure.[4]

The discount rate represents the degree of patience of the representative consumer, i.e. the rate at which the agent prefers the present over the future. Utility is discounted at the rate of 2 percent per period, which we view as corresponding to a quarter and in our empirical analysis quarterly data will be used. This represents a fairly high rate of discount and characterizes a fairly impatient agent. As a counterfactual exercise, we will also briefly consider the adjustment path that corresponds to a much lower discount rate (around 1 percent per year). We do not need to specify the function W, unless we wish to conduct explicit welfare analysis of the particular fiscal shock.

The production side of the economy is parameterized by the Cobb-Douglas technology, of the form

$$F(k,l) = k^{\alpha}l^{(1-\alpha)} \qquad (16)$$

where the exponent α is chosen to be 0.36. This corresponds to the share of output going to capital of 36 percent and is a widely accepted value in the literature. As recalled from the model, investment is subject to a convex cost of adjustment function. In these initial simulations, this is taken to be of the quadratic form

$$C(I) = I\{1 + (1/2)hI\} \qquad (17)$$

where h represents costs of adjustment. Initially we shall assume $h = 0.1$, in the parameterization, though we have also experimented with higher values ($h = 10$), with basically the same qualitative results.

The final function we need to specify is the export function, which we take to be of the constant elasticity form

$$Z(\sigma) = \sigma^\gamma \qquad (18)$$

where it will be recalled that σ is the real exchange rate measured as the price of the foreign good in terms of the domestic good and γ is the price elasticity of exports. As noted, the size of the elasticity γ is important in determining the behavior of the current account. Based on some recent estimates of Krugman (1989) we assumed a relatively high value of $\gamma = 1.4$. While this may seem unreasonably high, we should note that we also considered the much smaller value of $\gamma = 0.1$. While most of the results are relatively insensitive to the choice of this elasticity, values of $\gamma < 1$ imply responses of the current account that are inconsistent with that of the data.

Taking the amount of initial government expenditure on good x to be 0.4 and the net asset position is unity, implying that the country is a net creditor, these functions and parameter values suffice to determine the initial equilibrium, which has the following structure:

Domestic output (z)	2.2160	(100%)
Consumption of domestic output (x)	0.9173	(41.4%)
Export of domestic output ($Z(\sigma)$)	0.8987	(40.6%)
Government expenditure on domestic good	0.4000	(18%)
Capital stock	39.8894	
Employment	0.4360	
Marginal utility $\bar{\lambda}$	0.5050	
Consumption of import good	0.9899	
Real exchange rate	0.9266	
Balance of trade	−0.0185	
Capital account surplus	0.0185	
Net asset position	1.0000	

These numbers are not unreasonable. Something over 41 percent of domestic output is consumed and a similar share exported, while the balance of around 18 percent is claimed by the domestic government. Given that output is assumed to be measured in quarterly units, this implies a capital-output ratio (with output expressed at annual rates) of around 4.5 which is also plausible. The domestic economy is assumed to have a small balance of trade deficit of around 0.8 percent of total output, which again is a reasonable starting point.

Our policy experiment consists of raising government expenditure on the domestic good by 12.5 percent from 0.40 to 0.45. This increase is fully financed by nondistortionary lump-sum taxes. The magnitude of the increase in government expenditure is fairly substantial and we should think of the change as representing the accumulation of the increase in government expenditure that took place over say two to three years. This was of the order of 15–20 percent of the initial level of government expenditure.

We then fully characterize the dynamic adjustment from the initial steady state to the new one, consistent with higher government expenditure. The dynamic paths of the relevant endogenous variables are presented in Figures 2 and 3.

The effects of this expansionary government policy on domestic output are modest. In the short run real output expands initially by 1 percent, though during the subsequent transition it continues to increase further, to an eventual increase of around 1.4 percent. Consumption of the domestic good as a share of output initially decreases by 3.75 percent and then increases slightly over time, though it remains below its initial share. The consumption of the foreign good responds fully on impact. This is because of the additive separability of the utility function in the two consumption goods, with the response being a slight drop of only around 0.4 percent. The consumption of the foreign good as a share of domestic output actually falls by about 3.0 percent on impact. This is a consequence of the real appreciation of the domestic exchange rate, which appreciates on impact at around 1.5 percent and gradually depreciates thereafter, with its long-run appreciation being around 0.6 percent.

Turning to the behavior of assets, the increase in government expenditure leads to an initial increase in the shadow value of investment of around 0.1 percent, after which it gradually reverts to its stationary equilibrium level of unity. This leads to an initial increase in investment as a share of output, resulting in a modest long-run increase in the capital stock. Associated with this increase, the long-run net asset position n decreases substantially by about 7.7 percent. The trade balance, after an initial drop, gradually increases over time, though it remains in deficit.

The magnitudes of the initial adjustments are implausibly small. This is largely due to the small value for the adjustment cost parameter h. For larger values of h, the initial responses are increased, but the subsequent adjustment is slowed down. There is a tradeoff between these two dimensions of the dynamics that is characteristic of models of this type. Indeed, in a real business cycle context, Kydland and Prescott (1982) have criticized the adjustment cost model as yielding a pattern of covariances which is grossly at variance with the U.S. data. However, since our main concern is more with understanding general qualitative characteristics, rather than with a more precise calibration of the data, these parameter values suffice, though it is an aspect of the model that could be refined further.

These qualitative features of the model resemble some, but not all, of the characteristics of the U.S. experience during the decade of the 1980s. Starting

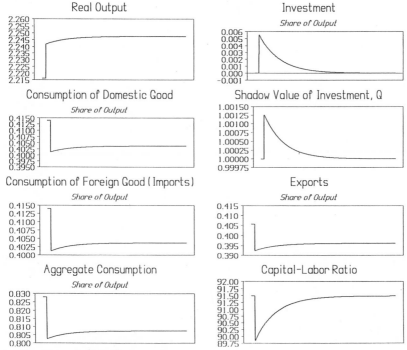

FIG. 2. Numerical simulation paths

from the second quarter of 1981 up to the end of 1982 we observe a consistent increase in government expenditures in the United States as a share of GNP. In the following years there is a consumption boom in the U.S. economy and a consistent deterioration of the current account. The model reflects reasonably well the behavior of the bilateral real exchange rate between the United States and Japan, over at least part of the period. During the first part of the decade the U.S. dollar appreciated in real terms, and after the Plaza Accord in 1985 it depreciated sharply. The model picks up the appreciation, but not the subsequent sharp depreciation. Furthermore, the general decline in the current account and the associated accumulation of foreign debt, characteristic of the period, is reflected by the model. It is not clear how pertinent the model is in explaining the growth rate of output in the U.S. economy, since after something of a spurt during 1981–83, the growth rate in U.S. GNP tends to drop off slightly. However, the model suggests very little impact on output, at least for these parameter values.

We turn to the implications for costs and competitiveness. The analytical model has the property that the capital stock is fixed instantaneously and adjusts only gradually over time. The short-run increase in output is therefore met by

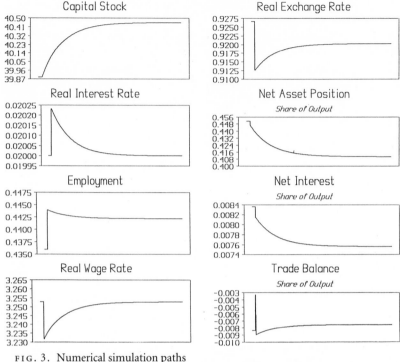

FIG. 3. Numerical simulation paths

an increase in employment, leading to an initial decrease in the capital-labor ratio of around 1.8 percent. Along the transitional path the capital stock increases and employment declines mildly, such that the capital-labor ratio eventually increases to its original level. The real interest rate is inversely related to the capital-labor ratio, while the real wage rate is positively related. The former increases initially by around 1 percent, while the latter decreases by approximately the same amount. During the transitional path, the real interest rate therefore declines, while the wage rate increases, both back to their original levels.

As noted, the model predicts a short-run behavior of the real exchange rate with an initial appreciation of about 1.5 percent and an almost flat profile along the transitional path to its new equilibrium. This is in accord with the large appreciation of the U.S. real exchange rate against a basket of goods from its major trading partners and with the bilateral rate between the United States and Japan.

It is well known that the nominal interest rate in the United States was high in the early 1980s, while the inflation rate was moderate. Real interest rates were very high at that time and tended to decline over the decade. The dynamics of the model correspond quite well to the actual data in this dimension, at least insofar as real interest rates are related to government expenditure.

However, the model does not do a particularly good job in explaining real wage behavior. U.S. data on unit labor costs show a consistent increase for the first half of the 1980s. By contrast, the formal model predicts an initial downward jump in the real wage rate, at the time of impact. This is due to the decline in the initial capital-labor ratio, associated with the initial increase in employment, together with the sluggish adjustment in the capital stock. However, over time, as the capital stock is accumulated, the capital-labor ratio rises, implying a steady adjustment in the real wage back to its initial equilibrium level. Not surprisingly, positive supply shocks are necessary to provide a more satisfactory explanation of real wage behavior over this period.

We conclude our discussion of this numerical analysis by briefly commenting on the sensitivity to alternative parameter values. First, we consider the case where the weight of leisure in the instantaneous utility function is increased to $\phi_1 = 1.67$. This value implies a long-run labor supply elasticity is about 1/3, as in Hansen and Wright (1992). The effect of increasing the relative weight on leisure is to change the initial allocation. For instance, the capital stock is smaller to accommodate for the lower labor supply in order to maintain the constant capital-labor ratio. But it does not change any of the responses to the government spending shock in any substantive way.

Second, we consider the case where the elasticity of labor supply is much lower, with $\phi_2 = 10$. In this alternative case, the initial labor supply decreases to about 1/5. The effect of the change in government spending is qualitatively the same, but quantitatively the capital stock and employment change very little.

Finally, we consider the case of the low discount rate, corresponding to the more patient economy. It has been documented that the saving rate in Japan is much higher than in the United States during the postwar period, see e.g. Horioka (1994). It is well known that with a lower discount rate the transition to the new steady state is much longer. In such an economy the impact effects of the fiscal shock are much smaller, but much more persistent. In particular, the initial investment boom is smaller, but more prolonged.

The pattern of transitional dynamic adjustment in the two economies is rather similar. However, the economy with the low discount rate is much less sensitive to the net asset position than is the more impatient economy. This has the consequence of a much smaller correlation between domestic government expenditure and the real exchange rate and the balance of payments. The implication is that if agents in the United States had been less myopic, a different pattern of interactions with the rest of the world would have emerged.

V. EMPIRICAL ANALYSIS

We turn now to discussing some empirical analysis we have performed based on the formal model.[5] This is divided into two parts. First, we present some regressions based on several models in the literature, including the present. Then we generalize this by extending the statistical analysis to dynamic vector autoregressions. In both parts we focus on the distinctive features of the U.S. economy relative to Japan, that is, its large government sector and its relatively large military expenditure.

Evidence on the Real Exchange Rate, Current Account, and the Transmission of Government Expenditure

In the economics literature there are a number of recent papers that develop one-country and two-country macroeconomic models of the international economy which are then used to test some theoretical propositions. Froot and Rogoff (1991) develop a one-country two-good model, very similar to the one outlined in Section III, to derive some testable hypotheses about the determination of the real exchange rate and to see the extent to which it responds to fiscal shocks. Bianconi and Turnovsky (1993) develop the transitional dynamics of a two-country one-good model and use it to derive testable hypotheses about the international transmission of fiscal policies.

In this section we pursue these two approaches to test some implications of the role of Japan in the determination of the U.S. real exchange rate and current account, as well as the international transmission of government expenditures across the two countries.

Tables 1–3 present regressions of the determination of the U.S. real exchange rate and the current account as a function of the share of government expenditures on GNP in the United States and Japan, controlling for lagged terms and one other relevant factor in the case of the current account equation, namely the real exchange rate. These equations are of the form

$$RE_t = \psi_0 + \psi_1 RE_{t-1} + \psi_2 SG_t^{US} + \psi_3 SG_t^{J}$$

$$SCA_t = \phi_0 + \phi_1 SCA_{t-1} + \phi_2 SG_t^{US} + \phi_3 SG_t^{J} + \phi_4 RE_t$$

where SG_t^{US} is U.S. government expenditure as a share of U.S. GNP (in logarithms), SG_t^{J} is Japanese government expenditure as a share of Japan's GNP (in logarithms), and SCA_t is the U.S. current account surplus as a share of U.S. GNP (in levels). The tables present results for total U.S. government expenditure, disaggregated into nonmilitary expenditures (Table 2) and military expenditures (Table 3) respectively.

TABLE 1
Real Effective Exchange Rate and
Current Account Regressions for USA
Total US Government Expenditure
Sample: 1975:2–1989:1

	Dependent Variable	
	Real Effective Exchange Rate	Current Account as a Share of GNP
Constant	−0.394	0.023
	(1.11)	(0.024)
RE(t−1)	0.991*	—
	(0.041)	
SCA(t−1)	—	0.925*
		(0.047)
$SG^{US}(t)$	−0.477*	−0.0025
	(0.165)	(0.0028)
$SG^{J}(t)$	0.362*	0.0042
	(0.128)	(0.0039)
$RE^{US}(t)$	—	−0.0022*
		(0.0006)
Rho	0.246	—
Adj-R^2	0.94	0.96
SEE	0.032	0.00069
Durbin-h	0.33	0.59
Nobs	55	56
D-Freedom	50	51
F-Statistic(4,51)	—	125.59*

* Significant at 5% confidence level.
Standard errors in parentheses.

The rationale behind the first equation is that in a symmetric two-country two-good world where a constant share of GNP is spent by the government, the real exchange rate (i.e., the relative price between the two goods) is determined, among other factors, by the differences in the share spent by the government in the two countries. It represents a generalization to two countries of the one-country analysis presented in earlier sections.

The results are revealing. Both U.S. and Japanese government expenditure impact significantly on the behavior of the real exchange rate, though not when U.S. military government expenditure is introduced. In Tables 1 and 2, an

TABLE 2

Real Effective Exchange Rate and
Current Account Regressions for USA
US Nonmilitary Government Expenditure
Sample: 1975:2–1989:1

	Dependent Variable	
	Real Effective Exchange Rate	Current Account as a Share of GNP
Constant	0.778	0.029
	(0.913)	(0.024)
RE^{US}(t−1)	0.914*	—
	(0.044)	
SCA(t−1)	—	0.927*
		(0.045)
SGNONMIL^{US}(t)	−0.478*	−0.003
	(0.159)	(0.002)
SG^J(t)	0.518*	0.005
	(0.155)	(0.004)
RE^{US}(t)	—	−0.002*
		(0.0007)
Rho	0.266†	—
Adj-R^2	0.95	0.96
SEE	0.032	0.00069
Durbin-h	0.27	0.43
Nobs	55	56
D-Freedom	50	51
F-Statistic(4,51)	—	363.14*

* Significant at 5% confidence level.
† Significant at 10% confidence level.
Standard errors in parentheses.

increase in U.S. government expenditure leads to an appreciation of the exchange rate, while an increase in Japanese government expenditure leads to a depreciation. Note that the coefficient on the lagged real exchange rate is close to 1, and that the coefficients on the two expenditure variables are of roughly equal magnitudes and of opposite signs. These results may therefore be interpreted as saying that changes in the real exchange rate respond to differentials in the share of government expenditure. Imposing the restriction $\psi_2 = -\psi_3$ leads to a common statistically significant coefficient of about −0.4, suggesting that a 1 percent increase in the differential shares of U.S. government expen-

TABLE 3

Real Effective Exchange Rate
and Current Account Regressions for USA
US Military Government Expenditure
Sample: 1975:2–1989:1

	Dependent Variable	
	Real Effective Exchange Rate	Current Account as a Share of GNP
Constant	−0.358	0.019
	(1.63)	(0.027)
$RE^{US}(t-1)$	1.019*	—
	(0.059)	
$SCA(t-1)$	—	0.932*
		(0.047)
$SGMIL^{US}(t)$	−0.219	−0.001
	(0.137)	(0.002)
$SG^J(t)$	0.184	0.002
	(0.135)	(0.003)
$RE^{US}(t)$	—	−0.002*
		(0.0008)
Rho	0.307†	—
Adj-R^2	0.94	0.96
SEE	0.033	0.00070
Durbin-h	0.10	0.51
Nobs	55	56
D-Freedom	50	51
F-Statistic(4,51)	—	356.04*

* Significant at 5% confidence level.
† Significant at 10% confidence level.
Standard errors in parentheses.

diture leads to a −0.4 unit real depreciation of the U.S. real effective exchange rate, consistent with the basic theoretical model.

The second regression shows that the U.S. current account is not sensitive to the discrepancies in government sizes in any of the three cases. However, it shows that the U.S. current account is very persistent and that the real exchange rate has a significant but small effect. In particular, a 1 percent appreciation of the U.S. dollar induces a 0.0022 deterioration of the current account as a share of GNP. This result is robust across all government expenditure types. This negative comovement of the real exchange rate and current account balance is

TABLE 4

US—Japan Real Exchange Rate Regressions

US Government Total, Military, and Nonmilitary Expenditure

Sample: 1975:2–1989:1

	Dependent Variable		
	Real Exchange Rate	¥ per US$*US	CPI/Japan CPI
Constant	−0.738	1.632	0.418
	(2.140)	(1.740)	(2.981)
RE(t−1)	0.936*	0.861*	0.925*
	(0.057)	(0.059)	(0.076)
$SG^{US}(t)$	−0.712*	—	—
	(0.282)		
$SGNONMIL^{US}(t)$	—	−0.655*	—
		(0.263)	
$SGNMIL^{US}(t)$	—	—	−0.258
			(0.212)
$SG^{J}(t)$	0.479*	0.760*	0.267*
	(0.222)	(0.277)	(0.260)
Rho	0.331*	0.358*	0.421*
Adj-R^2	0.92	0.92	0.52
SEE	0.050	0.050	0.052
Durbin-h	0.02	−0.54	−0.62
Nobs	55	55	55
D-Freedom	50	50	50

* Significant at 5% confidence level.
Standard errors in parentheses.

consistent with the predicted negative comovement of these two variables, implied by the theoretical model, in response to a domestic fiscal shock; see Figure 3.

Table 4 presents another set of regressions where the dependent variable is the U.S.-Japan bilateral real exchange rate. It confirms the result in the previous tables; i.e., the differences in government expenditure explain fairly well the real exchange rate, except for the case of military expenditures.

Tables 5–7 present the results of a small reduced form U.S.-Japan system, where the growth rate of GNP in the two countries is related to distributed lags of growth rates of different types of government expenditure *ARG* in the two countries. The rationale for this comes from the two-country generalization of the present model, developed by Bianconi and Turnovsky. These results provide

TABLE 5

Seemingly Unrelated Regressions (SUR) by Generalized Least Squares (GLS)
Total US Government Expenditure
Sample: 1973:2–1989:3

	Dependent Variable: *Rate of Growth of GNP*	
	USA	Japan
GNP(t−1)	0.773*	0.818*
	(0.060)	(0.049)
INV(t)	0.126*	0.074*
	(0.016)	(0.0088)
INV(t−1)	−0.062*	−0.046*
	(0.021)	(0.010)
ARG^{US}(t)	0.130*	0.025†
	(0.051)	(0.015)
ARG^{J}(t)	0.033	0.070*
	(0.021)	(0.023)
Adj-R^2	0.90	0.92
SEE	0.0018	0.00065
Durbin-h	0.36	0.25
Nobs	66	66
D-Freedom	61	61
F-Statistic(1,61)	2.16	2.54

Correlation of Residuals −0.636E−2
λ_{LM}=0.267E−2 (Matrix is Diagonal)
* Significant at 5% confidence level.
† Significant at 10% confidence level.
Standard errors in parentheses.

some interesting evidence of spillover effects of government expenditure. First, in Table 3A, there is evidence of spillover effects from the United States onto Japan, though not in the reverse direction. These results are confirmed in a recent paper by Bianconi and Turnovsky (1994), using the vector autoregression methodology. However, note that in Table 6 for the case of nonmilitary expenditure, the growth effects disappear. In contrast, Table 7 shows that for military expenditures, the growth effects of government expenditures are significant and the spillover effects occur in both directions.

In summary, U.S. government expenditure of the nonmilitary type seems to have a much more powerful effect on the real exchange rate, but has very little explanatory power for the current account and the growth of GNP. Government

TABLE 6

Seemingly Unrelated Regressions (SUR) by Generalized Least Squares (GLS)
Total US Nonmilitary Government Expenditure
Sample: 1973:2–1989:3

	Dependent Variable: Rate of Growth of GNP	
	USA	Japan
GNP(t−1)	0.845*	0.843*
	(0.057)	(0.048)
INV(t)	0.136*	0.078*
	(0.016)	(0.008)
INV(t−1)	−0.082*	−0.050*
	(0.020)	(0.010)
ARGNONMIL^{US}(t)	0.037	0.002
	(0.039)	(0.012)
ARG^J(t)	0.021	0.044*
	(0.015)	(0.016)
Adj-R^2	0.89	0.92
SEE	0.0019	0.00066
Durbin-h	0.31	0.26
Nobs	66	66
D-Freedom	61	61
F-Statistic(1,61)	1.98	0.042

Correlation of Residuals −0.0127
λ_{LM}=0.011 (Matrix is Diagonal)
* Significant at 5% confidence level.
Standard errors in parentheses.

expenditure of the military type seems to have significant spillover effects in Japan and in the rate of growth of GNP in the United States.

Dynamics and Vector Autoregressions (VAR)

In order to gain further insight into the data and how they relate to the dynamic adjustments implied by the theoretical model, we have estimated VAR systems with the relevant variables most prominent in the underlying theoretical model. The estimated models are unrestricted with four values of each variable, and identification of shocks obtained through a Cholesky decomposition of the variance-covariance matrix of the errors.

We have estimated the effects of the three types of U.S. government expen-

TABLE 7

Seemingly Unrelated Regressions (SUR) by Generalized Least Squares (GLS)
US Military Government Expenditure
Sample: 1973:2–1989:3

	Dependent Variable: Rate of Growth of GNP	
	USA	Japan
GNP(t−1)	0.809*	0.798*
	(0.053)	(0.048)
INV(t)	0.130*	0.073*
	(0.016)	(0.008)
INV(t−1)	−0.069*	−0.042*
	(0.020)	(0.010)
ARGMIL^{US}(t)	0.076*	0.026*
	(0.030)	(0.009)
ARG^J(t)	0.028†	0.054*
	(0.014)	(0.015)
Adj-R^2	0.90	0.93
SEE	0.0018	0.00062
Durbin-h	0.20	−0.19
Nobs	66	66
D-Freedom	61	61
F-Statistic(1,61)	3.60†	7.54*

Correlation of Residuals −0.0599
λ_{LM}=0.2375 (Matrix is Diagonal)
* Significant at 5% confidence level.
† Significant at 10% confidence level.
Standard errors in parentheses.

diture. The VARs include the following variables in order: U.S. real government expenditure (total, nonmilitary, and military), U.S. industrial production, U.S. real consumption, U.S.-Japan real exchange rate, and U.S. current account. Figures 4–6 show the impulse responses up to 24 quarters, of a one standard deviation in U.S. government expenditure, while Tables 8–10 show the decomposition of the forecast error variance (FEV) for these systems.

Several important results can be identified. First, a shock in any type of U.S. government expenditure has a persistent positive effect on U.S. industrial production and consumption, but smaller effects on the real exchange rate and the current account. The result that a positive shock in government expenditure has a positive persistent effect on domestic industrial production is consistent

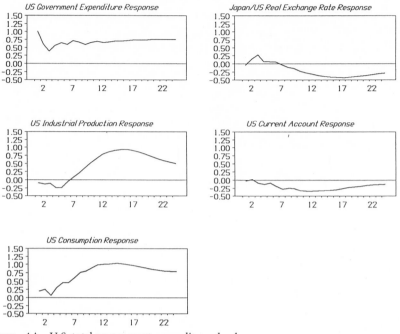

FIG. 4A. U.S. total government expenditure shock

with the predictions of the theoretical model. However, the accompanying persistent increase in domestic consumption is not, since the model implied that crowding out of private consumption should occur. This issue has been explored at greater length in a recent paper by Bianconi and Turnovsky (1994). That paper explains this empirical regularity using a two-country single-good general equilibrium model where government expenditure impacts on the productive side of the economy, rather than on the consumption side as is being assumed here; see also Turnovsky and Fisher (1995).

Second, the total nonmilitary government expenditure is much more persistent and has much more impact than does the military expenditure case. Third, in the cases of total and nonmilitary expenditure, the real exchange rate initially appreciates and then starts depreciating after three quarters. This is generally consistent with the theoretical predictions of the model. We should observe, however, that in the case of military expenditure the real exchange rate does not behave as the model would suggest; it depreciates initially and remains somewhat stable thereafter. Finally, the generally negative response of the current account reflected in the VARs is consistent with the underlying model.

The FEV decompositions in Tables 8–10 show that the current account

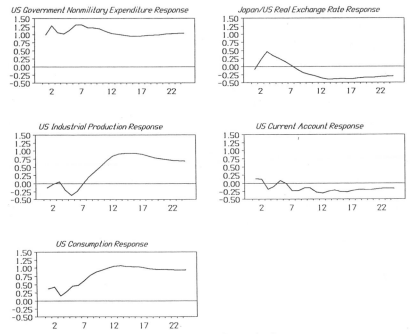

FIG. 4B. U.S. government nonmilitary expenditure shock

explains very little of the other variables, confirming the limited dynamic interactions between it and the other variables in the system. The real exchange rate has the highest standard error and explains more than two-thirds of its own FEV. At the same time, movements in the real exchange rate do contribute significantly to the FEV of U.S. consumption and industrial production. U.S. government expenditure contributes generally modest amounts to the FEV of most variables, particularly the exchange rate and the U.S. current account.

VI. CONCLUSIONS

The analysis undertaken in this paper is in some respects an overly ambitious one. It has been to use a tightly specified benchmark theoretical macroeconomic model to help interpret some of the recent growth performance of the U.S. economy and, in particular, emphasizing its external relationship with Japan. In many ways it is unrealistic to expect such a simple aggregate model to accomplish this task and in fact the representative agent framework has come under criticism for its unsatisfactory empirical performance.

Nevertheless, we feel that the representative agent model provides a useful framework for understanding the dynamic adjustments that took place in the

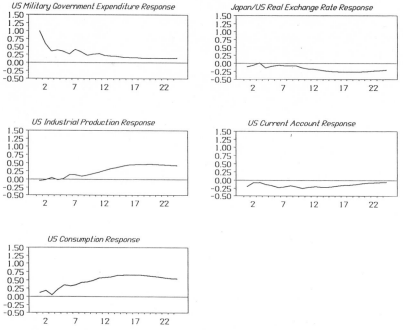

FIG. 4C. U.S. military government expenditure shock

1980s.[6] Many of the theoretical implications of the model are reflected qualitatively, if not quantitatively in the empirical data. And more importantly, the
model provides a framework for understanding the dynamic characteristics of
the data as reflected in the VARs.

In Table 11 we present a summary of the performance of the theoretical
model when compared to the raw U.S. data and the VARs. The raw data are
unconditional and the variables relating to the theoretical model and to the
VARs are conditional on the domestic government expenditure shock. The
model performs well in some basic dimensions. The behavior of real output,
exports, the real interest rate, employment, the real exchange rate, the net asset
position, and the current account are all tracked reasonably well. But it does
not do so well in other dimensions, most notably, aggregate consumption,
investment, imports, the real wage, and to a minor extent the trade balance.
Taking into account the fact that the only source of disturbance in the model
is the government expenditure shock, we believe that the model performs
credibly. Once other shocks are taken into account, and some of the benchmark
assumptions relaxed, the performance may improve significantly.

With this in mind, we conclude by noting that the government expenditure
shocks in the United States during the 1980s have contributed significantly to

TABLE 8

Decomposition of Forecast Error Variance (FEV):
United States Total Government Expenditure VAR (%)

Quarters Ahead	Std. Err.	US Gov. Exp.	US Indus. Prod.	US Consump.	Japan/US Real Ex. Rate	US Current Account
Decomposition of FEV for US Government Military Expenditure						
8	0.02	34.67	19.95	14.94	28.88	1.53
12	0.03	25.80	25.17	16.70	30.80	1.50
Decomposition of FEV for US Industrial Production						
8	0.03	2.36	40.69	42.48	12.47	1.97
12	0.05	9.32	19.74	44.26	24.20	2.46
Decomposition of FEV for US Consumption						
8	0.02	15.90	4.56	56.85	22.09	0.57
12	0.04	21.50	5.52	39.32	32.36	1.28
Decomposition of FEV for Japan/US Real Exchange Rate						
8	0.09	2.74	14.99	4.51	66.40	11.34
12	0.11	6.36	13.39	10.31	60.60	9.31
Decomposition of FEV for US Current Account						
8	0.07	5.10	19.93	13.86	30.07	31.00
12	0.10	8.90	18.85	15.22	37.46	19.55

explaining some of the imbalances of the United States against the rest of the world in general, and Japan in particular. In this respect we find an interesting difference between the response to military and nonmilitary government expenditures; the effects of the former tend to be more transitory, while the effects of the latter tend to be longer term. Our results also suggest that the channel of transmission between the two countries occurred more through the real exchange rate between the two countries rather than through the current account. Indeed, a significant fraction of the variance in both U.S. consumption and industrial production can be attributed to the movement in the real exchange rate.

NOTES

We gratefully acknowledge the helpful comments made by the participants of the Conference on International Capital Transfer and U.S.-Japan Economic Relations: Lessons

TABLE 9

Decomposition of Forecast Error Variance (FEV):
United States Nonmilitary Government Expenditure VAR (%)

Quarters Ahead	Std. Err.	US Gov. Nonmil. Exp.	US Indus. Prod.	US Consump.	Japan/US Real Ex. Rate	US Current Account
Decomposition of FEV for US Government Nonmilitary Expenditure						
8	0.02	53.02	2.94	3.43	28.41	12.17
12	0.03	38.13	1.79	11.09	36.11	12.85
Decomposition of FEV for US Industrial Production						
8	0.03	2.78	34.38	51.52	7.68	3.62
12	0.05	7.96	18.93	56.36	14.44	2.27
Decomposition of FEV for US Consumption						
8	0.01	14.02	7.22	76.50	1.70	0.54
12	0.04	17.05	3.51	52.88	26.31	0.23
Decomposition of FEV for Japan/US Real Exchange Rate						
8	0.09	9.99	11.70	6.24	65.36	6.68
12	0.12	11.45	7.93	14.85	59.14	6.61
Decomposition of FEV for US Current Account						
8	0.07	4.11	0.71	35.36	28.92	30.89
12	0.10	5.05	0.68	43.41	32.69	18.15

of the 1980s and Perspective for the Future, held in Langley, WA, June 1–4, 1994 and in particular the suggestions made by the editors of this volume, Yukio Noguchi and Kozo Yamamura.

1. The model is drawn from Turnovsky and Sen (1991). A more detailed discussion of its properties is available in that paper.

2. A reasonable alternative would be to set θ to the empirical share of domestic goods in expenditure on consumption.

3. In the real business cycle work of Hansen and Wright (1992), they calibrate the value of ϕ_1 such that a steady state value of l is about 1/3. We consider this alternative in the sensitivity analysis below.

4. In the sensitivity analysis below we consider the case where $\phi_2=10$, which corresponds to the much lower labor supply elasticity of 0.1, found in the study of MaCurdy (1981) and used in the simulations of Turnovsky and Bianconi (1989). Note also that the polar case where $\phi_2 \to \infty$ represents a perfectly inelastic labor supply. In this analysis it implies that the capital stock does not respond to changes in government consumption.

TABLE 10

Decomposition of Forecast Error Variance (FEV):
United States Military Government Expenditure VAR (%)

Quarters Ahead	Std. Err.	US Gov. Mil. Exp.	US Indus. Prod.	US Consump.	Japan/US Real Ex. Rate	US Current Account
Decomposition of FEV for US Government Military Expenditure						
8	0.04	34.32	21.94	21.02	19.71	2.98
12	0.05	24.34	25.56	24.63	17.27	8.17
Decomposition of FEV for US Industrial Production						
8	0.03	0.55	55.06	23.60	15.49	5.28
12	0.05	1.22	30.02	37.37	27.45	3.92
Decomposition of FEV for US Consumption						
8	0.02	6.33	4.51	65.37	23.15	0.61
12	0.03	7.55	2.51	56.32	32.65	0.94
Decomposition of FEV for Japan/US Real Exchange Rate						
8	0.09	1.40	9.69	6.12	72.54	10.23
12	0.11	2.70	7.34	13.27	67.93	8.74
Decomposition of FEV for US Current Account						
8	0.07	5.65	10.87	16.99	33.04	33.43
12	0.09	6.37	8.95	23.03	39.53	22.08

Instead, government expenditure completely crowds out an equivalent quantity of private consumption.

5. The statistical and econometric analysis is performed using RATS as in Doan (1992).

6. For example, one related paper that has been relatively successful in applying a general equilibrium framework to explain the data is the recent contribution by Yi (1993).

REFERENCES

Backus, David. 1993. The Japanese trade balance: recent history and future prospects. NBER Working Paper No. 4553, November.

Bianconi, Marcelo and Turnovsky, Stephen J. 1993. International effects of government expenditure in interdependent economies. Unpublished manuscript.

TABLE 11
Summary Model Performance

Variable: Domestic	Raw Data [Unconditional]	Theoretical Model [Conditional on Government Expenditure Shock]	VARs
Real output	+	+	+
Aggregate consumption	+	−	+
Investment	High Volatility	Low Volatility	NA
Exports	−	−	NA
Imports	+	−	NA
Real interest	+/−	+/−	NA
Employment	+	+	NA
Real wage	+/−	−/+	NA
Real exchange rate	+/−	+/−	+/−
Net asset position	−	−	NA
Current account	−	−	−
Trade balance	−	−/+	NA
Budget deficit and debt	+	NA	NA

NOTE: (+) increase in most of period; (−) decrease in most of period; (+/−)(−/+) increase(decrease) in early period, decrease(increase) in late period; NA=not applicable.

———. 1994. The international transmission of government expenditure shocks: theory and evidence. Unpublished manuscript.

Doan, Thomas. 1992. User's manual, regression analysis of time series (RATS) Version 4.0. VAR Econometrics, Evanston, IL.

Froot, Kenneth. A. and Rogoff, Kenneth. 1991. The EMS and EMU and the transition to a common currency. In *NBER macroeconomics annual 1991*, ed. Olivier J. Blanchard and Stanley Fischer, pp. 269–316. Cambridge, Mass.: MIT Press.

Hansen, Gary and Wright, Randall 1992. The labor market in real business cycle theory, *Federal Reserve Bank of Minneapolis quarterly review* 16:1–12.

Horioka, Charles Y. 1994. Japan's consumption and saving in international perspective, *Economic development and cultural change* 42:293–316.

Ito, Takatoshi. 1992. *The Japanese economy.* Cambridge, Mass.: MIT Press.

Kydland, Finn E. and Prescott, Edward C. 1982. Time-to-build and aggregate fluctuations. *Econometrica* 50:1345–70.

Krugman, Paul. 1989. Differences in income elasticities and trends in real exchange rates. *European economic review* 33:1031–46.

MaCurdy, Thomas E. 1981. An empirical model of labor supply in a life-cycle setting. *Journal of political economy* 89:1059–85.

Stockman, Alan and Tesar, Linda. 1990. Tastes and technology shocks in a two-country model of the business cycle: explaining international comovements. NBER Working Paper No. 3556, December.

Turnovsky, Stephen J. and Bianconi, Marcelo. 1989. Strategic wages policy and the gains from cooperation. In *Dynamic policy games in economics*, ed. Frederick van der Ploeg and Aart de Zeeuw. Amsterdam:North-Holland.

Turnovsky, Stephen J. and Fisher, Walter H. 1995. The composition of government expenditure and its consequences for macroeconomic performance. *Journal of economic dynamics and control* 19:747–86.

Turnovsky, Stephen J. and Sen, Partha. 1991. Fiscal policy, capital accumulation and debt in an open economy. *Oxford economic papers* 43:1–24.

Yi, Kei-Mu. 1993. Can government purchases explain the recent U.S. net export deficits? *Journal of international economics* 35:201–25.

Contributors

MARCELO BIANCONI is an associate professor of economics, Tufts University.

KOICHI HAMADA is a professor of economics, Yale University.

TAKATOSHI ITO is a Senior Advisor at the International Monetary Fund and a professor at Hitotsubashi University.

KAZUMASA IWATA is a professor in the Department of Social and International Relations, University of Tokyo, Komaba.

YUKIO NOGUCHI is a professor of economics, University of Tokyo.

JOEL SLEMROD is a professor of economics and of business economics and public policy at the University of Michigan.

STEPHEN J. TURNOVSKY is the Castor Professor of Economics, University of Washington.

KOZO YAMAMURA is the Job and Gertrud Tamaki Professor of Japanese Studies, University of Washington.

NAOYUKI YOSHINO is a professor of economics, Keio University.

Index